Understanding YOURSELF

With an introduction by Dr Christopher Evans

Hamlyn

LONDON · NEW YORK · SYDNEY · TORONTO
in association with Phoebus

INTRODUCTION

We all have a clear idea of the sort of person we think we are: dominant, assertive, unsure, weak even. And it may well be that this self-image, built up through childhood and adolescence, is accurate. But can we be sure? Robert Burns summed it up when he wished for the gift "to see ourselves as others see us." Does the personality others see really match our own mental picture?

This book of tests and questionnaires, all of which have been specially designed and developed by psychologists, will not overnight provide a new personality — nor is it intended to. But it will offer, to anyone tackling the questions with a frank and open mind, some fresh and fascinating slants on various aspects of his or her psychological makeup. Some of the tests are more or less entirely concerned with personality, others with skills and abilities, others with artistic and cultural matters. Some are complex, requiring concentration and self-discipline to complete, and demand an hour in a quiet place to get the best results. Others are light-hearted and less searching, and can be filled in at the odd moment. None are party games, however, and none are intended for administering to friends or acquaintances with "psychological problems" — anyone seriously troubled in this way should seek professional advice. Some will yield results which may be unexpected and, perhaps, a little jolting!

Fancy yourself as a good driver, for example? Do the questionnaire on page 41 and you may get a surprise. Do you do a lot of dreaming? Check how your own dreamlife matches up with other people's. Could you survive a catastrophe? The questionnaire on page 68 might prove you may be more indestructible than you think! One final point: in the field of psychological evaluation, there are no absolute rights or wrongs, and the questionnaires in Understanding Yourself *do not pretend to be infallible. You will however find them intriguing and revealing, and you may never see yourself in quite the same light again!*

Executive Editor: Nicolas Wright   **Editor:** Mundy Ellis   **Designer:** Jeff Gurney

Published 1977 by The Hamlyn Publishing Group Limited, London
New York . Sydney . Toronto
Astronaut House, Feltham, Middlesex, England
ISBN 0 600 39020 9

This edition © 1977 Phoebus Publishing Company/BPC Publishing
Limited, 169 Wardour Street, London W1A 2JX

This material first appeared in **Understanding Human Behavior**
© 1974 BPC Publishing Limited
Made and printed in Great Britain by Waterlow (Dunstable) Limited

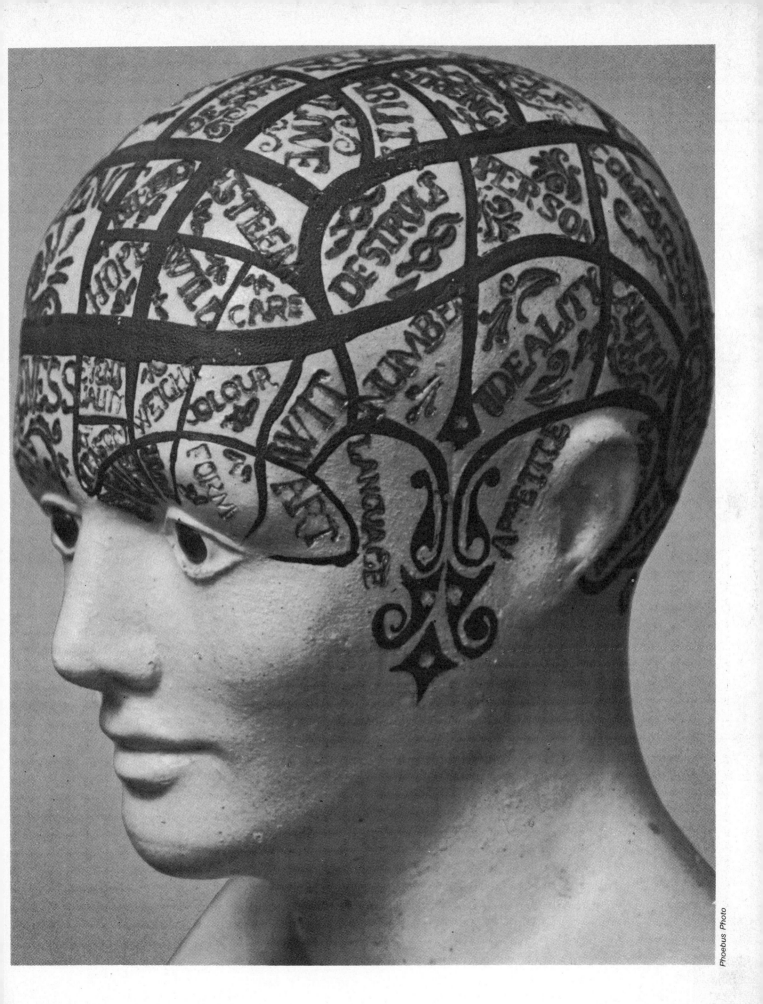

CONTENTS

Are you an introvert or an extrovert?	5
Analyzing your dreams	9
How well do you cope with stress?	13
How sexy are you?	17
How popular are you?	21
How brave are you?	25
How healthy a life do you live? I	28
How healthy a life do you live? II	31
You and anger	34
How superstitious are you?	37
What kind of driver are you?	41
Can you take a risk?	45
ESP and you I	48
ESP and you II	52
Are you a true leader?	57
Are you a hypochondriac?	61
How creative are you?	65
Could you survive a catastrophe?	68
Are you a happy human? I	72
Are you a happy human? II	75
How well do you cope?	78
How assertive are you?	81
How permissive are you?	85
How good is your self-image?	89
What are your social attitudes? I	92
What are your social attitudes? II	95
How imaginative are you?	98
How strong is your unconscious?	102
Are you in the right job?	105
Are you a slave to money?	109
Check your artistic IQ:	
How musical are you?	113
How visual are you?	116
Your literary IQ	120
How tolerant are you?	123
Are you a good judge of people?	127
Intuition and insight: How important are they to you?	131
Does time work for you?	135
What kind of parent are you? I	138
What kind of parent are you? II	141
Are you a victim of the blues?	145
What is your real age?	149
How emotional are you?	153
Test your self-confidence	157

Philip Castle

Are You an Introvert or an Extrovert?

The measurement of human personality is one of the dominating goals of modern psychologists. To anyone wanting to study human behavior, at whatever level, the striking fact emerges that whereas human beings clearly present a vast range of physical differences, differences in personality, which may be far more significant, are more elusive. Physical characteristics are fairly constant, altering only with the slow passage of the years and occasional bouts of physical ill-health, but the essence of personality seems altogether more fluid.

A man may be docile and good-natured one minute, a furious raging animal in the next. He may be apparently honest at one moment, fraudulent at the next; passionate and suddenly indifferent; cautious and impulsive. As if this were not enough, even the words which people use to describe their changing moods are ambiguous and uncertain.

Perhaps it is not surprising that, despite the fact that man has been looking at his own moods for thousands of years, he has only recently begun to develop techniques for measuring and describing them. Some of the first breakthroughs in what is generally known as modern psychology came from the early insights of psychoanalysis.

Psychologist Carl Gustav Jung was one of the first to note that people tend to direct the force of their personality—their psychic energy if you like—either outward to the world or inward to themselves.

The particular characteristics of such outgoing and ingoing personalities were, he felt, somewhat difficult to pin down but he gave them the blanket names of extroversion and introversion.

These personality types have turned out to be among the most useful psychometric measures and although Jung's original ideas have been modified somewhat and tests have become increasingly sophisticated, the personality dimensions of introversion and extroversion have endured and become more concrete with the passage of time.

We all know—or think we know—which of our friends and acquaintances are extroverts and we may even feel that we have a pretty good idea where on the sliding scale we ourselves lie. Actually, the categorization is not that easy. While there is a very good chance that the hearty, back-slapping, smiling salesman is in fact a high-level extrovert, and the retiring, bookish, mild-mannered clerk a clear-cut introvert, superficial appearances can be very misleading.

In order to be quite sure (or as sure as one can get at the present level of psychological knowledge) carefully prepared tests have been designed to filter people along this continuum of extroversion and introversion.

Many of these have to be administered and interpreted by psychologists with special training. But this test has been specially designed for self-rating and self-administration. Provided that you answer the questions honestly, you will find that your final score will give you an interesting insight into your own personality.

To achieve the best results, observe the following rules:

1. To keep your answers completely confidential, you should mark all your choices on a separate sheet, so have a pencil and paper ready. This will also mean that your family and friends can do the questionnaire without being influenced by your answers.
2. Do not mark any part of the test until you are quite clear that you have understood the question that is being asked.
3. You will often find that you are unable to agree exactly with any of the attitudes or statements expressed. You should in all cases therefore choose the one that is closest to your own attitude or belief. Conversely, you may feel that two or more attitudes correspond fairly closely to your own. In such cases you must choose the one which is closest to yours.
4. Mark as honestly as you can. Remember that no other person should see your answers or your score so there is no need to mark yourself in such a way as to present a favorable image to other people.
5. Do not score any part of the test until you have marked it completely.
6. You should also make a note of the time, to the nearest minute, you take to complete the test.

1. Here are five statements reflecting attitudes to conversation. Read them carefully and choose the statement which most closely matches your own feelings.
   a. I tend to be a talkative and forward conversationalist, perhaps too talkative and forward for a lot of people's tastes.
   b. I tend to be talkative and often take the lead in group conversations.
   c. I'm afraid I'm simply a bad conversationalist.
   d. I enjoy conversation but would as soon listen as talk.
   e. I find myself generally ill at ease in a situation where I am likely to be drawn into conversation.

2. Here are five statements reflecting attitudes to using the telephone. Read them carefully and choose the statement which most closely matches your feelings.
   a. I can conduct a good conversation on the telephone but much prefer to see people face to face if I am to really get across to them.
   b. The telephone fails for me principally because I cannot see the face of the person I am talking to.
   c. I can use the telephone when I have to but find it a limited instrument for communication.
   d. I find that when I use the telephone I can communicate very easily with people and get through to them in surprising depth.
   e. I feel positively ill at ease on the telephone.

3. You have won a choice of the following holidays in a competition, with all expenses paid. Look at them carefully and choose the one which you would *most* enjoy, and the one you would *least* enjoy.
   a. A month in a luxury holiday camp with sun, surf, music, communal eating and good company.
   b. A small but superbly comfortable hotel in a quiet, remote part of the country where walking, fishing or other gentle pastimes are possible.
   c. A house party at the villa of a wealthy author friend whose other guests are mainly writers, artists and people with creative interests.
   d. The opportunity to devote yourself entirely to doing something that you have always wanted to do—learning to fly, reading Gibbon's *Decline and Fall*, writing a book, visiting every theater you can.
   e. A quiet holiday with family or friend in a quiet hotel.
   f. A month's tour in a luxurious bus of historical and cultural centers in every country of Europe.

4. In an evening's television viewing, which of the following do you prefer to watch *most* and which *least*?
   a. An old feature film.
   b. A panel discussion on a serious topical issue.
   c. A lightweight talk show.
   d. An uninhibited comedy show.
   e. A modern play with psychological undertones.
   f. A live boxing match.

5. Here are various ways you might spend a spare evening. Indicate the evening which you would *most* and *least* enjoy.
   a. You and half a dozen friends in a cheery, lively bar where darts and perhaps some music are on hand.
   b. An evening with a close companion at the theater.
   c. A really swinging party with lots of good food, drink and company.
   d. An evening at home listening to music or reading.
   e. A small dinner party at a friend's home with plenty of stimulating conversation.
   f. An evening at home watching good TV.

6. Which most closely matches your own attitudes to taking decisions?
   a. I am scared sometimes about the consequences of decisions and tend to put off making them.
   b. I like to have time to think, but when I make my mind up I'm firm about it.
   c. I come to quick decisions but they are generally well-balanced and not over-hasty.
   d. If I make rapid decisions they tend to be wrong; if I consider them carefully they tend to be right.
   e. I can make decisions with great speed but sometimes wish that I was not so impulsive.
   f. I tend to find it difficult to make decisions.

7. Choose the statement which most closely matches your own feelings or experience.
   a. I would never hurt anyone physically unless I had to in self-defense, but then I would fight hard.
   b. I find the idea of human beings fighting each other repulsive.
   c. I do not deliberately seek out trouble but have had to resort to physical violence on more than one occasion.
   d. I have frequently been involved in arguments which could easily lead or have led to violence.
   e. I would never under any circumstances fight physically with another person.

8. Choose the statement which most closely reflects your own level of work or productivity.
   a. I am pretty average in the amount of work I get through, I suppose.
   b. I am capable of a high level of steady, productive work which doesn't vary too much from one week to the next.
   c. I am not very productive and most work for me is hard work.
   d. Sometimes I am highly productive, other times unproductive, but most times I'm fairly average.
   e. I find I can get through a tremendous amount of work if I want to, but it tends to come in bursts.

9. In this question you must try to rate yourself not according to how you feel about yourself, but how you believe *others* feel about you: On the whole other people probably view me as
   a. Good company sometimes, but decidedly poor company other times.
   b. Exceedingly active and outgoing, possibly even somewhat overactive and pushy.
   c. Pretty much of a bore for one reason or another.
   d. Active, friendly and pleasant, lively company.
   e. More or less average in terms of activity and friendliness.
   f. A rather restrained type of personality.

10. If I could "see myself as others see me" I'd be
    a. Disappointed at their poor image of me.
    b. Somewhat more pleased than I had anticipated.
    c. Very pleased and flattered.
    d. Horrified.
    e. Surprised at some aspects of my personality which I had been unaware of.
    f. Not surprised to find my own shortcomings clearly spotlighted.

11. Which of the following most closely matches your attitude to shopping or buying things?
    a. I tend to spend lavishly but what else is money for?
    b. I tend to be rather foolish when it comes to shopping and frequently end up buying things that I don't really want.
    c. I am a fairly responsible shopper and tend on the whole to buy within my means.
    d. I don't enjoy shopping for major items as I feel that the risk of making a mistake is too great.
    e. I hate shopping of any kind.

12. For each of the following statements say whether you agree or disagree or whether you are not sure.
    a. The world would be a better place if people were obliged to explain their decisions to someone else before they were able to carry them out.
    b. Man is an aggressive creature who must adjust, however, to the requirements of society.
    c. Credit cards are a menace on the whole as they make people spend more than they can afford.
    d. There is no surer way of getting a dull decision than by putting it to a committee.
    e. Neurotic people tend to be a bit self-indulgent of their own problems.
    f. Variety is the spice of life.

13. Which of the following (assuming you had to do one) would you enjoy doing *most* and which *least*?
    a. Tackle a vital cataloging task for a big library.
    b. Act as treasurer of a sports or social club.
    c. Take the lead in a theatrical presentation.
    d. Revive a failing local political party.
    e. Do an absolutely enormous jigsaw puzzle.
    f. Get thoroughly acquainted with the latest development in psychological theory.

QUESTIONS 14-16 FOR MEN ONLY

14. Forgetting purchase price, resale value, garaging and running costs, etc., which of the following cars appeals to you the most and the least?
    a. Rolls-Royce Corniche
    b. Ferrari
    c. Rover 3500
    d. Volkswagen
    e. Ford Mustang
    f. Ford Thunderbird
    g. Ford Granada
    h. Mercedes 200
    i. Jaguar E-type
    j. Mercury Cougar
    k. Not sure

15. Your closest friend has to choose a car from the above list which he feels suits your personality (not necessarily your pocket) best. Which would he pick?

16. Does your choice match your friend's choice?

QUESTIONS 17-19 FOR WOMEN ONLY

17. Forgetting your present job, training, background, which of the following jobs would appeal to you most if you had freedom of choice, and which the least?
    a. Head of a big university library.
    b. Secretary to a famous film producer.
    c. World-class athlete.
    d. A successful fashion model.
    e. Brilliant psychologist.
    f. Principal of a modern progressive school.
    g. Housewife with a happy home and family.
    h. Successful authoress.
    i. Film or stage star.
    j. Wife of a successful but rather reclusive author.
    k. Not sure.

18. Your closest friend has to decide which of the above jobs would be most suited to your character and personality (not necessarily to your age, ability or prospects). Which do you think he or she would select?

19. Does your choice match your friend's choice?

Now turn to page 8 and check your scores.

Analysis

Over 100 E An E score of more than 100, if the questionnaire has been frankly and honestly filled out, represents a quite abnormal degree of extroversion—so great in fact that it would suggest a distinctly unbalanced personality. All tests become very inaccurate at their extremes, but any score of a hundred or over would be quite remarkable. The most probable explanation of this is that you have either misunderstood some of the questions, or misinterpreted the scoring.

76 E to 100 E This is an unusually high score and if you have filled out the questionnaire and scored it correctly, then this suggests that you are exceptionally extroverted in comparison with most people and may be considered rather overbearing by some. The question now arises as to what you can or should do about it. If you are already aware that this side of your personality is hindering you to one degree or another then you will have to strive to curb it a little. The best and simplest strategy is to try to form a more accurate image of yourself. A slightly cruel but revealing technique is to arrange to make tape recordings of yourself talking at a party, in a bar or in an office. Listen to them carefully and you may see which aspects of your image you need to modify.

51 E to 75 E This high score indicates that your personality is marked by an unquestionable extroversion. The chances are that you have adjusted your job and/or life style to your personality. If not, then you should take steps to make this adjustment. Your present job might be too constraining, your friendships inhibiting. Only you can decide. Strong extroversion is often coupled with high drive to succeed and provided that you can avoid being pushy it is a useful trait.

31 E to 50 E You are clearly extroverted and most people will probably judge you to be so when they know you well. Those scoring in the 30s however may not be immediately recognizable as extroverts to others. No adjustment is required for this normal, healthy trait, but all extroverts should make the most of their special potential for good social relationships.

11 E to 30 E In balance your personality is extroverted. The bias is fairly mild however and you may not even be aware that it exists in yourself. If you have been considering yourself to be *introverted*, it may be that a few minor changes in your life style are called for! You may well also have a latent organizing ability and you will tend to be successful in any job which involves dealing with other people.

10 E to 10 i Your personality is neither introverted nor extroverted and along this dimension of personality you can be described as being "balanced." This is neither good nor bad but on the whole you gain because you are acceptable to both introverts and extroverts and you should find it easy to form relaxed social relationships.

10 i to 30 i On the whole your personality is introverted. It is a fairly mild bias however and it could be that you are not aware of it in yourself. For example, you may find some forms of social interaction, while not unenjoyable, to be somehow stressful, without knowing quite why. This stress can be alleviated by doing more what you want to do rather than what you think you ought to do.

31 i to 50 i This is a very clear introvert score and most people who know you will classify you as introverted or shy. If your score is in the 30s however you may have been able to conceal this aspect of your personality, consciously or unconsciously. This is fine as long as it does not cause you stress by exposing you to complicated social situations which you do not really enjoy.

51 i to 75 i The dominating feature of your personality is a marked introversion. The chances are that your work and life style have long ago been adjusted to accept the situation. You will not really enjoy large gatherings of people and social situations. Most introverts however tend to turn their energies towards intellectual pursuits which do not require interaction with other people —reading, appreciating music and creative hobbies. If you are in a job that makes great social demands then in the long run it would be in your interests to change it.

76 i to 100 i This very high score denotes a quite unusual imbalance towards introversion. Many people you know will probably consider you shy to an unusual extent. There is not a great deal that you can do about this except to come to terms with it. Do not be tempted to force yourself into social interaction which you do not really enjoy and you are never likely to enjoy.

Over 100 i Assuming that this questionnaire has been honestly filled out your i score of over 100 represents a quite abnormal bias towards introversion. You are certainly exceedingly shy and must lead a highly restricted social life. The most likely explanation though is that you have not filled out the questionnaire accurately.

Scores

For each answer give yourself either an *E* (Extrovert) score or an *i* (Introvert) score as indicated below. You will end up with a total *E* score and a total *i* score.

1. a. 3E b. 5E c. 3i d. 0 e. 5i
2. a. 3E b. 3i c. 0 d. 5E e. 5i
3. Most enjoy:
  a. 5E b. 3i c. 2E d. 5i e. 2i f. 3E
  Least enjoy:
  a. 5i b. 3E c. 2i d. 5E e. 2E f. 3i
4. Most of all:
  a. 0 b. 4i c. 0 d. 2E e. 2i f. 4E
  Least of all:
  a. 0 b. 4E c. 0 d. 2i e. 2E f. 4i
5. Most enjoy:
  a. 3E b. 1i c. 5E d. 5i e. 1E f. 3i
  Least enjoy:
  a. 3i b. 1E c. 5i d. 5E e. 1i f. 3E
6. a. 5i b. 1E c. 5E d. 3i e. 3E f. 1i
7. a. 0 b. 5i c. 3E d. 5E e. 3i
8. a. 3i b. 5E c. 5i d. 0 e. 3E
9. a. 0 b. 3E c. 5i d. 5E e. 0 f. 3i
10. a. 3E b. 2i c. 5E d. 5i e. 0 f. 0
11. a. 5E b. 3E c. 0 d. 3i e. 5i
12. Agree on the whole:
  a. 5i b. 0 c. 3i d. 2E e. 3E f. 3E
  Not sure:
  a. 2i b. 2i c. 2i d. 2i e. 2i f. 2i
  Disagree on the whole:
  a. 3E b. 0 c. 3E d. 5i e. 5i f. 3i
13. Enjoy most:
  a. 2i b. 2E c. 5E d. 5E e. 5i f. 5i
  Enjoy least:
  a. 2E b. 2i c. 5i d. 5i e. 5E f. 5E

14. MEN ONLY
  Appeals most:
  a. 4E b. 5E c. 5i d. 1i e. 1E f. 1E g. 5i
  h. 1i i. 4E j. 5i k. 5i
  Appeals least:
  a. 4i b. 5i c. 5E d. 1E e. 1i f. 1i g. 5E
  h. 1E i. 4i j. 5E k. 5i
15. Same score as in 14 "appeals most."
16. Yes 5E No 0.
17. WOMEN ONLY
  Appeals most:
  a. 2E b. 5E c. 2i d. 5E e. 5i f. 2E g. 5i
  h. 2i i. 5i j. 5i k. 5i
  Appeals least:
  a. 2i b. 5i c. 2E d. 5i e. 5E f. 2i g. 5E
  h. 2E i. 5i j. 5E k. 5i
18. Same scoring as in 17 "appeals most."
19. Yes 5E No 0.

You should now add on your special time score based on the amount of time taken to complete the test.

5 minutes or less	25E	16 minutes	5i
6 minutes	20E	17 minutes	10i
7 minutes	15E	18 minutes	15i
8 minutes	10E	19 minutes	20i
9 minutes	5E	20 minutes or over	25i
10-15 minutes	0		

Now add up your extroversion (E) and introversion (i) scores independently. Subtract the smaller of the two from the other, whichever it may be. For example, if you have an *E* score of 40 and *i* score of 25, you should take 25 from 40, which leaves you with an *E* score of 15. Refer your final score to the Analysis on page 7.

Brian Froud

Analyzing Your Dreams

This Personal Analysis is about your sleeping and dreaming habits. It concerns that vast area of your life—approximately one-third of it in total—in which you leave the world of consciousness and enter new and mysterious territory. There are no right or wrong answers to the questions, only the answers which you believe to be true about yourself. You can check how your answers compare with those given by other people by referring to the Analysis on page 10. The details given there were arrived at on the basis of a questionnaire completed by over 50,000 people. Some of the questions are about sleep, but most are about dreams. Even if you feel that you do not dream very much, you will still find it interesting to complete this Analysis. You may find that the act of filling it in makes you more aware of your dream life than you have ever been before!

Mark your answers on a separate sheet of paper.

1. On average how many hours do you sleep each night? In answering this question, please try to consider the total number of hours you sleep, even if you wake once or twice in the night.
    a. Less than 6 hours
    b. 6-8 hours
    c. More than 8 hours

2. Do you generally awake refreshed after an average night's sleep? (Please note the word "generally." Most people have the occasional "unsatisfactory" night's sleep. What you should really ask yourself is how you

feel most mornings when you wake up from your regular type of sleep.)

3. Do you ever use any drug in order to help you to get to sleep? For the purposes of this question, "drug" includes any kind of sleeping pill prescribed by a doctor, the use of alcohol *specifically* to help you sleep. It does *not* include such things as warm milk drinks, the occasional aspirin, etc.

4. Would you say that you sleep less now than you used to when you were younger?

5. Have you ever suffered from insomnia? For example, have you ever spent one complete night awake when you had been trying to get to sleep? (Remember, you may often *feel* that you have not slept all night, but make sure you are certain before you answer "yes.")

6. Have you ever had a vivid experience, *when awake*, which could be described as "I have done this before" or "I have been here before"?

7. When you wake in the morning, how long does it take before you feel completely "yourself"?
    a. Less than 5 minutes
    b. Up to 30 minutes
    c. Over 30 minutes
    d. Over an hour

8. On the whole do you enjoy dreaming?

9. Do you ever have nightmares?
  a. Never
  b. Occasionally
  c. Often

10. On average, what percentage of your dreams are generally:
  a. Pleasant
  b. Neither pleasant nor unpleasant
  c. Unpleasant
(Total percentages should add up to 100%.)

11. Here is a list of dreams, some common, some uncommon. Look down the list carefully, noting down each one that you yourself are sure you have *definitely* experienced.
  a. Dreams in which you find you can fly or float in the air
  b. Dreams in which you feel very anxious about something
  c. Dreams about the sea
  d. Dreams in color
  e. Sexual dreams
  f. Dreams about the future which came true
  g. Dreams about smoking cigarettes, pipes, etc.
  h. Recurring dreams
  i. Dreams about finding money
  j. Dreams in which you discover the "secret of the universe" or some similar revelation, only to forget it on waking
  k. Dreams about famous people, politicians, film stars, etc.
  l. Dreams featuring scenes of violence
  m. Dreams about falling
  n. Dreams in which you are being chased
  o. Dreams in which you are in a strange or unknown house
  p. Dreams in which you are at a party or social gathering
  q. Dreams in which your teeth are breaking or falling out

12. Have you ever felt that you were hearing music in your dreams?

13. Have you ever had any type of hallucination when you were awake?

14. Have you ever, to your knowledge, talked in your sleep?

15. Have you ever, to your knowledge, walked in your sleep?

Now read the analysis to see how your sleep and dream life compares with that of others.

Analysis

1. The amount of sleep that you need is related in the first instance to your personality. Some people inherit the disposition to need a great deal of sleep and others to need relatively little. The "average" range for the normal adult however lies between 5 to 6 hours, at the low end, and up to 10 hours at the top end. If you wrote down between 6-8 hours then you share the sleep habits of the vast majority (60%) of adults. If you wrote down over 8 hours then you are also in fairly normal company (36%). Only 4% sleep less than 6 hours on average. Incidentally, men and women require approximately the same amount of sleep, though children and young adults of course require more.

2. Most people (57%) state that they generally awake refreshed after a night's sleep. Men and women feel the same way about this though there is a tendency for sleep to seem somehow less refreshing as you get older. On the whole if you have to resort regularly to drugs of one kind or another to get to sleep, the sleep period itself tends to be psychologically less refreshing.

3. If you use a drug of any kind to help you get to sleep then you are in the company of 15% of the adult population. The frequency of drug usage rises sharply with age and is also related to business and personal anxieties, which also tend to increase with age. Among retired people, who may have fewer worries, the drug-taking habit is often quite unnecessary as our sleep requirement falls off with age. Many people however believe that when they are 65, they should still take the 8 or 10 hours which they used to when they were young and hence resort to drugs to "help them." This is quite unnecessary and old people should accept the fact that they simply need less sleep. Women (17%) are much more likely than men (10%) to use sleep-assisting drugs.

4. Not everyone seems to be aware that they sleep less than they did when they were young, for on average only 65% of people believe this. However the sleep requirement does not fall off noticeably until the late thirties or early forties and if may not be big enough to be noticed until even later on in life.

5. If you have had at least one night's complete insomnia despite all attempts to get off to sleep, then don't worry for you're in the company of 40% of the population. Incidentally if you are a woman you are far more likely (44%) to have suffered from insomnia than a man (35%). This of course ties in with women's greater tendency to use sleeping pills, etc., and seems to suggest that women on average have more to worry about than men —or are more likely to carry worries to bed with them.

6. This question deals with something not strictly to do with sleeping or dreaming but with a strange experience that has a dreamlike quality. Psychologists know it as *déjà vu*, which means literally "seen before." When experienced it is striking and memorable and often consists of a powerful sensation that you have been in an identical situation at some previous time in your life. There is no totally satisfactory explanation for this phenomenon but 80% of people report that they have definitely had it at one time or another in their life.

7. The transition period between sleep and waking varies enormously from person to person and there is very little that you can do to alter it. An alert 27% of people become fully awake within 5 minutes, 46% need more than 5 minutes but less than half an hour, and 17% need between half an hour and an hour. Even if you take over an hour before you come completely to, take comfort from the fact that 11% of the population are like you. This variation is physiological rather than psychological in origin.

8. If you enjoy your dreams on the whole then you are in the company of the vast majority of other people—75% on average. It is interesting to note that 80% of men state that they enjoy their dreams, as opposed to 72% of women.

9. If you have lots of nightmares you are obviously not going to enjoy your dreams so much. We have already established that women are somewhat less likely to have a pleasant dream life than men, and we find that the frequency of reported nightmares backs this up. Some 9% of women have nightmares often, 72% have them occasionally, and only 13% never. The comparable values for men are 4% often, 72% occasionally and 23% never.

10. You might find it interesting to compare your own breakdown of dreams, classified into the categories pleasant, indifferent and unpleasant. On average people feel that about 35% of their dreams are pleasant, approximately 50% indifferent and the remaining 15% actually unpleasant. Once again women tend to have a greater number of unpleasant dreams than men, though it is not clear why this should be. Such dreams, even if not of nightmare status, are not in themselves signs of psychological abnormality unless they occur with very great frequency. They tend to occur at critical or anxious times in one's life.

11. a. Dreams about flying or floating in the air are often considered to be related to an unconscious wish to escape from something. They are in fact reported by about 50% of dreamers.

b. Anxiety dreams are among the most common types reported and are particularly common among women (78%). Only 63% of men experience them.

c. Dreams about the sea, which are reputed to have a sexual interpretation by the Freudians and to represent the unconscious mind by Jungians, are very common indeed. Again however women (40%) are far more likely to experience them than men (27%).

d. Colored dreams tend to be very vivid when they are experienced and are much more likely to be reported by artistic and creative people. On average 55% of people have had color dreams at one time or another.

e. Many people feel embarrassed at having had sexual dreams, particularly when these feature sexual behavior of an "abnormal" type. In fact sexual dreams are quite normal and healthy, though more common in men (85%) than women (72%). Not surprisingly, one is far more likely to have sexual dreams if one is not leading an active sex life.

f. Dreams about the future which come true are very frequently reported though it is fair to say that scientists are very doubtful about whether these are simply coincidence or genuine peeps into the future. Almost 30% of people believe that they have had at least one such dream.

g. Smoking dreams are not in themselves very common, with only about 10% of people reporting them. However the frequency of smoking dreams goes up very rapidly indeed among ex-smokers and if you report this type of dream then it is almost certain that you are an ex-smoker. Such dreams of course are best explained in terms of the Freudian "wish fulfillment" theory: unconsciously, you may still wish to smoke.

h. Recurring dreams are very common—70% of people reporting them on average. In most cases recurring dreams are of a vaguely unpleasant kind and are almost certainly caused because the individual has a problem of a significant kind which he is unable to resolve in his waking life. The solving of his problem almost always leads to the disappearance of the recurring dream. Women are more likely to have recurring dreams than men.

i. This is a relatively common dream, often experienced by people when their finances are tight. Typically it involves finding coins showering from a slot machine or picking them up in great profusion from the ground. About a quarter of men have had this dream, but only 15% of women. This presumably relates to the fact that money matters are more likely to preoccupy the male than the female.

j. Dreams of this kind, which may be either pleasant or unpleasant, are often associated with recovery from a general anesthetic after having a tooth out or an operation. Such dreams, which are very hard to explain, are in fact surprisingly common with about 17% of people having had them.

k. Women are more likely to dream about famous

people, politicians, pop stars and the like (33%) than men (27%). Since dreams tend to reflect our daytime interests, perhaps this is not too surprising for women are notably more interested in the activities of famous people as relayed in magazines or TV than are men. One very common dream, which almost certainly falls into the wish fulfillment category, is when people report that they are actually meeting famous people in their dreams.

l. Dreams featuring scenes of violence are, perhaps predictably, much more common among men (50%) than among women (44%). However the differences are not very great. Perhaps men are simply more likely to talk about violent things and it must be remembered that women are often the most ardent fans of TV Westerns and wrestling programs.

m. Dreams about falling are very common with about a 75% scoring on average. The most frequently reported is one in which typically, one "trips over something," stumbles or falls and wakes up with a jump. Psychologists now believe that these dreams do not necessarily have any great emotional significance but are merely due to muscular spasms which take place on the threshold between consciousness and sleep.

n. Over 70% of people have dreamed that they were being chased or pursued by something, and often in the dream they find themselves unable to flee for one reason or another. These often occur during periods of great anxiety and may be related to frustrating situations which are frequently occurring in their waking life.

o. A very curious and common dream (31%) is one in which the sleeper finds himself wandering in a strange house full of empty rooms. The psychoanalytic interpretation that this is a disguised sexual dream is not generally accepted today and the present feeling is that this is another class of anxiety dream which reflects a general uneasiness in waking life. Often in such dreams one is looking for something which one never finds and is conscious of a pervading sense of worry.

p. About 31% of people have this dream, and it may take principally two forms. In one, the dreamer is happy and enjoying himself in the group. In the other he is ill-at-ease. Such dreams tend to relate to such personality variables as extroversion and introversion.

q. This bizarre dream, which may take a number of different forms, may also have a number of different explanations. In psychoanalysis the loss of the teeth is presumed to denote a loss of sexual potency or a fear of such loss. Some psychologists however believe that it is a memory dream referring back to that significant period in your baby life when teeth fell out. A third explanation is that you are suffering from low level toothache which is not enough to get through to the conscious mind but which trickles through into your dreams.

12. Most people tend to associate dreams with visual experiences only, but there is a growing body of evidence which suggests that there is a whole range of dreams featuring all the senses. The fact is that visual dreams are probably the most easy to describe and to remember. Auditory dreams, or "hearing" dreams, generally feature conversations but also quite commonly feature music, with 40% of people reporting them. Sometimes the musical dreams may be very vivid indeed with sharp, clear sound, sometimes apparently featuring a full orchestra. It is not difficult to explain such dreams when one considers the amount of time which most people spend listening to music, if only on background radio, in the course of the day.

13. Hallucinations are best described as "waking dreams" but must be clearly discriminated from so-called daydreams, which are fantasies under conscious control. In hallucinations what actually occurs is that the brain sets in motion a dream or fragment of one at an inappropriate time—i.e. when the brain is awake and conscious. Thus one sees an inner, mental picture projected vividly on the outside world. The hallucinogenic drugs, LSD, etc., act by stimulating the dream mechanism in the waking mind with results which may be psychologically unpleasant and dangerous. Hallucinations, incidentally, are relatively common with about 25% of people reporting them at one time or another in their lives.

14. Sleep talking is a harmless but common habit reported by about 70% of men and 75% of women. It is not in any way psychologically harmful and is more of a nuisance to one's sleeping partner than anything else of great significance.

15. Sleep walking is a much bigger nuisance than sleep talking but is fortunately far less common. Women (25%) experience it more than men (20%) and its cause is not properly understood. It does tend to be more common among children and adolescents and often vanishes in adult life.

Summary

If you've answered the questions carefully you will have been able to plot your sleeping and dreaming habits against the statistical background gained from a huge cross section of normal people. Please remember that there are no right or wrong answers and that if you find yourself consistently among the minority groupings this in itself is in no way abnormal. The act of filling out the questionnaire may have made you more aware of your own dream life. Many people find that their dreams offer interesting gateways to their unconscious minds and reveal a rich and exciting landscape of whose existence they had not previously been aware.

Zip Art

How Well Do You Cope with Stress?

Our bodies are equipped with an elaborate early warning system designed to detect and avert danger before it has actually caught up with us. This system has as its front rank the five senses—vision, hearing, touch, taste and smell—and behind this is a complex computer which samples and integrates information gathered by nerve receptors. Behind this again is another command and control device (the main part of the brain) which directs the body's neural and muscular responses after making the decision to stand and fight or turn and flee, depending upon the nature of the threatening situation. The various changes that take place in the nervous system as the result of the body's response to danger—or to any arising situation—bring in their wake distinct psychological changes. These we call our emotions—the "feelings" we have which tell us which state of arousal our nervous system has switched into.

In fact all animals including humans live in a dangerous, threatening or challenging environment, and therefore whether in love or hate, elation or depression, our nervous systems are for a large part of our lives in a high state of tune. In the days when the average life expectancy was a mere thirty years (or forty if you were lucky), this didn't matter too much, but today many people (particularly as middle age approaches) begin to feel their emotional defenses sagging somewhat as the pressures of the world around them pound on. But while everyone responds to threat and danger by exhibiting some degree of emotional response the variability in the degree of stress engendered by a particular situation is considerable. Not everyone is able to adjust satisfactorily and this failure to adjust often manifests itself in bodily symptoms or unusual attitudes of mind.

Broadly speaking these are the patterns of behavior which are loosely called "neurotic." The word unfortunately has acquired unsatisfactory overtones and in many people's eyes neuroticism and insanity are equated. In fact nothing could be further from the truth. Some degree of neuroticism is present in everybody—or at least everybody who leads an active physical or intellectual life and faces up to the fact that at no time is the world perfect or free from problems.

This Personal Analysis, which has been specially developed for *Understanding Yourself* by a consultant psychologist, allows you to undertake a frank assessment of the way in which you are responding to the complicated psychological, sociological and physiological stresses of modern living. The Analysis is based on a careful assessment of current clinical psychology. Nevertheless, it is intended as a guide *only* and not as a precise or comprehensive statement about your personality.

To achieve the most satisfactory result, you should obey the following simple rules:

1. Mark your choices on a separate sheet of paper so that you do not spoil the test for others, or influence them by your answers.

2. Answer each question as honestly as you possibly can. If you do not you will end up with a distorted and misleading picture of yourself.

3. Don't rush into the Analysis. Set aside a time when you can do it properly *on your own* and without discussing your answers or the questions with anyone else.

4. Don't rush through the Analysis, but on the other hand don't linger over it unduly. You should allow yourself a maximum of five minutes to complete it (not including scoring).

5. In many of the questions you will be asked to make a choice between a number of different views and attitudes. You may not find a perfect match on all occasions, but you must therefore pick the one that is *closest* to the way you feel on the subject.

6. Check your scoring carefully and don't peep at the score guide until you have completed the Analysis.

7. Do not administer the Analysis to anyone else. It is not suitable for this purpose and will give a misleading and inaccurate picture.

1. Try to imagine that you overhear two people whom you know very well talking about someone. After a while they say something which makes you realize that they are talking about you as what they say fits pretty closely with how you think other people see you. Which of the following statements is closest to the one that you "overheard"?

    a. "X" seems to be a pretty well-balanced person. Nothing much bothers him/her.

    b. I like "X" but I wish he/she wasn't so fussy and finicky.

    c. Poor "X" always seems to have something the matter with him/her!

    d. "X" is very moody, don't you think? I wish he/she was a bit easier to get on with.

    e. I simply don't understand "X." I wish I knew what made him/her tick.

2. Here's a question about your relationships with the opposite sex. Which of the following most commonly corresponds to your own case?

    a. I find it extremely easy to get on with members of the opposite sex and my love life is smooth and untroubled.

    b. I am quite unable to form a happy relationship with anyone of the opposite sex and I find this very worrying.

    c. On the whole I get on well with members of the opposite sex, but I have difficulties or upsets from time to time.

    d. Occasionally I get on well with men/women but most times it's not too easy.

    e. I lead an active love life but it's a very troubled and uncertain one.

    f. I cannot find any statement above that is anywhere near my own case.

3. Here are six statements. Show whether you strongly agree, agree, disagree, or strongly disagree with each.

    a. Politicians tend to be concerned with advancing themselves rather than helping ordinary people.

    b. Spare the rod and spoil the child may be an old-fashioned saying but there is certainly a good deal of truth in it.

    c. Most people who suffer from neuroses could benefit from more firmness and less sympathy.

    d. Homosexuality is basically wrong and is a matter for punishment rather than treatment.

    e. People who become alcoholics have only themselves to blame.

    f. An untidy house denotes an untidy mind.

4. Indicate which of the statements below most closely agrees with your overall picture of your attitude to life.

    a. I feel full of confidence about the future for most of the time.

    b. I'm pretty optimistic about things on the whole.

    c. Sometimes I feel optimistic, sometimes pessimistic about the way things are going to turn out.

    d. Occasionally I feel optimistic, but mostly I'm not too hopeful or happy about my future.

    e. The future looks pretty black to me most of the time.

5. Indicate the questions to which you answer yes.

    a. Are you having difficulty getting off to sleep at the moment?

    b. Do you tend to be troubled by "dizzy spells" or "shortness of breath"?

    c. Do you dislike the idea of foreign travel?

    d. Do you have what you feel to be an unreasonable fear of high places or open spaces?

    e. Do you often find yourself needing to cry?

    f. Do you dislike shyness in others?

    g. Do you have to check things that you do over and over again?

    h. Have you ever had the feeling that you are just about to "go to pieces" in your mind?

    i. Does the thought of being in a closed space like an elevator or a tunnel upset you?

    j. Do you tend to wake up unusually early in the mornings?

    k. Do you suffer from indigestion and upset stomach rather a lot?

l. Do crowds of people make you feel a bit panicky?

m. Are you interested in current affairs and politics?

n. Does life seem to you to be "too much effort"?

o. Do you often worry about mistakes you have made in the past?

p. Are you at your happiest when you are being kept really busy?

q. Have you been suffering from poor appetite recently?

r. Do you enjoy watching thrillers on TV?

s. Do you find it difficult to look at pictures of any creepy-crawly animal, spider or worm?

t. Do you get strange tingling or burning sensations in different parts of your body?

u. Does it worry you quite a lot if you see an untidy room or house?

v. Do you often have the feeling that you are going to faint?

w. Are you interested in crossword puzzles?

x. Are you really scared of heights?

y. Do you get unusually tired rather easily?

z. Do you suffer from palpitations or strong flutterings of the heart?

aa. Does the prospect of a journey or voyage of any kind unsettle you?

bb. Would you describe yourself as a person who worries a lot?

cc. Do you find that you get unusually annoyed if someone prevents you from doing something that you want to?

dd. Are you interested in athletics?

6. Here are some drugs that people take to help them when under stress of one kind or another. Say honestly whether you use them never, occasionally or regularly.

a. Aspirin or tranquilizers

b. Sleeping pills of any kind

c. Herbal tonics or medicine

d. Alcohol

Now turn to page 16 and check your scores.

Analysis

Table A: Total Score

0-10 This is a suspiciously low score. There could be two reasons for this—either you've misread the instructions or have made an error in your scoring in some way, or you have not been honest with yourself when filling out the questionnaire. In theory it would be just possible for someone to be so well-adjusted that he could produce the score as you have recorded, but he would certainly be leading a very dull and unchallenging life. Have a look at the questions again and try to be a bit franker with yourself this time.

11-25 This is the "normal" range of response. No human being is completely well-adjusted but the answers you have given reveal that you are striking a reasonably satisfactory balance between your personality and the stresses of the world around you. Some degree of irrational or "neurotic" behavior exists in everyone and in many ways helps to make their personality somewhat more interesting. You should look however at the distribution of your scores in the four personality strains A, B, C and D. If your score is fairly evenly drawn from each of the four personality strains then you are indeed "well-balanced." If the preponderance is within two strains, this will give you a clue as to those areas of your personality where the adjustment is somewhat less easy. A major contribution to your score coming from only one of the strains however denotes a more marked imbalance. To interpret this tendency see Table B.

26-45 No human being is totally free of emotional stress and most people compensate for this stress by a degree of irrational behavior. This irrational behavior is known as neurotic, and your score indicates that there is a measurable neurotic component to your psychological make-up. This in itself should not be a matter for worry but it does suggest that you do tend to be making rather heavy weather of life and some of its problems. This is largely a matter of personal adjustment and there is no known physical treatment, even assuming that you felt the need for one. Often such stresses as are reflected in your score are due to unresolved conflicts of a major kind—for example an unhappy married life, an unsatisfactory job, or financial troubles. But whatever the reason for it, you may gain some greater insight into your condition by looking at the relative balance of the four personality strains and these are further explained in Table B.

46-60 There's little doubt from your score that you lead an erratic and troubled emotional life. If you are young, say under 25, this could well be a passing phase brought on by the enormous stresses of the transition into adult life. If you are older it suggests that you are being faced with crises and conflicts which you are finding very hard to resolve. As long as these conflicts remain, the strong neurotic aspect of your character will also remain. It is important to realize however that neurotic responses do represent the fact that the individual is struggling to solve his problems. In that sense, therefore, your high score is nothing to be ashamed of. However, there's no doubt that life is giving you a bit of a hard time at the moment and there would be an obvious advantage to trying to resolve some of those conflicts. Perhaps It's not easy for you even to identify what they are. Have you a friend or member of your family that you can confide in? This often helps to highlight the route out of the problem. You should also look at the distribution of scores among the four personality strains (see Table B).

Over 60 This is an exceedingly high score by any standard and either you are passing through a highly critical time of your life, in which case the scores are probably inflated and will later decline, or you have been misscoring or misinterpreting the questionnaire. If after rechecking your scores you still retain the same high score then you should seriously set about trying to solve the problems which are obviously troubling you. A long chat with a close and trusted friend may help you to find out exactly what these are, and you might also consider seeing your family physician.

Table B: Individual Trait Scores
The four scores A, B, C and D represent four major personality traits. Each of these represents a method by which the individual attempts to deal with problems and difficulties in his life, which could be solved by "normal" means. The difficulty is that often the conflicts which bring about neurotic disturbance are unclear to the individual, and thus he is simply unable to take the correct steps to remove them.

Clinical psychologists recognize a large number of different "Neurotic strains," but for simplicity's sake we have grouped them in this questionnaire into four categories: Anxiety (A), Phobic (B), Obsessive (C) and Hysterical (D). Anxiety states tend to be dominated by feelings of depression and general uneasiness, Phobic states by irrational and unmeasurable fears, Obsessive states by a tendency towards a rigid personality and preoccupation with trivial detail, and Hysterical states by physical and psychological symptoms of one kind or another.

As a general guide to interpretation you can say that if your overall score is less than 25 and no individual trait score exceeds 15 your personality pattern in these areas can be described as normal. An individual score of over 15 does not at this level mean very much but it does give you a clear indication that any psychological stresses you experience will tend to be reflected in distortions in this particular area.

When overall scores lie between 25 and 40 there is again little to be said if the distribution is evenly balanced. Individual trait scores of over 15 are indicative of a particular strain and tension in that area whereas individual scores of over 20 in the case of Phobic, over 25 in the case of Anxiety and Hysteric and over 30 in the case of Obsessive suggest a marked imbalance in the way you cope with stress.

Much the same comments apply to those with higher total scores when of course any significant imbalance, for example an Obsessive score of over 30, would suggest that you are having very marked difficulties which are being compensated for to some degree by this obsessive behavior pattern. People with very high individual trait scores may well need to seek professional advice.

For those with lower total scores (and any individual score not more than half of the total) the following simple rules apply:

1. If moderate Anxiety score: Do the best you can (despite your inclinations) to mix with other people and engage in productive activities, such as hobbies or sport where possible.

2. If moderate Phobic score: Don't fight the phobias but merely try to avoid them. If they become severe seek professional guidance.

3. If moderate Obsessive score: Try to be a little less fussy and more tolerant of others; your intolerance is really intolerance of yourself.

4. If moderate Hysterical score: Try to realize that much of the troubles that appear to be affecting you are psychological in origin and will vanish if major conflicts in your life style can be resolved.

Scores

Add up your A, B, C and D scores separately, then add them together for your total score.

1. a. 0 b. 4C c. 4D d. 4A e. 0

2. a. 0 b. 3C c. 0 d. 3A e. 0 f. 3A

3.	Strongly agree	Agree	Disagree	Strongly disagree
a.	4D	2D	0	0
b.	4C	2C	0	2A
c.	4C	2C	0	2D
d.	4D	2D	0	0
e.	4C	2C	0	0
f.	4C	2C	0	2A

4. a. 0 b. 0 c. 2A d. 4A e. 6A

5. Scores are for yes answers only. a. 2C b. 2D c. 0 d. 4B e. 2A f. 0 g. 2C h. 2D i. 4B j. 2A k. 2D l. 4B m. 0 n. 2A o. 2C p. 2C q. 2A r. 0 s. 4B t. 2D u. 2C v. 2D w. 0 x. 4B y. 2A z. 2D aa. 4B bb. 2A cc. 2C dd. 0

6.	Never	Occasionally	Regularly
a.	0	1D	2D & 2A
b.	0	1C	2C & 2A
c.	0	1C	2C & 2A
d.	0	1C	2C & 2A

How Sexy Are You?

Camera Press

This questionnaire is less concerned with your attitudes and beliefs in sexual matters than with sexual practices and behavior. All human beings are equipped from birth with immensely powerful sex drives in order to ensure the survival of mankind as a species. The tremendous pleasure which most people experience from sexual intercourse is, in evolutionary terms, the bait which lures us into what would otherwise be something of a nuisance—the birth, feeding, care and upbringing of children. In physiological terms sexual behavior patterns are instinctive and automatic and, as Freud was the first to point out, spring into action from the moment of birth when the child blindly seeks gratification at the mother's breast. Mating patterns, including the full reproductive sex act, are also instinctive: animals brought up in isolation from others, and therefore, never having the opportunity to observe mating, still show normal sexual behavior when they mature.

But cultural factors are important in modifying these inbuilt behavior patterns, changing them according to social and cultural circumstances. Legal and moral taboos, for example, prohibit the sex act between brother and sister or mother and son. In most societies homosexuality is also frowned on and sometimes legislated against, as is rape, sexual intercourse with minors, and so on. Within any human society, sexual habits tend to vary considerably yet still be described as "normal" within that society.

This questionnaire explores your own sexual behavior within this dimension of "normality." As usual do your best to be totally truthful and score always what you *believe to be true in your case* rather than what you think you "ought" to score. Three dimensions of sexual life are represented in this questionnaire, and these will be explained to you *after* you have completed it.

Mark your answers on a separate sheet.
Read each of the following statements and check either "Yes" or "No" on a separate answer sheet according to whether you tend to agree or disagree with it. If you feel yourself in a bit of doubt, force yourself to decide whether *yes* or *no* is more applicable in your case.

1. The opposite sex will respect you more if you are not too familiar with them.

2. Sex without love is highly unsatisfactory.

3. All in all I am satisfied with my sex life.

4. Everything has to be "just right" before I can get sexually excited.

5. I do not feel that I am deprived sexually.

6. I do not need to respect or love a sexual partner in order to enjoy intercourse with him or her.

7. If I love a person I could do anything with them.

8. I know that I am sexually very attractive.

9. I have very many friends of the opposite sex.

10. It doesn't take much to get me excited sexually.

11. Sex contacts have never been a problem to me.

12. I would like to take part in a sex orgy.

13. I feel there is something lacking in my sex life.

14. I enjoy having sexual intercourse with a partner of a different skin color or racial background.

15. I have strong feelings but when I get a chance I can't seem to express myself.

16. A woman should sometimes take the dominant role or be sexually aggressive.

17. I believe in taking my pleasures where I find them.

18. My sex behavior often causes me unhappiness.

19. Young people should be allowed to behave more or less as they please regarding sexual matters.

20. My love life is just great.

21. I have never been involved with more than one sex affair at the same time.

22. Sex should be used only for the purpose of reproduction, not for personal pleasure.

23. I prefer to have intercourse under the bedcovers and with the light off.

24. I deliberately try to keep sex out of my mind.

25. It is alright to seduce a person who is old enough to know what they are doing.

26. I only get sexually aroused at night; not in the day.

27. My parents' influence did not inhibit me sexually.

28. Intercourse should not take place outside marriage.

29. I make lots of vocal noises during intercourse.

30. My religious beliefs are against sex.

31. I have had a number of both homosexual and heterosexual relationships.

32. There are some things I only do because they please my sex partner.

33. I wouldn't change my sex life in any significant way.
34. I would not enjoy watching my usual partner having intercourse with someone else.
35. I always know for sure when I have had an orgasm.
36. My sex partner does not satisfy all my physical needs.
37. I would never vote for a law permitting polygamy.
38. Being good in bed is very important in my partner.
39. Sex is not all that important to me.
40. I would like to have a new sex partner every night.
41. I don't enjoy a lot of precoital love play.
42. I find it difficult to tell my sex partner what I like or I don't like about love-making.
43. Sex is more exciting with a stranger.
44. To me physical factors in my sex partner are more important than psychological ones.
45. I would like my sex partner to be more expert.
46. I would never dream of taking part in group sex.
47. I sometimes feel like scratching or biting my partner during intercourse.
48. No one has ever completely satisfied me sexually.
49. Illicit relationships do not excite me.
50. I believe my sexual activities are average.
51. Romantic love is just childish illusion.
52. I can't stand people touching me.
53. I feel sexually less competent than my friends.
54. I would be bothered if my sex partner had sexual relations with someone else.
55. Physical sex is the most important part of marriage.
56. I am a bit afraid of sexual relationships.
57. I don't like to try different positions in love-making.
58. The need for birth control upsets my love-making because it makes everything so cold-blooded.
59. Physical attraction is not important to me.
60. I love physical contacts with the opposite sex.

Now turn to page 20 and check your scores.

Analysis

YOUR P RATING

0P to 5P This represents an average rating, which suggests that you are not in any sense of the word a promiscuous person, although you have a normal person's interest in the realities of sex and appreciate that it would be a peculiar person indeed who did not at sometime in his or her life feel a sexual attraction to more than one individual at any one time. If your score lies in this range and you also have a C rating greater than 2, the chances are that you are either happily married, or in the midst of a stable and satisfying relationship with someone you feel very close to.

6P to 10P Your sexual behavior is not far from average, though you have a slight but perfectly normal tendency to sexual adventuring. If you are under the age of 30 this is no more than characteristic human behavior, and if it is coupled with a C rating of greater than 4, you are probably enjoying a balanced and contented love life.

11P to 15P There's not much doubt that you have a promiscuous nature and the chances are that as a result you find your love life in a bit of a tangle. This may not upset you too much, and if you are scoring above 5 on the C rating, then there is not much doubt that you are enjoying yourself. If you have only a middling C rating, or one with some minuses in it, however, then it is very likely that your free and easy approach to sex is bringing domestic or personal problems with it.

Over 15P You have a decidedly promiscuous nature. Possibly this is the first flush of youth, and if you have a C rating of 6 or more then you have really nothing to complain about. It may be however that other people are suffering because of your exceedingly casual approach to sex, and this is almost certainly the case if your C score is in the low plusses or in the minuses. If it is in the high minuses, then your promiscuity might be a flight from something and may lead to conflict.

YOUR C RATING

7C to 10C Congratulations on having what is almost certainly a balanced and contented love life. Long may it remain so. The chances are that this is coupled with a relatively low P rating (say under 10) and very likely a plus rather than minus S rating. If your wife, husband or lover has filled out this questionnaire too he or she is likely to have come out with a rather similar score.

3C to 6C These denote a high measure of contentment in one's sex life, which at any age is a bonus to life happiness in general. Like all human pleasures, sex is never 100 percent perfect, but your rating suggests that you have learnt to accept these imperfections.

−2C to 2C Perhaps this is best described as an average score, suggesting that your love life is on the whole happy, though sprinkled occasionally with difficulties and small disappointments. Very possibly you move from moments of ecstasy to moments of relative indifference in your love-making, and this may be part of your nature and unlikely to change as the result of any conscious efforts on your part. A more passionate lover might stir things up a bit, but if you have a high P rating and also a high S rating the chances are that you have tried this without success. This may not

be particularly useful advice if you are already married, except to say that perhaps you could persuade your husband or wife to return to the passion of the past.

−3C to −6C Clearly there is some measure of disappointment and dissatisfaction in your love life. This could be due to a large number of reasons of which you are probably yourself aware. If you have a high P rating as well then it may be that you are seeking sexual contentment in the wrong way—through a series of whizzbang affairs which come to nothing and are in the long run deeply unsatisfying. If your low score is also coupled with a low S score (say less than minus-2) then the problem may be that you are a bit inhibited and disinclined to let go of your emotions. If you are married or have a lover the best tactic by far will be to talk over your dissatisfaction in as open a way as you can.

−7C to −10C It is quite evident that you are leading a disappointing love life, perhaps to the extent that it is overflowing to make the rest of your life a bit unsatisfactory as well. There are so many possible reasons for this that one cannot offer specific advice, but if you are married you should certainly talk about this immediately and quite openly with your partner. The problem may be one of inhibition (do you have a low S rating as well?) or of sheer incompatibility and boredom—this may be reflected in a high P rating as well. Perhaps also you are trying too hard, for it is certainly true that contentment in love comes naturally and not at anyone's command. If your life is being made unhappy through disappointing love relationships, then you might consider seeking qualified medical or psychological advice.

YOUR S RATING

5S to 10S This denotes that you have a strongly developed nature which makes the physical side of love-making tremendously important to you. There are clearly no traces of sexual inhibition in your nature, and if this is coupled with a high C rating (say over 4) then you have probably found yourself a perfect partner as well. It would be rather surprising if these high scores are also coupled with a very high P rating, unless you are a young person just experiencing the first joys of sex. If you do have high scores on all three ratings then love may well be the most important aspect of your life. Fine, as long as you still find time and emotional energy for other things.

4S to −4S Most people will find themselves falling into this category, and scores in this range will almost invariably be coupled with plus C scores and P ratings no higher than 15. If your S score lies between 1 and 4, then you have a healthy appreciation of the physical side of love; if between 0 and minus-4 you may be a bit on the inhibited side. If you have an inhibited partner too then this will be reflected in a C score in the minuses rather than in the plusses.

−5S to −10S In physical terms you are a cool person and are not likely to be described as a passionate lover —unless you happen to meet exactly the right partner for you! Very likely there is some psychological inhibition here, possibly because when you were younger you were taught to believe that sex was improper and immoral. It is not easy to overcome such prejudices from the past, but the first step might be to realize that without love and sex (two of the most important drives), the human race would soon cease to exist.

Scores

	Agree	Disagree			Agree	Disagree
1.	−1S	0		31.	1P	0
2.	0	1P		32.	−1S	0
3.	1C	0		33.	1C	0
4.	−1S	0		34.	0	1P
5.	1C	0		35.	0	−1S
6.	1P	0		36.	0	1C
7.	1S	0		37.	0	1P
8.	1P	0		38.	1S	0
9.	1P	0		39.	−1C	0
10.	1S	0		40.	1P	0
11.	1C	0		41.	0	1S
12.	1P	0		42.	0	1C
13.	−1C	0		43.	1P	0
14.	1P	0		44.	0	−1S
15.	−1C	0		45.	−1C	0
16.	0	−1S		46.	0	1P
17.	1P	0		47.	1S	0
18.	0	1C		48.	−1C	0
19.	1P	0		49.	0	1P
20.	1C	0		50.	1C	0
21.	0	1P		51.	1P	0
22.	−1S	0		52.	−1S	0
23.	−1S	0		53.	−1C	0
24.	−1C	0		54.	0	1P
25.	1P	0		55.	1S	0
26.	−1S	0		56.	0	1C
27.	0	−1C		57.	0	1S
28.	0	1P		58.	−1C	0
29.	1S	0		59.	0	1S
30.	−1C	0		60.	1S	0

Evaluating Your Score

Three dimensions of your sexual behavior are marked by the letters P, S and C. Add up all the P points you score, and next all the S and C points. Then from your S and C totals subtract all the minus-S and minus-C points. For example, if you collect 5C points and 3 minus-C points, your score will be 2C.

This questionnaire allows you to evaluate your sex life and behavior along three important dimensions: Promiscuity, Contentment and Sensuality (P, C and S) which are considered by psychologists to be important aspects of an individual's sex life.

Remember, when you assess your score, that there is nothing "right" or "wrong" about any score you achieve —this merely gives you an indication of what kind of person you are in the important field of sexual relationships. An extreme score will simply mean that you are not characteristic of the *majority* of other people in this respect. It does not mean that you are bad, good, moral or immoral, mentally balanced or unbalanced.

On the whole, the higher your P score the more promiscuous a person you are—the more likely you are to be involved in large numbers of sexual relationships. Bear in mind however that while this means you are leading an *active* sex life, it does not necessarily imply that you are particularly *happy* with this. Often a high

level of promiscuity brings more problems with it than pleasures in the long run!

The C, or contentment, scale gives a closer picture of whether your love life is a happy and satisfactory one. Most people will end up with a lowish C score (whether on the plus or minus side) and it is fair to say that those scoring very high in Cs really are having a satisfactory love life, while those with high minus-Cs are certainly disappointed or discontented.

The S score refers to the dimension of sensuality, a term in some ways exchangeable with "sexiness," but which all in all is probably related to the individual's interest in the purely physical side of sex. Of course sexual intercourse is impossible without a strong physical component, but psychological factors are important as well. People vary in the amount of weight that they attach to the physical and psychological aspects, and those with a high S score tend to find the former dominant in their lives, while the opposite is true for those with a high minus-S score. For more specific information on how you rate, look at the detailed comments on page 19. You will end up with three scores of course, which may all be high, all low or a balance between them. There are no hard and fast rules as to how to interpret the combination of scores: the best person to do this is yourself.

How Popular Are You?

Marshall Cavendish

In our society human beings are taught that one of the most important requirements in life is that one should be liked. We like people to smile welcomingly when they see us; we like to hear people say flattering things about us; we like to be admired, loved, desired, wanted.

But people differ in their need for popularity and admiration. And often those who need it most of all are those who simply do not know the technique for getting it. On the other side of the coin, there are those who really prefer their own company and yet find themselves very much in social demand. It would be simple, and very satisfactory, if one could lay down a set of rules which would tell everyone how to achieve popularity precisely to the extent that they require it but, unfortunately, no single type of behavior or single aspect of personality *guarantees* popularity.

What do you believe is the real essence of popularity? Is it simply to be the life and soul of the party? Or would you say that you are more likely to be popular if you are consistently thoughtful and considerate? This questionnaire, provided that you answer it as accurately and honestly as you can, may help you to work out what kind of popularity *you* want. It may also help you to find out how far you have achieved it.

Mark your answers on a separate sheet.

1. When you go on holiday, do you
   a. Usually make friends easily?
   b. Prefer to spend time alone, or with the person accompanying you?
   c. Have the wish to make friends but find it difficult?

2. You have made an arrangement to meet a friend, but you are very tired. When you try to call and explain, there is no reply. Would you
   a. Not turn up, hoping that he will understand?
   b. Turn up and try to enjoy yourself?
   c. Turn up to ask if he minds if you go home early?

3. Which statement is true for you?
   a. I accept every invitation I get.
   b. I am choosey about invitations and only accept if I am sure I will have a good time.
   c. I only accept invitations from old friends or family.

4. A guest who came for two days has stayed for ten, and you are longing for him to go. Would you
   a. Ask him to go directly?
   b. Invent another guest, or work to be done, as a pretext for getting rid of him?
   c. Be a bit frosty and hope he will take the hint?

5. How long do you usually keep your friends?
   a. Years mostly.
   b. It varies a lot; if you still have something in common, it can be for years.
   c. Not long as a rule, you keep moving on.

6. An old acquaintance, who can be relied on to drink all your liquor without ever replacing it, is dropping over. This time you are determined not to let him get away with it again. Would you
   a. Hide the bottles?
   b. Say, "Fine, how about bringing a bottle"?
   c. Tell him you are not going to be home?

7. A friend tells you of a highly interesting personal problem. Would you
   a. Long to tell someone else, but try to resist?
   b. Treat it as confidential and not even consider passing it on?
   c. Call up someone else to discuss it as soon as the first friend had left?

8. When you have a problem, do you
   a. Usually feel able to cope by yourself?
   b. Turn to friends you can rely on?
   c. Only turn to your friends if it is really bad?

9. Have you considered joining a dating service, marriage bureau or any kind of club providing introductions to other people?
   a. No, your pride could not take it.
   b. No, you have never been lonely enough.
   c. Yes, it seems a good idea.

10. If you were asked to sing, or join in some game, at a party, would you
    a. Make an excuse to get out of it?
    b. Join in with relish?

c. Simply refuse outright?

11. When you feel anxious or depressed, do you
a. Find that you cannot help being irritable with others around you?
b. Tell your friends that you feel lousy?
c. Manage to cover up?

12. When a group of friends plays a practical joke on you, do you
a. Join in the laughter?
b. Feel angry and show it?
c. Possibly either a or b, depending on your mood and the circumstances?

13. Your new boss (or your husband's), a rather aloof man, invites you to dinner at his place. Would you
a. Go feeling nervous and timid?
b. Go determined to make a good impression?
c. Go expecting to have a good time?

14. When your friends have problems, do you find
a. That they come to you for help?
b. That only those close to you come for help?
c. That they do not tend to bother you for help?

15. Last time you had friends over to your place, was it
a. Because you find them entertaining and interesting to be with?
b. Because they like you?
c. Because you thought you had to?

16. An old friend is going out with a new man and asks your opinion of her dress. You think she has made a big mistake. Would you
a. Tell her straight?
b. Say "You look fine" in an unenthusiastic way?
c. Suggest a constructive change?

17. How do you usually make friends?
a. Through people you already know.
b. From all kinds of encounters.
c. Only after a long time and with some difficulty.

18. Which of these qualities do you think is most important in a friend?
a. The ability to make you feel happy.
b. Reliability.
c. Interest in you.

19. When you are with someone you dislike, do you
a. Manage to be friendly and polite?
b. Just about manage to be polite?
c. Show coldness or dislike, unless there is a pressing reason for concealment?

20. Which statement is true for you?
a. I can usually make people laugh.
b. I usually make people think.
c. People seem to feel comfortable with me.

21. Do you welcome people to your place
a. Only when you have made a specific arrangement?
b. Any time they want to come?

c. Only when you feel the need for company?

22. How often do you get in touch with friends who live a long way off?
a. Once a year, at Christmas or some other special occasion,
b. Whenever they get in touch with you.
c. Quite often—whenever you feel like it.

23. Which statement is true for you?
a. I usually wait for friends to call me before seeing them.
b. If I want to see my friends I call them and don't worry about whether it is my "turn" or not.
c. I do not usually take the initiative in contacting friends unless I have a particular reason to do so.

24. Which is true for you?
a. I like to praise my friends as much as possible.
b. I believe in honesty, so I sometimes have to make negative comments to my friends.
c. I do not really either flatter or criticize my friends.

25. Do you find
a. That generally you can get on with almost anyone?
b. That sometimes you would like to get on with someone who is unresponsive to you?
c. That you only get on well with people who share your interests?

26. Which would you prefer to be?
a. An interesting person who knows a lot about many varied things.
b. A person who makes life fun.
c. A warm and sympathetic person.

27. Would you prefer to spend an evening
a. Giving a dinner party?
b. Going to someone else's dinner party?
c. Reading a good book?

28. Which statement is true for you?
a. I always put my family before my social life.
b. My family is my social life.
c. My friends are as important to me, sometimes, as my close family.

29. Which statement is most true for you? (Answer this question as honestly as you can.)
a. I am a tactful person in general.
b. I seem to find myself saying the wrong thing rather a lot of the time.
c. I occasionally upset people when they misunderstand what I say.

30. How do you feel about others depending on you?
a. Fine, I like to be the kind of person who can be dependable.
b. A bit wary, I would prefer to keep clear of some responsibilities.
c. Up to a point I do not mind, but I like a certain amount of independence in my friends.

Now turn to page 23 and check your scores.

Scores

(Total your scores to find your analysis below.)

1. a. 3	b. 2	c. 1
2. a. 1	b. 3	c. 2
3. a. 3	b. 2	c. 1
4. a. 1	b. 2	c. 3
5. a. 3	b. 2	c. 1
6. a. 2	b. 3	c. 1
7. a. 2	b. 3	c. 1
8. a. 1	b. 2	c. 3
9. a. 1	b. 2	c. 3
10. a. 2	b. 3	c. 1
11. a. 1	b. 2	c. 3
12. a. 3	b. 1	c. 2
13. a. 1	b. 2	c. 3
14. a. 3	b. 2	c. 1
15. a. 3	b. 2	c. 1
16. a. 2	b. 1	c. 3
17. a. 2	b. 3	c. 1
18. a. 3	b. 2	c. 1
19. a. 3	b. 2	c. 1
20. a. 2	b. 1	c. 3
21. a. 1	b. 3	c. 2
22. a. 2	b. 1	c. 3
23. a. 1	b. 3	c. 2
24. a. 3	b. 1	c. 2
25. a. 3	b. 2	c. 1
26. a. 1	b. 3	c. 2
27. a. 3	b. 2	c. 1
28. a. 2	b. 1	c. 3
29. a. 3	b. 1	c. 2
30. a. 3	b. 1	c. 2

For a rough guide and answer to the question "How Popular are You?" mark your level on the Popularity Thermometer over the page and read off the comment that applies to your popularity rating. Then get your friends and family to mark theirs, and see if you all agree with the results shown on the thermometer!

But as you compare your scores, bear in mind that the thermometer does not take account of the fact that some people *prefer* to be solitary. For a more detailed discussion of your individual score, refer to the analysis below.

Analysis

71–90

You enjoy having people around you, and get a good deal of fun out of life. You are probably popular with a wide circle of friends, though you may avoid more intimate relationships. Are you sociable and gregarious, or do you need others to establish your own identity? Only you can tell. Perhaps you could combine more attention to close friends with your outgoing acceptance of larger numbers of more superficial acquaintances.

51–70

Does your popularity fluctuate? It could be that, while you want to be liked, you try too hard and others are not always relaxed in your company. Your choice of friends could be motivated by ambition, or social aspirations; if this is true, are you missing out on the company of people you would really like?

30–50

You may be a rather solitary person. This does not mean that you are not popular; you prefer the good opinion of a small number of people you respect to the admiration of many acquaintances. Popularity in the usual sense of the word may not interest you, but if it does, you need to revise your relationships with those outside your usual circle; they may have more to offer than you suspect.

Marshall Cavendish

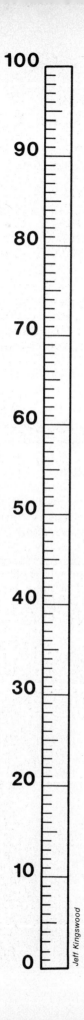

Popularity
Thermometer

You are almost at boiling point on the popularity gauge. Strangely enough you may be so popular that you wish people would cool down a bit!

You are a really popular person, almost certainly because you have a naturally easy way with people.

You are a popular person. You will have lots of friends and you very likely enjoy their company as much as they enjoy yours.

You are probably not the life and soul of the party but on the whole people like you.

You are less popular than you would like to be, almost certainly. There is possibly just one thing keeping you out in the cold. Bad temper? Tend to be a bore? Have a good think about it.

You are not a very popular person. There may be all kinds of reasons for this and you should try to find out what they are. It is warmer and nicer further up the scale!

When the thermometer falls below 30° it's too cold for comfort. Check your score once more: no one can be that unpopular!

How Brave Are You?

Everyone experiences fear to some degree or another —any animal or human being which was incapable of the emotion would not survive long in what is essentially a hostile and dangerous world. However there are marked differences in the degree to which people respond to "fearful" situations, and psychologists also often distinguish between appropriate and inappropriate fear responses. These responses can, broadly speaking, be broken down into "rational" or "irrational" varieties. This questionnaire, if you answer it honestly and objectively, will give you some idea of how fearful a person you are: it will also reveal whether your fears tend to be biased towards the rational or irrational—the real or the imagined.

To get the best results from this questionnaire you should go through it in one sitting, answering as honestly and quickly as you reasonably can and *not* spending a great deal of time trying to "work out" what the questions are trying to get at. You should also do the questionnaire on your own, mark your answers on a separate sheet of paper, and not discuss them with anyone else. Needless to say, do not examine the score sheet until you have completely finished the questionnaire. You may find the scoring a little complicated so you will need a pencil and paper handy.

Mark your answers on a separate sheet.

For Questions 1-10, indicate whether you would be seriously frightened, frightened, neutral, pleasurably thrilled, or definitely thrilled by each of the situations.

1. You are being driven in a sports car by a friend whom you know to be a reckless driver. Suddenly he sees someone he knows in another car and they agree to have a race.

2. You are just setting out for a ride on the biggest and fastest roller coaster in the world.

3. A friend whom you know to be a top-notch pilot and keen on aerobatics offers you a ride in his own light airplane.

4. You are staying overnight in a hotel and there is a fire alarm. The fire itself is not threatening you, but you are ordered to evacuate from your sixth-story window by a fire engine ladder.

Popperfoto

5. You are riding home late at night in a train in an empty car. Just as the train begins to pull out of the station an unpleasant looking man, who is very obviously drunk, gets in.

6. You are given the opportunity to have a ride in a midget submarine.

7. For a bet you have agreed to spend the night on your own in a wax museum. Your bed has been set up in the dimly-lit chamber of horrors.

8. You are walking on your own on a beach. You suddenly realize that the tide has cut you off in a cove which is obviously going to be completely covered when the tide is full.

9. Your car has broken down in the country near a large private house. You walk up the driveway to ask for help and you see a large dog coming towards you.

10. Your doctor tells you that you must go into the hospital for an operation. The operation is not risky in itself but it is essential.

11. When you were a child were you particularly "scared of the dark"?

12. Are you still scared of the dark?

13. Do you find the following things very frightening, slightly frightening, or not at all frightening?
a. Thunderstorms
b. Snakes
c. Ladders
d. Fire
e. The sea
f. Knives
g. Blood
h. Bridges
i. Tunnels
j. Elevators
k. Rowing boats
l. Forests
m. Cats
n. Spiders
o. Moths
p. Motorcycles
q. Fireworks
r. Zoos
s. Crowds
t. Bats

14. If you had the opportunity to attend a séance at which a genuine attempt would be made to conjure up spirits from the dead, would you attend?

15. Would you take a ride in an untethered balloon if you had the opportunity?

16. If you were offered the opportunity for a guided tour of a really deep mine would you take it?

17. Would you like to learn a "dangerous sport," such as sky-diving, motor racing, or shark hunting?

18. Do you find the idea of standing in the center of a wide open space unsettling?

19. If you look out of the window of a really tall building do you feel a little uneasy?

20. Would you mind if you were called upon to give a public speech?

21. Do you feel nervous at the thought of having to take an exam or test of any kind?

Now turn to page 27 and check your scores.

Analysis

R (Rational) SCORE

All human beings are fearful to some degree and if they were not they would not survive very long. The R score which you have arrived at gives an index of the degree of rational fear that is built into your makeup.

Over —20 This is an extraordinary score, and the chances are that you have arrived at this by not marking the questionnaire properly or misinterpreting results in some way. Check your answers again, for a score of this kind would imply that you were too reckless for your own safety!

—16 to —20 The questionnaire reveals that as a person you are rash to the point of being somewhat irresponsible. This is fair enough, as long as it is only yourself that you put at risk. Try to remember, however, that people like yourself may be able to do all kinds of frightening things without turning a hair—and yet seriously scare other people by doing so.

—11 to —15 There is little doubt that one of the marked characteristics of your personality is a streak of daring. It would be surprising if it has not already involved you in one or two complications of a mild kind, for your daring will border on rashness occasionally. Provided that you bear this in mind, you should be able to steer clear of trouble.

—6 to —10 On the whole this is fairly close to the normal range of reaction, but in your case the balance tips slightly towards the fearless, or perhaps one should say the daring. This is nothing to worry about for risk taking (in moderation) is part of life.

—5 to 5 This is the "normal" range of response and indicates that you have a balanced and satisfactory approach to the genuinely frightening aspects of the world around you. You are sensitive to danger but not obsessed with it, and you are able to keep in a proper perspective the things that threaten you.

6 to 10 This is not far outside the "normal" range and on the whole you show a reasonable balance. There is a basic timidity about you—not strong but enough to make you draw back slightly where most people would go ahead.

11 to 15 There is not much doubt that you are the nervous type. Time and time again your answers denote that you will withdraw from a threatening situation more rapidly than most other people. This facet of nervousness or timidity is sufficiently strong for you to have always been aware of it in yourself, though you may have been able to disguise it from your friends.

16 to 20 Your answers to the questionnaire reveal that on the whole you are a fearful and indeed perhaps overcautious person. It would be surprising if you did not find that this hyper-nervous side to your personality interfered to some degree with your social life and perhaps even with your work. If this high score also correlates with a high i score, you will be seriously handicapped. If your i score is low, however, you could probably conquer the "rationally nervous" side of your nature with will power and help from a close friend.

Over 20 This score is so extreme that you probably have not marked the questionnaire properly, but if your score *is* as high as this then you may well be passing through an upsetting and troublesome period in your life and should consider seeking professional medical or psychological advice.

i (irrational) SCORE

No fear is absolutely irrational, for all fears have their roots somewhere in the past. Many phobic responses are amplified versions of instinctive behavior patterns which appear inappropriately and handicap individuals in their daily lives. Other phobias, or "irrational" fears, may have their origins in the traumatic experiences in childhood. Such fears which relate to the *past* and handicap people unconsciously in the *present* can be a big nuisance. Your i score tells you how much your personality is biased towards irrational fear.

0 If you have really scored zero on the i scale, you are so well balanced that it is remarkable! Human beings with literally no phobic tendencies are very rare indeed. Congratulations if you have come out with a zero score—but are you sure that you answered the questionnaire honestly and accurately?

1 to 5 You have slight phobic tendencies but absolutely at the "normal" level of human response. If you want to know how to get rid of the irrational fear that you have, the answer is that there is probably not much you can do about it. It certainly will not be marked enough to interfere with your life.

6 to 10 You have slightly more phobic tendencies than most people. Whether this matters or not depends entirely upon whether you feel that your life is affected by them in any way. If you picked up this relatively high score by collecting a few low i scores here and there then you probably will not be troubled. If the i scores were concentrated, however, then you might find that some aspects of your life are interfered with.

11 to 15 You have at least one fairly marked and definite phobia. It is very likely that this is an active nuisance to you in some particular aspect of your life. If not, it means that you are somehow able to avoid the fear-causing situation. Phobias can be treated, and if you do find yours a real nuisance you can seek professional advice from your doctor.

16 to 25 You seem to have more than your fair share of phobias and irrational fears. If these are troubling you and you have not been able to get any advice or help up to now, you should certainly have a talk with your family doctor. There are organizations which help people

suffering from certain phobias and he may be able to advise you on how to contact them.

Over 25 This is such a high score that you have either a seriously phobic personality or are passing through a difficult and stressful time. The most probable explanation of this score, however, is that you have made an error in answering the questionnaire or marking it.

Scores

As you check your answers against the score sheet you will note that you accumulate R (Rational) scores and i (irrational) scores. The R scores may have plus or minus values. Total up your R and i scores separately, subtracting any minus —Rs you have collected from any Rs. You should arrive at some total between about —25R and 25R. Your i score should total between 0 and 25, or thereabouts.

	Seriously frightened	Frightened	Neutral	Pleasurably thrilled	Definitely thrilled
1.	2R	1R	0	—2R	—4R
2.	5R	2R	0	—1R	—2R
3.	3i	1i	—1R	—2R	—3R
4.	5R	3R	—1R	—2R	—3R
5.	3R	2R	—1R	—3R	—5R
6.	5i	3i	0	—1R	—3R
7.	5R	3R	—1R	—3R	—5R
8.	1R	0	—2R	—3R	—5R
9.	1i	2R	0	0	0
10.	1i	2R	—1R	0	0

11. Yes 0   No —3R
12. Yes 3i   No 0

13.	Very	Slightly	Not at all
a.	3i	0	—2R
b.	2i	0	—1R
c.	3i	1R	0
d.	3i	0	0
e.	3i	0	0
f.	1i	0	0
g.	3i	0	—1R
h.	5i	2i	0
i.	3i	0	0
j.	5i	1i	0
k.	5i	3i	0
l.	3R	0	—2R
m.	5i	1i	0
n.	2i	0	0
o.	5i	1i	0
p.	3R	1R	—2R
q.	1R	0	—2R
r.	5i	2i	0
s.	2i	0	0
t.	3i	0	0

14. Yes —2R   No 2R
15. Yes —2R   No 1i
16. Yes —1R   No 2i
17. Yes —2R   No 2R
18. Yes 3i   No 0
19. Yes 0   No —2R
20. Yes 0   No —2R
21. Yes 0   No —2R

How Healthy a Life Do You Lead?
Part I

Marshall Cavendish

This two-part questionnaire "How Healthy a Life Do You Lead?" explores one of the most important – perhaps the most important – aspects of man's life: his adjustment to his environment, to his work, to the people he lives with and to his own inherited physical and mental capabilities. The trouble is that when people speak of good health they always assume it to be sheer physical fitness – the sunburned, muscular figure is the focal point of much of our society's self-expression, both in the fictional world of TV, movies and magazines, and the commercial world of advertising.

But true good health, as psychologists and physicians have realized for decades, perhaps even centuries, is the sum of a variety of features of which physical vitality is but one. The two parts of the questionnaire are designed to build up a profile of how healthy you really are, as expressed in terms of eight key factors. These factors and their relationship to each other will be explained when you come to analyze your scores at the end of Part II. It is important to remember that the tests are in no way a substitute for a physical checkup by a doctor, and a high score on the tests should not lead you to be incautious about your physical health or neglect medical advice or treatment. They will, however, give you a really interesting and informative picture of the balance of these factors in your case – a useful guide to how healthy a life you lead. As usual, you must answer the questions honestly to get any real value from the tests, refrain from peeping at the scoresheet before finishing, and, if possible, do the questionnaire on your own without discussing the results with anyone afterwards.

Mark your answers on a separate sheet.

1. Do you take sugar in your coffee or tea?

2. Do you take more than two spoonfuls?

3. Do you regularly take aspirin and nonprescription painkillers more than once a week? (Women exclude painkillers for period pains.)

4. Do you play, on a regular basis (more than twice a month), any active competitive sport such as tennis, squash, football (but not including golf)?

5. If yes, do you play more than once a week?

6. If you are a cigarette smoker do you have a morning cough? (Nonsmokers score "No.")

7. Do you use, even occasionally, any illegal drug such as marijuana?

8. Do you tend to bolt your food?

9. Do you walk or jog a minimum of a mile every day? (Include golf, but not walking around the house or office.)

10. Do you drink (including tea and coffee) at least 3 pints of fluid a day?

11. When suffering from relatively minor illnesses and infections, do you go to the doctor for antibiotics or other medication as a matter of course rather than try to "ride it out" on your own?

12. Do your eating habits frequently give you painful indigestion?

13. If you own a bicycle, do you use it whenever you can? (If you have no bicycle, answer "No.")

14. Do you find yourself frequently nibbling snacks or chocolates between meals?

15. Are you constantly finding that you have to squeeze yourself into clothes?

16. Do you have to use pills of any kind to help you sleep?

17. Does your diet include regular helpings of salads and fresh vegetables?

18. Do you make a point of regularly visting your doctor and dentist for checkups – say once a year?

19. Do you tend to skip meals because "you are busy" and substitute filling snacks?

20. Has anyone ever said to you that you drink too much?

21. Do you feel that you could, with just a little practice, take up a really strenuous sport such as mountaineering, long distance running or competitive swimming? (Answer "Yes" if you already do so.)

22. When eating out at restaurants or with friends do you frequently end up feeling rather overfull?

23. Do you tend to have a definite weakness for sweet, sticky foods?

24. Do you smoke?

25. Do you regularly smoke more than a pack a day or its equivalent in pipe tobacco?

26. Do you do regular daily exercises (including exercise machines at home)?

27. If you stand in front of a mirror without clothes on, do you notice definite areas of excess fat?

28. Do you find it a real strain to carry bags or heavy parcels upstairs?

29. Do you drink alcohol regularly?

30. Do you ever drink enough alcohol to give you unpleasant side effects of any kind?

31. Do you tend to keep very late hours, even when you feel physically tired and fatigued?

32. Do you have any false teeth, other than crowns or cosmetic replacements?

33. Do you have fresh fruit or fruit juice (not canned) at least once a day?

34. Do you regularly use tranquilizers or antidepressant drugs as prescribed by your doctor?

35. Do people tend to comment spontaneously on "how well you look"?

36. Do you swim regularly (say at least twice a week in the summer months, or at other times when you have the opportunity)?

37. Do you avoid, wherever possible, fatty foods such as French fries?

38. If you are a smoker, do you feel uneasy if you do not have cigarettes always to hand or if you find yourself in a place where you cannot smoke? (Nonsmokers score "No" for this question.)

39. If you take regular exercise, have you been doing so for at least the last two years?

40. Do you allow clothing styles or fashions to interfere with your physical comfort significantly – for example, uncomfortable shoes or clothing unsuitable for the weather?

41. Do you regularly eat more than two cooked meals in the day?

42. Do you plan your own or your family's meals so as to make sure that you or they have a balanced diet?

43. Is your weight within 10 pounds of that recommended for your build? (If you do not know, answer "No.")

44. Do you weigh more than 20 pounds over the recommended average?

45. Do you find yourself taking a car for short journeys when you could just as easily have walked?

46. Do you receive prescription medicines on a regular basis from your doctor?

47. Do you spread butter liberally on toast or pastries?

48. Would you honestly describe yourself as a physically lazy person?

49. Do you brush your teeth properly and vigorously at least twice a day?

50. Do you walk or jog over two miles regularly each day? (Include golf, but not walking around the house or office.)

51. Do you *regularly* take alcohol (even a glass of beer) at lunchtime?

52. Do you tend to eat out more than you eat at home?

53. Do you find yourself short of breath after climbing a flight of stairs?

54. Has anyone ever said to you that you smoke too much? (Nonsmokers score "No.")

55. When potato crisps, salted nuts and cocktail savories are around, do you find them impossible to resist?

56. Would you say that on the whole your life-style leads you to abuse or ill-treat your body?

Now turn to page 30 and check your scores.

Scores

Now check your score according to the answer sheet. You will find, as you score, that you begin to accumulate four sets of values – F, D, E, and C factors. These refer to food, drugs, exercise and care, and your maximum score for each will be 14.

	Yes	No		Yes	No		Yes	No		Yes	No
1.	0	1F	15.	0	1C	29.	0	1E	43.	1C	0
2.	0	1F	16.	0	1D	30.	0	1D	44.	0	1C
3.	0	1D	17.	1F	0	31.	0	1D	45.	0	1E
4.	1E	0	18.	1C	0	32.	0	1C	46.	0	1D
5.	1E	0	19.	0	1C	33.	0	1C	47.	0	1F
6.	0	1C	20.	0	1D	34.	1F	0	48.	0	1E
7.	0	1D	21.	1E	0	35.	0	1D	49.	1C	0
8.	0	1C	22.	0	1F	36.	1E	0	50.	1E	0
9.	1E	0	23.	0	1F	37.	1E	0	51.	0	1D
10.	1F	0	24.	0	1D	38.	1F	0	52.	0	1F
11.	0	1D	25.	0	1D	39.	0	1D	53.	0	1E
12.	0	1C	26.	1E	0	40.	1E	0	54.	0	1D
13.	1E	0	27.	0	1C	41.	0	1C	55.	0	1F
14.	0	1F	28.	0	1E	42.	0	1F	56.	0	1C

Keep a careful note of your scores for these first four facets of your physical well-being. When you have completed the second part of the questionnaire you will be able to com-bine the two sets of results, and draw up your own personal Life Chart — a very graphic and revealing answer to the question "How Healthy a Life do You Lead?"

How Healthy a Life Do You Lead? (Part II)

This is the second part of a multifactorial questionnaire, and the instructions for completing it are the same as for Part I. You will notice that some of the numbered questions in this part are prefixed by an A and some by a B. Others have no prefix at all. Those without a prefix should be answered by everyone taking the test, those with an A by men and women in full-time employment only, and those with a B by women not in full-time employment, house-wives for example.

Mark your answers on a separate sheet.

1. Are you taking any part-time study or self-improvement course?
2. Would you describe your childhood as having been a happy one?
3. (B) Do you feel that your personality has evolved and matured in a satisfactory way since you left school?
4. Do you find it difficult to introduce yourself to people and converse with them?
5. Are you a good letter writer?
6. (A) Do you find your work really enjoyable?
7. Do you watch television on average for less than two hours a day (say 15 hours a week)?
8. Do you tend to jump from one hobby or pastime to another without ever getting deeply into one?
9. Do you have any unusual fears or phobias?
10. (A) Would you honestly say that your work gives you the challenge and opportunity which you deserve?
11. Would you say that you lead an active social life?
12. Have you got any domestic hobbies of a practical kind – for example, woodwork, dressmaking, decorating or handicraft of any kind?
13. Do you have any domestic hobbies of a creative but not necessarily practical kind – for example, painting, stamp or coin collecting, modeling, embroidery?
14. Do you feel happy and confident most days?
15. (B) Do you find the things that you do in the course of the day really enjoyable?
16. Do you have trouble sleeping?
17. Are you married? If not, do you have a lover or fiancé?
18. If so, would you describe your relationship with this person as a happy one?
19. (B) If you could give up your present life and take a more interesting job at a reasonable salary, would you gladly do so?
20. Do you make a point of taking at least one holiday per year when you are two weeks away from your work and usual surroundings?
21. Do you always seem to be in financial difficulties?
22. Do financial problems worry you unduly?
23. (A) Do you tend to push yourself harder than most other people in your working environment?
24. (B) Would you say that the working aspects of your life – housework, children and so on – provide you with the kind of challenge that really satisfies you?
25. Do you make friends easily?
26. Do you tend to find yourself bored and restless when not working?
27. Have you ever had a nervous breakdown or been treated for severe depression?
28. Would you prefer an evening watching television or reading to an evening out with friends?
29. Would you describe yourself as basically quite a happy person?
30. (Men only answer this question.) Do you enjoy tinkering with your car or motors of any kind?
31. (B) Do you tend to push yourself harder than most other people in the work that you do?
32. Do you regularly read books (other than magazines and newspapers)?
33. If so, would you say that you really enjoy reading?
34. Do you wish that your sex life was fuller and happier?
35. Do you sometimes feel that everything is getting to be too much for you?
36. Would you say that most people think of you as a sociable person?
37. (A) Do you feel that other people have seriously handicapped you as far as your job or profession is concerned?
38. (Women only answer this question.) Do you enjoy cooking, and the serving of food?
39. Do you enjoy going out to dinner with friends?
40. Do you regret having missed out on any educational opportunities?
41. (A) If you were offered a more interesting job than your present one, at three-quarters of your existing salary, would you take it?
42. Do you get unnecessarily anxious and worried about things?
43. On balance, are you content to do things on your own and be on your own if neccessary?
44. Have you more than one close friend whose company you really enjoy?
45. Do you enjoy actively listening to music?
46. (A) Have you made steady progress and advancement in your job – for example, with promotion or business successes?
47. Do you find it difficult to switch off and relax at the end of the day?
48. Do you have any regular outdoor hobbies or pastimes, such as playing sports or watching them?
49. Do you enjoy parties?
50. Would you describe yourself as sexually attractive?
51. (B) Do you feel that people or circumstances have prevented you from fulfilling yourself in the way that you would have liked to?
52. Do you get irritable or short-tempered for no good reason rather more than you would like?
53. Do you watch television regularly for more than four hours a day, or say 25 hours a week?
54. Does untidiness and carelessness at work or home trouble you unduly?
55. Do you really enjoy sometimes just "loafing around doing nothing"?
56. Have you always got friends or relations who will be glad to have you visit them on a vacation?

Now turn to page 32 and check your scores.

Scores

Now check your score according to the answer sheet. You will find, as you score, that you accumulate four sets of values, as you did in Part I of the questionnaire. In this case the four letters – W, L, S and M – refer in general to work, leisure, social and mental factors, and your maximum score for each will be 14.

	Yes	No			Yes	No			Yes	No			Yes	No
1.	1L	0		15.(B)	2W	0		29.	1M	0		43.	1M	0
2.	1M	0		16.	0	1M		30.	1L	0		44.	1S	0
3.(B)	2W	0		17.	1S	0		31.(B)	2W	0		45.	1L	0
4.	0	1S		18.	1S	0		32.	1L	0		46.(A)	2W	0
5.	1S	0		19.(B)	0	2W		33.	1L	0		47.	0	1M
6.(A)	2W	0		20.	1L	0		34.	0	1S		48.	1L	0
7.	1L	0		21.	0	1M		35.	0	1M		49.	1S	0
8.	0	1L		22.	0	1M		36.	1S	0		50.	1S	0
9.	0	1M		23.(A)	2W	0		37.(A)	0	2W		51.(B)	0	2W
10.(A)	2W	0		24.(B)	2W	0		38.	1L	0		52.	0	1M
11.	1S	0		25.	1S	0		39.	1S	0		53.	0	1L
12.	1L	0		26.	0	1L		40.	0	2W		54.	0	1M
13.	1L	0		27.	0	1M		41.(A)	0	2W		55.	1L	0
14.	1M	0		28.	0	1S		42.	0	1M		56.	1S	0

Analysis

A healthy life involves more than sheer physical strength and vitality. It relies on striking an adequate balance among a number of facets of life. For the purpose of this two-part questionnaire we have broken these down into eight key factors, the first four of which we tested in Part I. When you have completed Part II gather your scores from both sections together and, bearing in mind your personal rating, read the analysis below.

Food
For true good health one needs nutritious food and a balanced diet, all taken in moderation. Overeating is generally more harmful than undereating (except in extreme cases) and the type of food you eat is also important. Fourteen questions in part one were devoted to "food factors" and your score will therefore lie somewhere between 0 and 14. The higher your score the better your eating habits.

Drugs
Drugs are substances taken into the body which are essentially alien to it; they may be taken for a number of reasons which vary from the psychological changes they induce to their physical effects, including of course the treatment of disease or illness. But a dependence on drugs in any form is not conducive to good health. A *high* "drug factor" denotes a relative freedom from their harmful effects.

Exercise
The body is a highly flexible machine which for maximum health should be kept finely tuned. There is no better way of assuring this fine tuning than by lots of exercise in a variety of forms. The higher your score in this factor the more healthy exercise you probably take, and this will be reflected in the Life Chart.

Care
The body's machinery not only needs to be exercised and stoked with the appropriate fuel, but it also needs to be protected from unnecessary ill treatment. Just as ceaseless revving of a motor car's engine, lack of attention to its electrical system and bodywork will cause it to come to grief before its time, so the same applies to your own biological system. The "care factor" gives an indication of how well you are treating your body.

Work
To continue the parallel with mechanical devices, which are tailormade to do work and cease to function smoothly if they are underused, so the body, and in particular the nervous system and the brain benefits from a satisfactory output of intellectual effort, generally reflected in a positive and happy attitude to work. A high "work factor" score suggests that you are probably well integrated into your worklife and this will be reflected in your overall health.

Leisure
"All work and no play makes Jack a dull boy" is an old saying which has a deep ring of truth in it. And play is not just physical exercise. The healthy active mind feeds on diversions and activity which extend beyond the working day, and the more active and instinctive the activity, in the long run the greater the contribution to psychological well-being and health in the broadest sense. A high rating on the "leisure factor" means that you are probably employing your brain to the full at all times and reaping the rewards in terms of psychological satisfaction as a result.

Social
Man is a social animal who is unable to live a full and normal life without some measure of positive interaction with other members of his species. This interaction need not necessarily be in the form of love relationships, though these obviously represent a significant part of the picture. And while it is true that some people are essentially (and contentedly) more solitary than others, the higher you score on this social rating the more likely it is that you are making a satisfactory adjustment to the world around you and the people in it, again with benefits to your overall health.

Mental
All physical factors aside, in the long run it is the mind that rules the body, and it is in our mental life that true contentment lies. If mental forces are out of balance and conflicts of one kind or another dominate our behavior, then it is impossible for us to be truly healthy and happy. "M factor" questions are geared to discovering your own state of mental contentment and stability. A high score on this factor indicates a very satisfactory adjustment.

Plotting and Interpreting Your Scores

Follow the example below to draw up your own Life Chart using a pencil and a compass if you have one. Then take your individual scores for the eight Health Factors and, with a colored pen or pencil, draw over the line appropriate to your score in each segment. For example, if you scored 10 in the "F factor", fill in the line between the two number 10s in the F segment; if 8 for the "D factor" fill in the line that represents 8 in the D segment. To make the balance of the various factors easy to recognize, we suggest that you shade in the interior sectors in a color.

Clearly there are a vast number of possible combinations — some segments will be higher than others (some considerably so) and in other cases the segments may appear roughly equal. No two people are likely to end up with identical profiles. For this reason it is impossible to give a clearcut interpretation for every possible profile, but the following tips will be helpful in allowing you to make your own personal interpretation.

1. The chart itself is broken up into three distinct rings — 0-5, 6-10 and 11-14. On the whole, scores lying between 6 and 10 are average or normal for that factor, scores lying between 0 and 5 are below normal and scores between 11 and 14 are superior or above normal. You should congratulate yourself therefore for any occasions when your profile enters the outer segment.

2. While outer segment scores may be gratifying and spectacular in themselves, in general their effect is weakened if they are accompanied by an equivalent number of scores in the inner segment, suggesting an erratic profile, good in some factors and poor in others. On the whole the "best" type of profile is one in which the segments are all roughly equal, suggesting a more balanced general picture. The only exception to this of course is if all one's scores fall within the inner ring, which, assuming the questions have been answered honestly, and correctly, would be a very unsatisfactory picture.

3. Your Life Chart will give you a graphic and helpful indication of your strong and weak points. Think carefully about them – in particular try to consider what you can do to correct the weak ones.

4. Some account should be taken of age for, generally, the older you are the more likely it is that your scores in some or all segments will be squeezed in towards the center. A generally low profile in a young person, for example, would be much more disturbing than the equivalent profile in someone over the age of 60.

5. Note that, on the whole, the segments on the right half of the graph are those concerned with physical factors while those on the left are more concerned with psychological ones. Most people will be seen to be somewhat stronger on one side than on the other.

Life Chart (How Healthy a Life Do You Lead?)

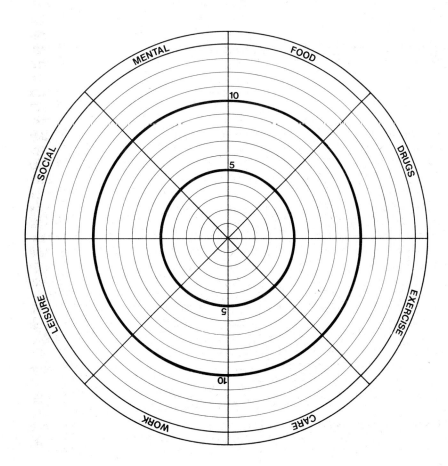

You and Anger

Man is a dominating, dangerous animal—perhaps the most dangerous on earth. He has reached his position of power over all other animals by skillfully but ruthlessly combining his enormously flexible intellectual powers with his excellent muscular coordination and manual dexterity. But even these characteristics on their own would not be sufficient to ensure his survival and general dominance. Behind it all there lies a thrusting dynamic force which urges him to compete, to conquer and to succeed. Whenever this force is blocked or hampered in any way it responds by becoming amplified rather than by weakening. The end product of this amplification we know as anger. Unfortunately, while the forces which lie behind angry behavior ensure that man competes with the world rather than withdraws from it, they have their roots further back in our evolutionary past than those which underly our much prized intellectual powers. It is for this reason that sometimes all common sense, good manners, respect for law and society are flung to the winds when anger takes over.

This questionnaire seeks to determine how much you are the master of your anger and how much it is the master of you. Anger can be used constructively or destructively. Do you tend to dam it up? The psychiatrist Dr. Anthony Storr has pointed out that blocked anger can hit back at you in the form of depression, tension and other physical ailments. Answer this questionnaire, which is divided into a series of subsections, with as much care as you can.

Mark your answers on a separate sheet.

Section 1: How angry do you feel?
Indicate which statement is most true for you.
 1. **a.** I often get angry, even over small things. I know I am sometimes in the wrong, but nevertheless I find it hard to apologize.
 b. It takes a lot to make me angry, and when I blow up I usually feel a bit ashamed of myself.
 c. I do not lose my temper. I never feel really angry and it upsets me when other people behave in such a stupid, childish way.

 2. **a.** I enjoy angry scenes in movies. I would not throw things around myself, but it somehow satisfies me to watch when it's not real.
 b. I don't like angry scenes in movies, just as I don't like angry scenes in life.
 c. I identify strongly during angry scenes in movies—in fact they sometimes give me ideas about expressing anger in my own life.

 3. **a.** When I get mad, I really yell and let everyone know just how angry I'm feeling.

 b. When I get mad, I go very quiet.
 c. I try not to get mad, but to do something about what is bothering me instead.

 4. **a.** When my feelings are hurt I need a few hours before I can talk about it.
 b. When my feelings are hurt, I say so on the spot.
 c. It cuts me up so much when my feelings are hurt that I may never say anything about it.

 5. **a.** Angry people frighten me; I always try to placate them, or get out of the way.
 b. When someone gets mad with me, I listen to what they have to say and try to calm them down so that we can talk about it.
 c. Angry people don't frighten me—I enjoy giving as good as I get.

Do not check your scores on this section until you have completed Sections 2 and 3.

Section 2: Anger in personal relationships
This section tests whether you are more or less inclined to express anger in your personal life. Sometimes people are oddly contradictory, meek at work, raging at home, or vice versa.
 6. Do you row with your partner, family or close friends
 a. Often?
 b. Sometimes?
 c. Never?

 7. If your partner was unfaithful, would you want to
 a. Attack the third party?
 b. Make your partner feel guilty and miserable?
 c. Ignore the whole business?

 8. Do you believe in saying exactly what you think?
 a. Yes, always.
 b. No—you are pretty careful about saying negative things.
 c. Not if what you think is going to cause trouble.

 9. After a couple of drinks, do you
 a. Usually feel carefree and relaxed?
 b. Become silent and gloomy?
 c. Turn nasty and say unpleasant things which you would hold back when sober?

 10. Have you smacked a child in anger?
 a. Yes, several times.
 b. Only occasionally under severe provocation.
 c. No, never.

 11. In a row at home, do you throw things?

a. Yes, sometimes.
b. Only when you go off alone after the fight.
c. No, you never have.

12. You have done something that you know will infuriate your partner or best friend but you do not think that you have behaved badly. Would you
a. Keep quiet about it?
b. Tell them and accept their anger?
c. Tell them defiantly?

13. Your partner persistently nags you on a particular theme. Do you
a. Lose your temper, then calm down quickly?
b. Row every time the theme crops up?
c. Endure it, but feel long-lasting resentment?

14. Do you think that anger destroys love?
a. Yes
b. No—a good fight can enhance love.
c. Not necessarily, but it could happen.

15. When you have had a rough time at work, or away from home, do you take out your annoyance on the people who are closest to you?
a. Never
b. Often
c. You try not to, but you are sometimes unable to stop yourself being irritable with them.

Do not check your score on this until you have completed Section 3.

Section 3: Anger in social situations
It is often easier for men to express anger outside close personal relationships than it is for women. In this section you can check how far you inhibit your anger in front of people you do not know particularly well.

16. You have bought a new and expensive gadget which goes wrong after a week. Would you
a. Call up the store and stay sweetly reasonable?
b. Do your best to get someone else to do your complaining for you?
c. Send an angry letter or call round personally to have a few strong words with the manager of the store?

17. You have just missed a train you particularly wanted to catch because the person in front of you in the ticket line fumbled for change and asked the clerk lots of questions. Would you
a. Feel angry but say nothing?
b. Tell him that his dithering has made you late?
c. Shrug the incident off as just one of those many hazards of life?

18. You are wakened at 3 a.m. by loud music from your next-door neighbor's house for the third time in two weeks. Would you
a. Go straight round and yell at them to shut up?
b. Put a polite note through the door next morning?
c. Feel mad, but do nothing?

19. Have you ever shown anger towards people at work?
a. Yes, mostly to those working under you.
b. Yes, mostly to those working over you.
c. Not at all.

20. Last time you saw a movie that you found highly offensive did you
a. Walk out?
b. Sit through it?
c. Complain to the management, write to your local newspaper or carry through your protest in some public way?

21. Someone pushes ahead of you in a long line at the bank. Would you
a. Tap him on the shoulder and ask him to move back?
b. Say nothing but glare at him?
c. Complain loudly to someone else in the line?

22. What would you say if a waiter at an expensive restaurant spilled sauce in your lap?
a. "Please don't worry" (genuinely).
b. "Please don't worry" (through gritted teeth).
c. "You idiot, you can damn well pay the cleaning bill!"

23. You have been kept waiting for your appointment at the doctor's and you are in a rush. After twenty minutes would you
a. Go on waiting?
b. Explain politely that you must go, and make a new appointment?
c. Complain loudly and walk out?

24. If a storekeeper is rude to you, do you
a. Reckon he must have had a bad day and forget it?
b. Feel humiliated, but say nothing and resolve never to go there again?
c. Display equal rudeness in return?

25. You get drawn into a discussion with a comparative stranger who annoys you. Would you
a. Withdraw from the discussion as soon as possible?
b. Refuse to lose your temper, and humor him?
c. Tell him how wrong you think he is?

Now turn to page 36 and check your scores.

Scores

(Total your scores to find your analysis below.)

Section 1
1. a. 5L   b. 3L   c. 1L
2. a. 3L   b. 1L   c. 5L
3. a. 5L   b. 1L   c. 3L
4. a. 3L   b. 5L   c. 1L
5. a. 1L   b. 3L   c. 5L

Section 2
6. a. 5P   b. 3P   c. 1P
7. a. 5P   b. 1P   c. 3P
8. a. 5P   b. 3P   c. 1P
9. a. 3P   b. 1P   c. 5P
10. a. 5P   b. 3P   c. 1P
11. a. 5P   b. 3P   c. 1P
12. a. 1P   b. 3P   c. 5P
13. a. 3P   b. 5P   c. 1P
14. a. 1P   b. 5P   c. 3P
15. a. 1P   b. 5P   c. 3P

Section 3
16. a. 3S   b. 1S   c. 5S
17. a. 1S   b. 5S   c. 3S
18. a. 5S   b. 3S   c. 1S
19. a. 5S   b. 3S   c. 1S
20. a. 3S   b. 1S   c. 5S
21. a. 3S   b. 5S   c. 1S
22. a. 3S   b. 1S   c. 5S
23. a. 1S   b. 3S   c. 5S
24. a. 3S   b. 1S   c. 5S
25. a. 1S   b. 3S   c. 5S

Analysis

The nature of anger is complex and there are various ways it can manifest itself and affect personal and social relationships. Because of this your scores on this questionnaire are rather more difficult to evaluate than those of the average questionnaire in this series. For this reason you must be particularly careful to check that your scores are correct.

Section 1

These questions relate to the level of anger that you feel when an angry-making situation presents itself. You will find yourself with an L score somewhere between 5 and 25. Check your score against the appropriate category below and then proceed to look at the analysis of Sections 2 and 3.

5L-10L   This low score indicates, without much doubt, that for some reason you are afraid of anger, not only in yourself but also in others. If you have a score of 7 or below, you may even believe that you are the kind of person "who never gets angry." The chances are, though, that you are fooling yourself.

11L-17L   This is a solid average and "normal" score. You tend to be aware of your anger and you express it appropriately. In general you are not an angry person.

However, because you try to be reasonable, you could be slightly inhibited about expressing forcibly enough what you feel.

Over 17L   One thing is beyond doubt—you have no difficulty whatsoever in expressing anger. This means you are uninhibited, which is often a good thing, but you could appear threatening and hostile to others. At times you may even sense that your feelings are really out of control. Watch it!

Sections 2 and 3

In scoring these you will collect P and S scores. The P (personal) scores refer to the degree to which you can control or express anger in your personal, family life, and your S (social) scores to the degree to which you can control or express it in social, non-family situations. Now add your P and S scores together and you should come out with a total between 20 and 100. Self-administered questionnaires such as this can never give you entirely foolproof answers, but on the whole, the higher your score, the higher your level of overt, readily expressed anger; the lower your score the higher your level of suppressed anger. Medium scores suggest that you have anger generally under control. To gain the most benefit from this questionnaire you need to check all the questions where you picked up 5 points (overt anger) and all those where you picked up single points (suppressed anger). These are the areas worth identifying if you are to gain a greater level of personal control in this aspect of your character. Now study them to see which fall in the personal and which in the social spheres. This kind of identification of your *reasons* for anger may well be helpful and instructive.

If your total score (P+S) is over 75 you are in an overt anger group; if less than 50 you are in a suppressed anger group. Scores between 51 and 74 inclusive are in the controlled anger group. Now, if you fell in either the overt or suppressed groups, answer the following series of questions:

  a. Do you suffer from feelings of tension and anxiety?
  b. Do you have fantasies of violence and revenge?
  c. Do you think that anger is a sign of weakness?
  d. Can you stay calm in the face of someone else's outspoken anger?
  e. Are you ever surprised by your own feelings?

This series of questions was designed to check how much anger dominates you. Give yourself one point each time you answered *yes* to a, b and c and one point each time you answered *no* to d or e. If you find you have scored 3 points or more, it is very likely that anger does indeed dominate you, whether or not you consciously experience it.

Try to remember that anger is a natural reaction to some situations but not to all. Because we live in a society which is bound together by mutual cooperation and help, it is often essential that we suppress some of our instinctive feelings. Of course it is important that we acknowledge that we do have feelings—and that others have them too—but that is no excuse for simply "letting it rip" whenever we feel like it.

How Superstitious Are You?

In popular terms we tend to define superstition as any kind of belief in the supernatural, in the existence of the power of witchcraft or magic, the reality of "luck," "fate," and so on. This in fact is a rather imprecise definition and means that what is superstition in one society may be solid fact and common sense in another.

Once the phenomenon of hypnosis was considered by "experts" to be superstitious mumbo-jumbo, and yet now it is recognized as one of the most interesting and perhaps revealing areas of modern psychology. It is clear that we must be cautious in deciding what exactly constitutes superstitious belief, and it is equally clear that we can be "superstitious" without necessarily believing in the supernatural. Psychologists have in fact realized for some time that a tendency to hold superstitious beliefs is a definite facet of many people's personality and may be significantly correlated with their psychological make-up and life style.

The following questionnaire is designed to assess your own tendencies in this direction, and if you fill it in carefully and honestly you will arrive at a figure which we could describe as a "Superstition Quotient." The key to understanding this quotient is given at the end of the questionnaire together with some comments on its significance. The questionnaire has been designed for self-administration, but it is only valid if filled in as honestly and accurately as possible. Needless to say you should *not* look at the scores before doing the questionnaire. You should in all cases answer the questions as they apply to you and not as they apply to other people or as you *feel* they should apply to you—and mark your answers on a separate sheet of paper so that you do not influence others filling in the test. It is not suitable for administering to any other person, and you should complete it on your own when no one else is present or watching you. Do not try to work out the "hidden meaning" of any of the questions, nor try to decide what are the "right" answers. The only right answers are those which you honestly give for yourself.

1. Which of the following most closely describes the kind of person that you believe yourself to be?
  a. I tend to hold rather strong ideas about things and it has to be a pretty good argument to convince me to change my mind.
  b. I tend to hold quite strong views but I do not find it difficult to change them.
  c. I do not often hold strong views about things, but when I do I stick with them.
  d. I tend not to have strong views about things and I change my mind quite easily.

2. Here are some beliefs which are considered superstitions by some people and not by others. Indicate in each case whether you strongly believe, tend to believe, tend to disbelieve or strongly disbelieve the statement.
  a. It is unlucky to walk under a ladder.
  b. Red-headed people tend to be more intelligent than others.
  c. Bad luck tends to go in cycles.
  d. "It's an ill-wind that blows no one any good."
  e. Bright sunlight will put out a fire.
  f. Very intelligent people tend to be mentally less stable.
  g. People's personality can be affected by the phases of the moon.
  h. Cancer is a hereditary disease.
  i. Most people succeed in business more by luck than by judgment.
  j. Women have a greater capacity to withstand pain than men.

3. If you tell someone about something that you hope is going to happen do you *ever* "touch wood" or feel a strong urge to?

4. Do you feel *at all* uneasy about the number 13?

5. Suppose that you were due to make a long car journey and the night before you had a dream of a highway accident. Which of the following would be closest to your reaction?
  a. To cancel the trip or make the journey by some other means.
  b. To consider cancelling the trip but go ahead with it in the end.
  c. To get in the car feeling somewhat more nervous than usual.
  d. To pay no attention to the dream and treat the journey like any other one.

6. Suppose that you were planning to move. You visit a fortuneteller or clairvoyant and she strongly advises you not to move. What would you do?
   a. Do everything you could to avoid the move.
   b. Go to a different fortuneteller to seek her advice.
   c. Reconsider your plans for moving to see whether there was any reason why you should not move.
   d. Go ahead and move without worrying.

7. Do you have a "good luck" token or talisman which you like to have with you whenever you can?

8. In your opinion is astrology
   a. A serious science with real predictive value?
   b. A mixture of truth and mysticism with some slight predictive value?
   c. A bit of fun with perhaps just some truth in it?
   d. A bit of fun with no truth in it?

9. Indicate whether you feel the following statements are definitely true, probably true, probably untrue or definitely untrue.
   a. Some human beings have telepathic ability.
   b. Flying saucers are spaceships from some other part of the universe.
   c. The power of prayer can affect plants.
   d. Animals can somehow sense when someone is frightened of them.
   e. If a sick man gets it into his head that he is going to die, then he may well do so.

10. You are in a gambling casino and a friend of yours seems to be having a remarkable run of luck. Would you
   a. Copy his bets in order to ride his lucky streak?
   b. Refrain from betting in case you upset his run?
   c. Start betting on a different color because you know his luck will change?
   d. If you bet at all, bet purely on your own hunches?

11. You visit a clairvoyant who tells you that someone close to you will shortly die in a plane crash. Do you
   a. Tell the other person about the prediction?
   b. Keep quiet but secretly worry?
   c. Say nothing unless they plan an air journey?
   d. Dismiss the prediction as sheer nonsense?

12. Do you believe that in life you have had
   a. More than your fair share of good luck?
   b. Less than your fair share of good luck?
   c. Just about the average amount of good luck?

13. You are at a wishing well where it is considered to be good luck if you throw in a coin. What do you do?
   a. Pass it by without wishing or parting with a coin.
   b. Throw a coin and wish for wealth and happiness.
   c. Throw a coin in and wish for something simple.
   d. Throw a coin in without making a wish.

14. Here are some more beliefs which are considered superstitions by some people and not by others. Check whether you strongly believe, tend to believe, tend to disbelieve or strongly disbelieve the statement.
   a. You can judge a person's character from his face.

   b. You can sense somehow whether a house has had a tragedy associated with it.
   c. It is possible to tell fortunes with playing cards.
   d. People can occasionally be "possessed" by evil.
   e. If only you could believe in something strongly enough, then you could make it happen.
   f. The ancient Egyptians and other vanished civilizations may have had supernatural powers.
   g. There are such things as ghosts.
   h. It is possible to tell anything about an individual's future by examining the lines on his hand.
   i. You can make a person turn around if you stare long enough at his back.
   j. It is possible by an effort of will to influence dice.
   k. Some people have the ability to detect hidden water or minerals by "dowsing."

15. You have been looking for a used car of a particular model and color. You find exactly what you want in excellent condition and at an unusually low price. The person offering it to you explains frankly that the reason for the low price is that its previous owner committed suicide in the car. Which of the following most closely matches your reactions?
   a. Despite the strange story you buy the car.
   b. You buy the car with some hesitation anticipating that you will soon forget about its associations.
   c. You buy the car determined not to drive it but planning to sell it at a profit to someone who doesn't know its history.
   d. You decide not to buy the car.

16. Do you feel that you have a particular day of the week which is usually "lucky" or "unlucky" for you?

17. Do you have a particular number which you believe is usually "lucky" or "unlucky" for you?

18. Do you have a "pet" name for your family car?

19. Do you read newspaper horoscopes?
   a. Regularly
   b. Occasionally
   c. Never

20. If you do read horoscopes regularly or occasionally, have you acted upon the advice given to you?
   a. Regularly
   b. Occasionally
   c. Never

21. Have you ever taken part, even if only for fun, in a seance, table tapping or something similar?

22. If yes, did anything supernatural take place?

23. Do you own any book or books on occult matter, astrology, extrasensory perception or fortunetelling?

24. If you were suffering from some annoying illness which had resisted all forms of medical treatment, would you consider going to some nonmedically qualified individual using techniques such as "faith healing"?

Scores

Camera Press

1. a. 5 b. 0 c. 5 d. 0

2.	Strongly believe	Tend to believe	Tend to disbelieve	Strongly disbelieve
a.	5	2	2	0
b.	3	0	0	3
c.	3	1	0	0
d.	0	0	0	2
e.	5	2	1	0
f.	3	0	0	3
g.	3	1	0	2
h.	3	1	0	2
i.	3	1	0	2
j.	3	1	0	2

3. yes 3 no 0 **4.** yes 3 no 0 **5.** a. 5 b. 2 c. 2 d. 0

6. a. 5 b. 5 c. 2 d. 0 **7.** yes 3 no 0

8. a. 5 b. 4 c. 3 d. 0

9.	Definitely true	Probably true	Probably untrue	Definitely untrue
a.	3	1	0	2
b.	3	1	0	2
c.	5	1	0	2
d.	3	0	0	3
e.	3	0	0	3

10. a. 3 b. 5 c. 5 d. 0 **11.** a. 2 b. 3 c. 5 d. 0

12. a. 3 b. 3 c. 0 **13.** a. 0 b. 2 c. 5 d. 1

14.	Strongly believe	Tend to believe	Tend to disbelieve	Strongly disbelieve
a.	3	1	0	2
b.	3	1	0	1
c.	5	2	1	0
d.	5	2	1	0
e.	5	2	1	0
f.	5	2	1	0
g.	5	2	1	0
h.	5	2	1	0
i.	5	2	1	0
j.	5	2	1	0
k.	3	1	0	1

15. a. 0 b. 2 c. 3 d. 5 **16.** yes 3 no 0 **17.** yes 3 no 0

18. yes 3 no 0 **19.** Regularly 5
Occasionally 1 Never 0

20. Regularly 5 Occasionally 3 Never 0

21. yes 1 no 0

22. yes 5 no 0

23. yes 3 no 0 **24.** yes 3 no 0

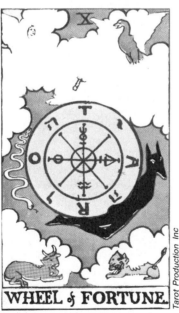

DEATH. WHEEL of FORTUNE.

Tarot Production Inc

Does she hold the key to the future? Would you believe this woman if she told your future according to the cards? Tarot cards are supposed to reveal the truth about people if handled by adepts. Are you a believer or a disbeliever?

Analysis

In the introduction we pointed out that being superstitious does not necessarily imply that you believe in the supernatural. Furthermore a belief that might be described as superstitious today might well be considered to be "normal" or even common sense in some other time or some other society. A more precise and useful definition currently employed in psychology is that a superstition is any strongly held belief or set of beliefs which are not adequately supported by facts. Even this needs some qualification, for to be true superstitions the beliefs should endure through time and persist often in the face of apparently conflicting evidence. This discriminates between superstitions and hunches—the latter being perhaps looked upon as "short-term" superstitions.

To find out how superstitious you are in comparison with the average person, and for some general comments on what this says about your personality, take your total score and check it against the explanatory table below. If you have filled in the questionnaire honestly this will give you a reasonable guide, though as in all self-administered questionnaires, you need some flexibility in interpretation.

Under 10   If you have scored under 10, this would imply that you had virtually no trace of any superstitious tendencies or beliefs. Frankly one would not expect to find many human beings registering such a low score and the most probable explanation is that you have either not filled out the questionnaire with complete honesty or misread the scoring in some way. Go through the questionnaire again and double check!

10-25   This is a very low rating in terms of the average response and implies that you have few superstitious beliefs and tendencies. On the face of it this may seem to suggest a commendably hard-headed approach to life. This could be coupled with a highly practical personality, suggesting that you might be very successful in any profession where facts and figures (as opposed to hunches and inspiration) are at a premium. On the other hand your inherent skepticism may make you overcautious and to some degree intolerant of other people's ideas. If you fall in this bracket you might find life a fraction more exciting if you broadened your imagination and intellectual horizons a little.

26-50   People scoring in this bracket reveal that they are equipped with a reasonable mixture of skepticism and flexibility in the way that they relate to the mysterious universe which we live in. Your attitude strikes a balance between two poles. On one hand you realize that scientists have been enormously successful in mapping the universe and that psychologists have made some way towards understanding the nature of the mind. On the other, you also feel that there are vast undiscovered territories in which the fantastic could still occur. You are probably consciously or unconsciously aware that today's superstition could become tomorrow's fact.

51-75   Scoring in this bracket defines you clearly as a person with marked superstitious tendencies, though you share these beliefs with a very substantial section of humanity. If your score is in the upper end of this range—say over 65—you may be considered by many people to be a bit *too* superstitious and overinclined to let your hunches mature into convictions without good evidence. This could be disastrous in business (though sometimes wild hunches pay off) but it might be a decided advantage if you are in a creative or artistic profession. As a general rule, however, you might try to be a little more skeptical than you are at present.

76-100   This marks you down as a very superstitious person indeed. You still keep company with a large number of people, but the signs are that you are a bit overenthusiastic about the supernatural and about fantastic claims made by people on insufficient evidence. If these interests of yours are merely a hobby, then all right, enjoy them as much as you can. On the other hand you might find yourself easy game for confidence tricksters of one kind and another, and if you are actively involved in the investigation of psychic phenomena or spiritualism, for example, then you should take care to keep your eyes open for frauds of all kinds. A score this high would also indicate that you should catch up with your reading on the topics that you are interested in, or if you already read a lot, you should be a bit more discerning in the books that you buy.

Over 100   This is a very high score indeed and either you are quite exceptionally superstitious or you have made some error in filling out or checking the questionnaire. Your score would suggest that you hold a multiplicity of beliefs considered quite unusual by most people, many of which are contradictory to a high degree. Holding such unusual beliefs with great conviction is sometimes a characteristic of people passing through a stressful period of life. If in fact you have scored over 125 then it could well be that you are passing through a period of psychological uncertainty and it might help you to confide in some close friend whom you trust or have a chat with your family doctor.

What Kind of Driver Are You?

In the modern world most people find themselves involved in driving motor cars, and even those who don't drive are personally involved with them at some stage as passengers. Driving is one of the major skills of late twentieth-century man, but the authorities – while they do pay some attention to physical characteristics in selecting people as suitable to drive and do impose a fairly simple test of driving ability before giving a license – pay amazingly little attention to the psychology of those who handle motor cars. Most European countries, it is true, are now proposing that a psychological examination should feature permanently in the basic driving test but far-reaching schemes of this kind have made predictably little headway – perhaps because few drivers would welcome a searching examination of their own motives, skills and driving habits.

Clearly this is an area which badly needs deeper, bolder and more forthright investigations. Road casualties in the Western world alone claim tens of thousands of lives every year, and literally millions of people suffer from injury of one kind or another. In many ways a country can suffer more damage to its population and to its economy through road accidents than it can through a full-scale war. But how can one set about investigating the psychology of driving? Psychologists have recently been devoting more and more thought to this problem and have devised a number of tests which at least make a start at distinguishing the safe from the unsafe driver. The test below leans on some of their established methods, and, if filled in conscientiously and above all honestly, it could be a useful and perhaps a surprising pointer to you as to how you measure up as a driver. One cannot of course draw absolutely firm conclusions from tests of this kind, which really should be administered and interpreted personally by a skilled psychologist. However this test will still give useful pointers which may yet help you to be a safer driver.

Mark your answers on a separate sheet.

1. On the whole, how would you rate yourself as a driver? Indicate honestly which statement seems most appropriate to the way you feel about your own driving.

- **a.** I believe myself to be a very good driver, skilled in the handling of motor cars on the road.
- **b.** I have my lapses, but I am pretty confident that my driving is better than average.
- **c.** As a driver I am probably no better and no worse than the average person.
- **d.** If I am really honest about this, I suppose my driving is a bit worse than average.
- **e.** I am afraid there is no doubt that I am not a good driver and I am conscious of this when on the roads.

2. Here are some statements about the use of alcohol and driving. Show which is closest to your own views. (If you are a strict teetotaller do not score this question.)

- **a.** It is not unusual for me to drive after I have been drinking and there are occasions when I am aware that my skill and judgement have been seriously impaired by alcohol.
- **b.** I often drive after I have been drinking, but I feel that in many cases my driving is improved by alcohol.
- **c.** I have driven after drinking, but really don't care to.
- **d.** I try to avoid driving after even as little as one drink.
- **e.** It would have to be very unusual circumstances indeed before I would drive after drinking.
- **f.** I have never, and would never, drive after drinking.

3. Here are a number of statements about driving habits, attitudes and behavior with which you may or may not agree and which you may or may not feel apply to you. Indicate whether, on the whole, you definitely agree, slightly agree, slightly disagree or definitely disagree with each.

- **a.** There are far too many pedestrian crossings.
- **b.** There are more bad drivers than good drivers.

c. Cautious, nonaggressive driving is safer than aggressive driving.

d. There are too many trivial restrictions on driving, particularly in towns.

e. Family cars and weekend drivers are the biggest menace on the roads.

f. The higher the speed, the more risk of accident.

g. It is OK to ignore speed limits if one really has to get somewhere in a hurry.

h. The roads should be better policed than at present.

i. Bad roads, and not bad drivers, are the principal cause of accidents.

j. A good driving rule is "Never let anyone get the better of you."

k. There is nothing more aggravating than someone showing off in a flashy car.

l. People over 70 should be banned from the roads.

4. Have you ever been punished for speeding?
   a. Yes, more than once.
   b. Yes, once.
   c. No, but only because of my good luck.
   d. No, I would never speed.

5. Have you ever been convicted of drunken driving?
   a. Yes, more than once.
   b. Yes, once.
   c. No, but only because of my good luck.
   d. No.

6. Have you ever been involved in an accident as a driver when someone was injured?
   a. Yes, more than once.
   b. Yes, once only.
   c. No.

7. Here are a number of questions about attitudes to driving. Indicate whether the answer in your case is most accurately described as often, sometimes, rarely or never.

a. It distracts me if someone talks to me as I drive.

b. I tend to cut in and out of traffic.

c. I get very annoyed if the lights change to red as I approach them.

d. I get nervous when changing lanes in heavy traffic.

e. I enjoy the sensation of driving fast.

f. I find window stickers on other vehicles annoying.

g. Wet roads make me worry about skidding.

h. I swear under my breath at other drivers.

i. Night driving scares me.

j. When driving I tend to picture myself in an accident.

k. I feel relaxed and confident when driving.

l. The idea of brake failure worries me on a journey.

m. The thought of driving far makes me nervous.

n. I dislike being overtaken.

o. I find it hard to control my temper on crowded roads.

8. Have you ever
   a. Shouted, shaken your fist or made any other aggressive sign at another driver?
   b. Put on your brakes to "shake up" another driver who is driving too close behind you?
   c. Got out of your car to argue with another driver?
   d. Found yourself in a scuffle with another driver?
   e. Accelerated to prevent another car from overtaking?
   f. Felt so nervous as the result of heavy traffic that you have had to stop to take a break?
   g. Overtaken in a dangerous spot someone who has overtaken you?
   h. Driven closely behind a slow driver and hooted your horn to make him speed up?
   i. Become so annoyed with another driver that you felt as though you could kill him?
   j. Worried about a tire blowing at high speed?

Now turn to page 43 and check your answers.

Scores

(Total your score to find your analysis below.)

1. a. 3A b. 1A c. 0 d. 1N e. 3N
2. a. 3A b. 5A c. 0 d. 0 e. 1N f. 3N

3.	Definitely agree	Slightly agree	Slightly disagree	Definitely disagree
a.	5A	2A	0	0
b.	3A	0	0	3A
c.	1N	0	1A	5A
d.	5A	2A	0	0
e.	5A	2A	0	1N
f.	2N	0	1A	5A
g.	5A	2A	0	1N
h.	2N	0	1A	5A
i.	5A	2A	0	1N
j.	10A	5A	1A	0
k.	3A	1A	0	0
l.	5A	2A	0	0

4. a. 5A b. 2A c. 2A d. 1N
5. a. 5A b. 2A c. 2A d. 0
6. a. 5A b. 2A c. 0

7.	Often	Sometimes	Rarely	Never
a.	5N	2N	0	1A
b.	5A	2A	0	1N

c.	3A	0	0	0
d.	5N	2N	0	1A
e.	3A	0	1N	5N
f.	5A	2A	0	0
g.	5N	2N	0	5A
h.	1A	0	0	2N
i.	5N	2N	0	0
j.	5N	2N	0	2A
k.	2A	0	2N	5N
l.	5N	2N	0	0
m.	5N	2N	0	0
n.	5A	2A	0	1N
o.	5A	2A	0	1N

8.
a.	yes 3A	no 0
b.	yes 3A	no 0
c.	yes 5A	no 0
d.	yes 10A	no 0
e.	yes 3A	no 0
f.	yes 5N	no 0
g.	yes 5A	no 0
h.	yes 5A	no 0
i.	yes 5A	no 0
j.	yes 5N	no 0

Analysis

After scoring the questionnaire you will find that you end up with separate sets of scores, one for A values and the other for N values. Your A score illustrates the amount of aggression in your driving behavior, and the N score the amount of nervousness or anxiety. To these scores you should add:

    10A if you are a woman
    5N if you are a man

When you have made this addition you can proceed to the evaluation below.

Psychologists who have studied the driving behavior of adults and compared accident statistics with personality variables now believe that both aggressive and anxiety tendencies are coupled with a high risk of accident or injury on the roads. The degree to which these factors are present in your own personality could be clearly revealed by this questionnaire, and while the usual reservations need to be borne in mind about self-administered questionnaires, if you are a person who takes driving seriously it would certainly be worth checking your score carefully against the evaluation given below.

A SCORES

Under 25A There is a normal and in no way excessive amount of natural aggression in your personality which will be reflected slightly in your driving habits, but only to the extent that this makes you a positive rather than a negative driver. The act of driving itself involves certain definite skills and a basic amount of dynamism – one needs to be capable of overtaking in a confident manner when the moment is right for example. If your A score is less than 10, then you may perhaps be a little too cautious. This will certainly be the case if your low A score is combined with a high N score – say over 25N. If so, it could either be that you are a novice driver, or that you could do with a course of driving lessons to boost your confidence a bit.

25A to 50A You are a slightly aggressive driver, inclined to take chances under certain circumstances and possibly some unjustified risks from time to time. On the whole however your driving is probably reasonably safe and you are unlikely to get into trouble unless weather conditions or circumstances are against you. It is most likely that your N score is less than 20, but if it is above 20 this suggests that your driving is probably erratic and varies in quality from time to time. Remember that it is never too late to learn. If you wish to take a pride in your driving you might consider having a refresher course at a driving school, or even taking one of the advanced driving courses. This would be particularly recommended if your N rating is over 20.

51A to 75A There is a strong streak of aggression and recklessness about your driving which could well get you into, at best, a brush with the law and, at worst, an injurious accident. A score in this range, particularly if it leans towards the seventies, should be taken as a definite warning to remind you to brush up on your driving. Try to treat road conditions for what they are and not get frustrated by them. Also try to avoid the temptation of being provoked by other drivers' stupidity and bad habits. In all probability you will have an N score of less than 20, but if it is higher than this then there is something very amiss with your driving and you should certainly take this opportunity to take a cool, hard look at the way in which you use motor cars.

76A to 100A For one reason or another you are too personally involved in driving and are treating it as a challenge in the wrong sense. The amount of aggression revealed by a score in this range is considerable, and if it has not already got you into trouble with the law and accidents, then it very likely will in the future. You should do everything that you can to cool down a bit. Perhaps road conditions in your part of the world are so bad as to introduce unreasonable frustration, which in turn is channeled into aggression. Is there any way in which you could use more public transport – or even give over a share of the driving to someone else – in order to avoid this frustration? Your N score will almost certainly be less than 20, but if it is higher then your driving is probably bad, even dangerous.

Over 100A If you really are scoring as high as this and haven't misunderstood the questions or miscounted, you are a dangerous driver, and the sooner you face up to this the better for you and other road users. For some reason the motor car brings out a distinctly aggressive streak in you and you are using the vehicle more as a weapon than a means of transportation. These may seem hard words, but you should consider taking them very seriously indeed and asking yourself whether you are prepared to face the possible consequences of really bad driving habits. You should certainly consider driving less. You will definitely have a low N rating, but it is of secondary importance to your abnormally high rating on the aggression scale.

N SCORES

Under 10N This is a normal score. You have some measure of caution and uncertainty about the roads, and this is probably just as well. The key to your driving personality will probably be revealed by your A score, whatever that is. If it is low then you are very likely a safe driver and should be congratulated for it!

10N to 20N There is a definite edge of nervousness or uncertainty about your driving, which probably makes you overcautious on occasions. If this is coupled with a very low (say under 10) or very high (say over 75) A score, then the nervousness is probably a factor which could put you at risk. It could of course be due to simple lack of practice and experience. Were you given proper driving instruction? Could you perhaps use some now?

21N to 40N You are definitely a nervous driver. It is doubtful if you even enjoy driving at all and probably the less you do of it the better. This is certainly true if you also have a very high A score (say over 75). Possibly the best thing is to do as little driving as possible, though some competent professional driving instruction might help.

Over 40N A score at this level denotes a degree of nervousness and anxiety which probably makes you a dangerous driver. One can only hope that your work or social life does not require you to use a car extensively! You will very likely have a low A score as well but, if by chance you have a high A score, then there is something seriously the matter with your driving and you should consider whether you ought not to give it up entirely. High anxiety scores may well indicate however that you have been badly taught or have had insufficient practice at driving. A course with a good professional driving school might do something to correct your dangerously nervous approach.

Can You Take a Risk?

The human brain is a computer, built to process information about the environment and to judge which of a large number of possible courses of action is the most likely to be successful. In a complex environment, decision making at high speed is going to be one of the necessary requirements of any animal if it is to survive and prosper. Some animals, of course, protect themselves from having to make too many momentous decisions by covering themselves with a thick armor so that the world can change around them while they plod on unheedingly. Fine, if you like to be an armadillo, a tortoise or a hermit crab, but for animals that wish to *interact* with the world or even conquer it, this kind of physical—or psychological—armor-plating will not do. It is for this reason that the higher animals—including man —get such satisfaction out of manipulating the environment, out of play, out of taking chances and out of risk.

Man is the greatest risk taker of them all. Human beings even have the extraordinary capacity for *enjoying* danger (we will never know for sure whether other animals do). People *like* to take rides on roller coasters, to drive fast cars, to engage in highly competitive sports, and, of course, they also like such intellectually risky practices as gambling. There is no person on earth who cannot take a risk and who does not enjoy it at least to some degree. Life presents us with risks every day: take too many and you are in trouble, take none and you will stagnate. How much of a risk taker are you? Fill in this questionnaire to find out.

Mark your answers on a separate sheet.

1. Is your gambling experience
   a. Limited to buying reluctantly a raffle ticket for church funds?
   b. Of betting small sums, or of a friendly card game played for a dollar or two?
   c. Of large wagers, covering a range of expensive pastimes?

2. You have worked overtime to save a substantial sum when you are invited to invest in a risky but interesting concern that will either bring big returns or lose your investment. Would you
   a. Invest the lot?
   b. Put your money into something safe?
   c. Risk half your capital?

3. If the same sum of money were an unexpected legacy, which choice would you make? (Answer a, b or c as in question 2.)

4. Can you enjoy watching a horse race if you have not put a bet on it?
   a. Yes, just as much as if you had.
   b. No, it would lose its point.
   c. Yes, but it wouldn't be so much fun.

5. Have you played a fruit machine?
   a. Yes, quite often
   b. Never
   c. Occasionally

6. If you got the jackpot first go at a fruit machine, would you be more likely to
   a. Feed the coins straight back in?
   b. Pocket the money and walk away?
   c. Play for a while, but end up with some of your original winnings?

7. Which of these reasons would be the likeliest one for you to risk your money?
   a. The sheer excitement of gambling.
   b. The possibility of increasing your stake.
   c. Nothing would induce you to risk more than a small sum.

8. Have you as a driver
   a. Never been responsible for any kind of accident?
   b. Been responsible for one or two minor scrapes but nothing serious?
   c. Been responsible for one or more accidents where vehicles or people have been damaged?

9. Would you take a new job which offered less money initially but with better prospects if you did really well?
   a. No
   b. Yes
   c. You would consider it, but might not take the risk.

10. Which statement is most true for you?
   a. I am pretty close about my feelings and wishes.
   b. I do confide in some people, but I choose my confidants carefully.
   c. I can't help being open—I tell most people what I'm thinking.

11. For some time one of your friends has been behaving in a way that you dislike. Would you
   a. Try to find a nice way of telling him?
   b. Suffer, or avoid his company, rather than tell him?
   c. Tell him straight?

12. Which of the following sports would you most like to try if you had the chance?

a. Mountaineering
b. Stock car racing
c. Skating
d. Fencing

13. Do you find it difficult to break out of a familiar routine?
a. No
b. Sometimes
c. Yes

14. If you had the chance to work in a strange city for six months, which would please you but annoy your partner or family, would you
a. Go anyway.
b. Turn down the chance.
c. Go, but try to minimize the annoyance.

15. A stranger asks you for a loan and tells you a hard luck story. Would you
a. Give him what you could?
b. Give him a small amount?
c. Refuse to give him anything?

16. Do you wonder if your partner really loves you?
a. Often
b. Sometimes
c. Not really

17. If you found that you no longer agreed with a group of friends and wanted to do things they disapproved of, would you
a. Feel frightened of being alone, and forget it?
b. Phase out your dependence on the group?
c. Do exactly what you want and let them disapprove?

18. Before taking a major decision in your life, do you
a. Agonize over the alternatives?
b. Make up your mind quickly and stick to it?
c. Think it out carefully, then decide with as few regrets as possible?

19. You decided to try a completely different holiday and everything goes wrong—weather, food and traveling are all disastrous. Would you feel
a. Ruefully amused?
b. Furious?
c. Determined never to do anything like that again?

20. Which would make you feel worst?
a. Making a fool of yourself.
b. Letting others down.
c. Failing to accomplish something after trying.

21. Have you stopped yourself from becoming involved with someone else in case of rejection?
a. No
b. Occasionally
c. Often

22. Women only: Have you ever risked an unwanted pregnancy?
a. Never
b. Only in love or urgency.
c. More often than you care to think.

23. Men only: Have you ever risked getting a woman pregnant?
a. Often
b. Occasionally
c. Never

24. Would you stand bail for your best friend?
a. Yes, without question.
b. It all depends on the amount.
c. No, never.

25. If you saw your child climbing a high tree would you
a. Stop him instantly?
b. Feel proud of him?
c. Let him try, but with your heart in your mouth?

26. Did you, at the beginning of your working life, make provision for retirement?
a. No
b. Yes
c. Only because it was part of your company's policy.

27. Would you be more likely to choose
a. A lover who delighted you, even if you thought it wouldn't last?
b. A lover who adored you and would stay with you?
c. To avoid close relationships?

28. Are you happiest when you
a. Start something new?
b. Are doing something you know well?
c. Achieve something difficult after practice?

29. Answer yes or no to whether you would risk the following for a person or cause very important to you.
a. Your life.
b. Your money.
c. Your reputation.
d. None of these.

Now turn to page 47 and check your scores.

Scores

(Total your scores to find your analysis below.)

1. a. 1	b. 3	c. 5	
2. a. 5	b. 1	c. 3	
3. a. 5	b. 1	c. 3	
4. a. 1	b. 5	c. 3	
5. a. 5	b. 1	c. 3	
6. a. 5	b. 1	c. 3	
7. a. 5	b. 3	c. 1	
8. a. 1	b. 3	c. 5	
9. a. 1	b. 5	c. 3	
10. a. 1	b. 3	c. 5	
11. a. 3	b. 1	c. 5	
12. a. 5	b. 5	c. 3	d. 1
13. a. 5	b. 3	c. 1	
14. a. 5	b. 1	c. 3	
15. a. 5	b. 3	c. 1	
16. a. 1	b. 3	c. 5	

17. a. 1	b. 3	c. 5	
18. a. 1	b. 5	c. 3	
19. a. 5	b. 3	c. 1	
20. a. 1	b. 3	c. 1	
21. a. 5	b. 3	c. 1	
22. a. 1	b. 3	c. 5 (Women only)	
23. a. 5	b. 3	c. 1 (Men only)	
24. a. 5	b. 3	c. 1	
25. a. 1	b. 5	c. 3	
26. a. 5	b. 1	c. 3	
27. a. 5	b. 3	c. 1	
28. a. 5	b. 1	c. 3	
29. a. yes 5	no 0		
b. yes 5	no 0		
c. yes 5	no 0		
d. yes 0	no 0		

Analysis

Check your score against the table below for an indication of how you rate as a risk taker.

Under 50 This is an unusually low score and if you have answered the questionnaire accurately and honestly it means that you are a person who has a very definite tendency *not* to take risks. In fact, one might almost say that you have an *inability* to do so. This will handicap you greatly in life and you should do everything that you can to be more adventurous.

51-70 You are somewhat inhibited as far as risk taking is concerned. This is a pity because not only will you be missing out on a lot of the fun of life, but also, paradoxically, you may actually be doing some harm to yourself. For example, your job or career may be made superficially secure by not taking risks, but it may also mean that you do not take *enough* risks to give you any chance of promotion or advancement. You may also find your relationships with other people frozen because you are slow to commit yourself to them. Steel yourself to take a few more chances—you will benefit.

71-100 You are not a high risk taker, but you are prepared to take chances from time to time. Actually you have a rather balanced approach to risk taking, tempering your natural human inclination to take a chance with a good measure of common sense. No matter how tempting a prospect it may seem to you, you will generally withdraw if your better judgement advises you against the idea.

100-120 You are a risk taker, and what's more you are aware of it. You will seldom turn down the opportunity to "take a chance" and you like risky things in general. If you are a car driver you are probably aggressive and may be incautious. You may well be intrigued by gambling though you respond more to the thrill of gambling itself rather than to any hope of gaining real financial reward from it. People may think of you as being a bit erratic and a bit unreliable, but in all probability you have enough common sense to mean that your risk taking does not damage you too seriously. But make sure that you hang on to your practical common sense—someone like you really needs it.

Over 120 A score this high indicates that you are a very definite risk taker, to the extent that it may well be endangering your social, domestic or financial life. It is very likely that you are attracted to gambling and if so your pocket probably suffers as the result. You may get a lot of fun out of risk taking, but those closest to you may feel that you are foolhardy and reckless. Perhaps it is all right if it is only your head that is on the chopping block. But have you no others to think of?

ESP AND YOU

Most people at one time or another in their life have had some sort of experience, often of a highly personal kind, which seems difficult to explain according to normal, accepted scientific laws: those occasions when you and someone emotionally close apparently "share" a common thought or when a dream seems to have given some warning or information about the future; peculiar "coincidences" when you are telephoned by a person whose name has just crossed your mind for the first time in weeks. Experiences like this are enormously common and many people believe that they reflect mental powers or faculties generally classified under the heading of the "psychic" or "paranormal." Though the existence of these faculties is still a matter of scientific dispute, many psychologists and other scientists believe that there is now clear evidence that they are real, and that possibly they can even be exploited. Furthermore there's little doubt that even people who are highly skeptical about human psychic powers still find the topic interesting: there are very few scientists who would argue that ESP is not a subject worthy of discussion and experimentation.

The tests which follow attempt to explore your own psychic potential in two ways. The first part is a questionnaire which sets out to establish how you feel about your own psychic or ESP (extrasensory perception) abilities. The second part is a practical experiment which allows you, both on your own and with someone else, to test for any objective evidence that you do have such powers. As with any reliable questionnaire, the results are only meaningful provided that you follow the instructions carefully. This is particularly important in the ESP tests, where the results will be completely distorted and inaccurate if there is any form of cheating or carelessness. There is no way in which we can prevent you from peeking at the answers and thus getting a "high" score in the ESP test. We assume, however, that if you are really interested in the topic you will want a *true* picture of your ESP ability rather than a *false* one! You should do the two tests in the order they are presented, and preferably not on the same day. Remember that the first questionnnaire gives a picture of your own beliefs and psychic experiences, and not specifically about whether you actually *have* such powers, and when you have established your level of belief, you should then go on to perform the practical test to determine whether your belief is supported by any experimental evidence.

Part I: Do You Believe You Are Psychic?

Mark your answers on a separate sheet.

1. It is a commonly held belief that people can have dreams which let them foretell the future or give warning about some future event. On the whole how surprised are you that so many people claim that they have had such dreams?
- **a.** Very surprised.
- **b.** Slightly surprised.
- **c.** Not at all surprised.

2. Have you ever had a dream or dreams in which you seemed to have gained some information about the future? Indicate which statement *most closely* matches your own personal experience.
- **a.** I have never had any dreams about the future which subsequently came true.
- **b.** I have had a dream (or dreams) about the future which seemed to come true but I am inclined to treat them as coincidence or chance.
- **c.** I have had one or two dreams which definitely seemed to have come true and I find it difficult to dismiss them as being chance or coincidence.
- **d.** I have had a number of dreams about the future which definitely came true and consider this to be evidence of some psychic or ESP ability.

3. Irrespective of whether you have had any dreams about the future which came true, suppose that tonight you had a vivid dream that good fortune would befall you if you telephoned an old friend whom you had not spoken to for years. Would you
- **a.** Pay no attention to the dream and not contact the friend unless you had some other definite reason for doing so?
- **b.** Wonder seriously whether to telephone the friend and decide to do so as soon as you could think of a reasonable excuse?
- **c.** Manufacture an excuse to telephone and do so as soon as possible?
- **d.** Be alarmed about the dream and refrain from telephoning in case it really implied bad luck?

- **e.** Telephone the friend immediately and recount your dream?

4. Have you ever had a very powerful sensation which could best be described as "I have been here before" or "I have done this before"?
- **a.** Yes
- **b.** No
- **c.** Not sure

5. If you *have* had this sensation, which of the following possible explanations seems to you to be the most likely to be correct?
- **a.** This has something to do with psychic powers or with ESP, possibly because the mind is looking slightly ahead in time and is able to predict what is going to happen a few seconds ahead.
- **b.** This is some peculiar aspect of the brain's function which no one understands properly yet, but which need not have anything to do with psychic matters.
- **c.** This is related to reincarnation and the memory is in fact of some other life you have lived in the past.
- **d.** You have done something rather like that before, but your brain is slightly confused and "believes" that the present and the partly remembered experiences are identical.

6. Which of the following most closely approximates your views about ghosts?
- **a.** Ghosts of one kind or another do occur from time to time and they could well be manifestations of a psychic or spiritual force.
- **b.** Ghosts certainly exist, and in many cases they are the spirits of the dead trying to communicate with us.
- **c.** No one has ever seen a ghost, and those who claim they have seen them are either liars, possibly mentally disturbed or may simply have been suffering from a hallucination or form of suggestion.
- **d.** I am very skeptical about the evidence for the exis-

tence of ghosts, but I suppose it is just possible that they could exist.

7. Irrespective of how you answered question 6, have you ever seen a ghost?
   a. Yes
   b. No
   c. Not sure

8. Have you any friends or close acquaintances who have told you that they have seen a ghost or some similar kind of apparition?
   a. Yes
   b. No

9. If you have answered yes to question 8 do you believe them?
   a. Certainly believe.
   b. Inclined to disbelieve.
   c. Definitely disbelieve.

10. Some people claim that by speaking to plants or "thinking" kind thoughts about them, they can be induced to flourish and grow unusually well. Indicate which statement most closely matches your feeling about this belief.
   a. Possibly something in it but only because of the special attention and extra care the plant is given and not because of any psychic powers.
   b. Could well be something in it. Plants and humans are both forms of life and there is no reason why the plants shouldn't be sensitive to human thoughts.
   c. A lot of nonsense which just shows how silly and superstitious some people can be.
   d. Definitely something in it and merely more evidence of the power of the human mind and spirit.

11. Irrespective of how you answered question 10, have you ever tried improving your plants by talking to them or deliberately thinking about them in a positive way?
   a. Yes and have got definite results.
   b. No, but might give it a try.
   c. Yes, but more for a joke than anything.
   d. Definitely not, and wouldn't waste the time.

12. Have you had an aunt, grandmother or other member of your family who was reputed to have "psychic powers" of some kind?
   a. Yes
   b. Not sure
   c. No

13. If you answered yes to question 12, show which of the statements below most closely corresponds to your attitude regarding these "special powers."
   a. Our family has always had a reputation for being psychic.
   b. I am not sure whether there was any real evidence for this person's psychic powers, but it could well be true.
   c. I am not surprised. Every family probably has someone in it who claims to have psychic powers, whether they have them or not.
   d. I have heard about these psychic powers but I have no reason to believe that they were genuine.

14. Have you ever been tested for ESP in a scientific experiment?
   a. Yes
   b. No
   c. Not sure

15. If yes to question 14, what were the results?
   a. About average and didn't show any evidence of ESP.

   b. Showed some evidence of ESP.
   c. Don't know or can't remember.
   d. Showed definite evidence of ESP.

16. Here are some terms used to refer to various types of alleged psychic powers. In each case you should indicate, honestly, whether you know what the terms mean or not. (Short definitions are given in the scoring sheet, but you should only refer to these *after* you have completed the whole questionnaire.)

a. Scrying		**f.** Dowsing
b. Precognition		**g.** Telepathy
c. Clairvoyance		**h.** Faith healing
d. Psychokinesis		**i.** Spirit mediumship
e. Psychometry		**j.** Palmistry

17. Indicate whether you feel you have any of the following powers.

a. Scrying		**f.** Dowsing
b. Precognition		**g.** Telepathy
c. Clairvoyance		**h.** Faith healing
d. Psychokinesis		**i.** Spirit mediumship
e. Psychometry		**j.** Palmistry

18. Have you ever had any of the following kinds of experiences?
   a. You and some other person suddenly discover that you have been having exactly the same thoughts at the same time.
   b. When driving a car or in some similar situation you suddenly get a warning of danger ahead which turns out to have been correct.
   c. You pick up the phone to call someone and the first thing they say is "I was just going to call you."
   d. You get a definite feeling that you are in contact with the mind or thoughts of a pet or other animal.
   e. You have had a dream of some disaster which subsequently came true.
   f. You will someone in a crowded room or on a street to turn round and look at you, and they do.
   g. You get the feeling that a particular day is going to be "unlucky" – and it turns out to be just that!
   h. You go to totally unfamiliar surroundings and yet seem to know exactly where everything is.
   i. You have a presentiment or strong feeling that someone you know is going to come to harm, and this actually happens.
   j. You have a strong sense of contact and a feeling of the real presence near you of someone who has died.

19. Have you ever been told quite seriously by someone else that you are psychic or have extrasensory powers?
   a. Yes, often.
   b. Yes, once or twice.
   c. Not sure.
   d. Never.

20. How confident are you that you have psychic powers or extrasensory abilities of one kind or another?
   a. Absolutely certain.
   b. Definitely inclined to believe.
   c. Sometimes think I have.
   d. Really don't know.
   e. Inclined to be doubtful.
   f. Very doubtful.
   g. Quite certain that I have not.

Now turn to page 50 and check your scores.

Scores

(Total your score to find your analysis below.)

1. a. 0   b. 1   c. 2
2. a. 0   b. 1   c. 3   d. 5
3. a. 0   b. 2   c. 2   d. 5   e. 2
4. a. 1   b. 0   c. 0
5. a. 3   b. 0   c. 5   d. 0
6. a. 3   b. 5   c. 0   d. 1
7. a. 5   b. 0   c. 2
8. a. 1   b. 0
9. a. 5   b. 2   c. 0
10. a. 1   b. 3   c. 0   d. 5
11. a. 5   b. 2   c. 2   d. 0
12. a. 2   b. 1   c. 0
13. a. 5   b. 3   c. 1   d. 0
14. a. 1   b. 0   c. 1
15. a. 0   b. 3   c. 0   d. 5

16. Score one point in each case where you were correct in your definition of the word.

   a. Scrying: attempting to see the future by gazing into a crystal ball or similar object.
   b. Precognition: ability to predict the future.
   c. Clairvoyance: knowledge about something which is not in the mind of any other human being (for example, the order of cards in a shuffled pack).
   d. Psychokinesis: the ability to move an object at a distance by the power of thought.
   e. Psychometry: the ability, by holding an object, to discover something on its history, its previous owners, and so on.
   f. Dowsing: water divining by rod, pendulum or other device.
   g. Telepathy: mind-to-mind contact without using any of the known senses.

   h. Faith healing: healing employing the power of faith or some kind of supernatural force.
   i. Spirit mediumship: communication between a living individual and the spirit or soul of a dead person.
   j. Palmistry: predicting the future or judging character by examining the lines on the palm of the hand.

	Definitely yes	Possibly yes	Don't know	Certainly no
17. a.	5	3	1	0
b.	5	3	1	0
c.	5	3	1	0
d.	5	3	1	0
e.	5	3	1	0
f.	5	3	1	0
g.	5	3	1	0
h.	5	3	1	0
i.	5	3	1	0
j.	5	3	1	0

	Several times	Once or twice	Not sure	Never
18. a.	3	1	1	0
b.	3	1	1	0
c.	2	1	1	0
d.	5	3	1	0
e.	5	3	1	0
f.	3	1	1	0
g.	3	1	1	0
h.	5	3	1	0
i.	5	3	1	0
j.	5	3	1	0

19. a. 5   b. 3   c. 1   d. 0
20. a. 10   b. 5   c. 3   d. 1   e. 1   f. 0   g. 0

Analysis

Under 25   You are hardheaded, distinctly down-to-earth and clearly you are very skeptical indeed about psychic matters in general and certainly resist the suggestion that you yourself have such powers. Parapsychologists (those scientists who study extrasensory perception in research laboratories) describe people like you as "black goats"! This implies that you have a very negative attitude to psychic matters – even to the extent that you might damp out any ESP in an experiment and even inhibit psychic powers in others. According to their predictions you should not score highly in the ESP tests which follow in the second part of this questionnaire, and might even end up performing *worse* than chance. Perhaps it would do no harm if you were a tiny bit more openminded. You may think it very unlikely that there is such a thing as ESP and be quite positive that you don't have it yourself – but ought you not to keep an open mind? Incidentally, parapsychologists contrast "goats" or disbelievers like yourself with believers, whom they call "sheep."

25 to 50   It is fairly clear that while you are not completely intolerant of psychic matters, you don't have any real tendency to believe in them and are pretty skeptical about whether you yourself possess them. Many people would consider this to be a balanced and healthy approach to the topic, and it is certainly true that for any evidence to impress you it would have to be very good. Parapsychologists (scientists who study ESP) divide believers and disbelievers in ESP along a scale which they have named the "sheep/goat continuum." At one end are the extreme skeptics ("black goats"), while somewhat less definite skeptics like yourself would be classed as a "gray goat." You would not normally be expected to do well on ESP tests, but you can check this for yourself in the experimental tests that follow in Part II of the questionnaire.

51 to 80   On the whole you are favorably disposed towards the idea of psychic powers and extrasensory perception and it is quite clear that you believe that you have a share of these powers yourself. Your attitude is shared by a very large number of people, and it is because of people with beliefs like yours, and the kind of phenomena that they report, that scientists have felt it to be worthwhile investigating psychic phenomena. While you have a high measure of confidence that some psychic powers exist, you have probably not reached the point of absolute commitment and if it could somehow be shown quite definitely that psychic phenomena were not real, you would be very surprised indeed but your world would not fall apart. Parapsychologists (scientists studying ESP) would classify you as a "gray sheep." They divide people up into "black goats" (extreme skeptics), "gray goats" (moderate skeptics), "gray sheep" (moderate believers) and "white sheep" (extreme believers). "Gray sheep" are supposed to be reasonably good at ESP tests: check this for yourself in Part II of the questionnaire.

81 to 115 You are one of those people who, for one reason or another, have made up their minds that psychic powers exist but you are also convinced that you have them yourself in some definite measure. You probably also believe that you can demonstrate them, in which case the tests in Part II will give you a chance to do this. Parapsychologists (scientific ESP researchers) classify people into four groups according to their attitude to ESP. The extreme skeptics are known as "black goats," the moderate skeptics as "gray goats," the moderate believers as "gray sheep" and the extreme believers as "white sheep." You are, without doubt, a "white sheep," and sheep are supposed to perform better in all ESP tests than are goats.

Over 115 This very high score suggests that you not only have a considerable interest in psychic matters, but also that you have a very definite belief in your own psychic or ESP ability. Of course no one can criticize your belief and it may well be that you do have these powers. However, a score as high as yours tends to be associated with an attitude of mind which is somewhat more than openminded – in fact you may not be quite as critical and discriminating as you should be. If you have not already taken part in some tests to determine whether or not you have ESP ability, then you should certainly attempt to see whether your belief is supported by scientific evidence. You could, as a start, take a stab at the tests which follow in Part II, but whatever the outcome there is no doubt that a small dose of skepticism in your outlook would do no harm. Parapsychologists classify believers in ESP as "sheep" and disbelievers as "goats." On their scale you would rank as the whitest of white sheep!

Below: the "sixth sense" is not the prerogative of human beings alone. Russian scientists found that a mother rabbit showed strong electrical responses at the moment when her young were killed – even though they were far away from her, submerged in a submarine at the time.

Graham Dean

Part II: Test Yourself for ESP

Caution! Read this introduction thoroughly before you turn the page – or you may jeopardize the tests!

Part II of the questionnaire consists of a brief introduction to the scientific approach to extrasensory perception and gives you an opportunity to test yourself to see whether you appear to have any genuine psychic powers.

It is absolutely vital that you follow the instructions most carefully, and more important than ever that you do not peek at the results or tables in advance. If you do even so much as glance at the scoring, the ESP tests could be spoiled and will not tell you anything about the phenomenon you are hoping to explore. But if you follow the instructions to the letter, and do not cheat in any way, then a high score on either of the two tests would be genuinely indicative of ESP, certainly to the extent that it could be worth your while repeating the experiments, possibly being tested by a university department researching into these matters. Read the following points carefully: they explain the background to the tests and how to conduct them to achieve the most accurate results.

The ESP Symbols

In the 1930s parapsychologists attempted to simplify the experimental situation and devise a standard experiment which would be easy to perform, to score and to evaluate. Our tests follow these general lines, and the target symbols that we employ were designed at Duke University in North Carolina for use in the laboratory of the eminent Dr. J. B. Rhine. The symbols, known as Zener Cards, consist of five bold, simple and distinct drawings – a star, a circle, a plus sign, a square and wavy lines – shown below in the photographs of five actual Zener Cards.

Before starting either of the experiments you (and your companion if you are conducting a telepathy test) should look at these symbols closely and get a clear image of them in your mind. When you are sure that you could copy each shape with reasonable accuracy from memory (it should take you a few minutes to learn them thoroughly) then you are probably sufficiently familiar with them to go ahead on the tests.

The Purpose of the Tests

The two tests aim to see whether you have the powers of (a) clairvoyance and (b) telepathy. The clairvoyance test you can conduct and score entirely on your own. For the telepathy test you will need someone else to help you. It is important that you choose someone who is seriously interested in doing the experiment properly and will also play the game "according to the rules." If there is someone with whom you have what you believe to be a good psychic or telepathic rapport, then by all means use him or her, but the experiment must be conducted with great care in order to guard against bogus and misleading results. Each test involves making 120 separate guesses, and allowing for time to pause between guesses you really should give yourself a minimum of half an hour to perform each test. Make sure that you and your helper have enough time and will not be disturbed at any time while you are performing the experiments.

Important note

For both the Clairvoyance and the Telepathy tests you will need to make yourself a separate experimental sheet on which to record your answers. We have provided an example of an experimental sheet on page 56, and you should copy this carefully, using a different sheet of paper for each test.

You can do this quite simply with a pencil and a ruler, making sure you get the right number of squares and that you make the boxes big enough to draw the symbols clearly and comfortably.

Do not use the example to mark in your answers. If you do, this may unconsciously influence anyone doing the test in the future. Catching a glimpse of your answers could invalidate the whole test.

These symbols – or "Zener Cards" – were devised to investigate ESP. Study them carefully before embarking on the clairvoyance or telepathy test.

Clairvoyance test

Clairvoyance is the perception by paranormal means of something which is neither in someone else's mind at the time, nor available to the normal senses. A classic example of clairvoyance would be the ability to read "in the mind's eye" down a deck of cards which had been shuffled and whose order no one had yet seen. Clairvoyance therefore can be practiced on your own (whereas telepathy is mind-to-mind contact and therefore requires two people to be present – the sender who thinks of something, and a receiver who tries to guess what the sender is thinking).

For the clairvoyance test your task is to attempt to visualize a set of 120 Zener Card symbols as they have been laid out on the clairvoyance target grid (printed sideways on page 54). **Do not look at the target grid until you have finished the experiment!** The cards are laid out in a series of 12 lines with 10 squares per line and there will be a roughly similar number of each symbol, though there might be slightly more of some than of others. They might be distributed in any order – you could get a number of symbols clustered together – for they are arranged entirely at random.

Before beginning the experiment make sure you have read these brief instructions carefully.

1. Write your name and the date and also the time at which the experiment begins and ends at the top of the experimental sheet you have copied from the example on page 56.
2. Do not feel that you have to hurry the test. Pace it out to suit yourself. You can take a short break from time to time if you please, but of course you should not check any of your results until you have completed the test.
3. Draw your symbols as clearly as you can so that there will be no doubt in your mind when you come to score as to which symbol you had drawn in.
4. Start at symbol number 1 and work down to symbol number 120 in sequence.
5. Use any method that you please for visualizing the target sequence.

After you have completed the test and not before, turn to page 10 to check your results.

Telepathy Test

In this your task is to guess at a sequence of symbols that are in the mind of the person collaborating with you in the test. There are two alternative target sequences printed out on pages 54 and 55 but **you should not look at or even glance at either** until the experiment is completed. Your colleague however will need to look at one of the sequences and will concentrate on each image in turn while you do your best to guess what is in his mind. For the telepathy test we have provided two random target grids so that both people involved in the test get a chance to guess at a sequence which is completely new to them.

Ideally the sender and the receiver should not be close to each other physically while the experiment is being conducted, and most modern parapsychological experiments tests of this kind are conducted in different rooms or even different buildings. This presents problems in coordinating guesses however, and for this pilot study – which should be treated as a guide only – it will be acceptable for you and your friend to be seated at opposite sides of a room, with your backs to each other and with no mirror or reflecting surface on hand which would allow one party to see the other. Before starting the experiment the receiver should draw up his own blank grid on a sheet of paper, and then read these brief instructions.

1. Write down the name of the sender and receiver, indicating which is which, and also the time, date and time taken at the top of the sheet you use. Note down also which target grid the sender is using.
2. Make sure that the sender has his chosen target grid and is seated in a position where the receiver cannot, even by mistake, see the sequence.
3. Make sure the receiver is seated comfortably with his back to the sender and has a pen handy.
4. Once the experiment is started, no words other than those given below should be spoken until the entire experiment has been completed.

5. When both sender and receiver are ready the receiver will say "Ready—1." At this point the sender should concentrate on the first symbol and attempt to "transmit" it in his mind to the receiver.
6. After the receiver has drawn whatever symbol he believes is being transmitted, and *only* when he has completed the drawing, he should then say "Ready—2" in a clear voice – and so on throughout the complete sequence of 120 symbols.
7. Either the sender or the receiver may call a short break by saying "Break" at any time, but no word should be exchanged between the two until the experiment continues, when one of the party says "Break over."
8. Under no circumstances should the receiver indicate to the sender what symbol he has drawn at any time, and if the sender does by chance discover what the receiver has drawn he should under no circumstances indicate whether the choice was correct or incorrect.
9. The pace of the experiment should be, within reason, determined by the receiver. If the sender feels that the receiver is calling too fast for him to be able to focus on the symbols he should say "Slow down," but no more.
10. Start at symbol number 1 and work down to symbol number 120 in sequence.
11. Use any method that you please for visualizing or transmitting the target sequence.
12. Draw your symbols as clearly as you can so that there will be no doubt in your mind when you come to score as to which symbol you had drawn in.
13. **In the telepathy test it is absolutely vital that both sender and receiver are working on the correct target number.** For this reason calling out "Ready—1," "Ready—2," "Ready—3" and so on, is essential.

After you have completed the test, and not before, turn to page 54 or 55 to check the results against target grid I or II, whichever you have been using.

TELEPATHY GRID I

CLAIRVOYANCE GRID

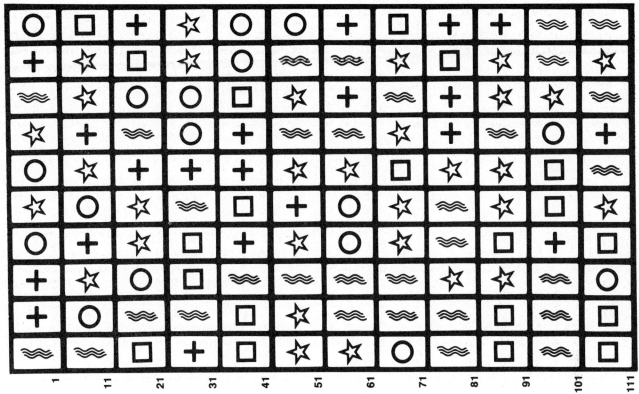

TELEPATHY GRID II

Your Score and What It Shows

These comments apply equally to both the clairvoyance and the telepathy tests.

After you have completed either the clairvoyance or the telepathy test, then and then only should you refer to the target series and note the number of correct hits you have achieved. If you want to be exceedingly cautious about this ask a friend to do the checking or double-checking. You will find the test is quite fatiguing, so if you wish to do two on the same day make sure that you leave an hour or so between them. Needless to say *you should not score or mark any part of the test until the whole of it has been completed*. It is most important in the telepathy test that the sender does *not* say whether you are right or wrong after each guess, and you should draw the symbols in silence.

The first step in evaluating your results is to deduct from the total that you have correct, in any one experiment, any "hits" that you got on the *first* or the *last* line of the grid (that is, numbers 1-10 and 111-120). To give an example, suppose that your total number correct for all 120 guesses is 25, and that 2 of these fell on the first line and one on the last line. This makes 3 hits that have to be eliminated from your score, leaving you with a final total of 22. This pruning process is to reduce the likelihood of your having unconsciously picked up some information about the answers, possibly by glancing at the grids by mistake when opening the test brochure. Too bad if you had 5 right on the first line and 5 right on the last line! You will now find yourself with a score of between 0 and 100, and most likely it will lie between 15 and 25, as the number correct out of 100 that would be expected by chance in this experiment has been calculated to be 20. If you have a result outside those figures, then it is interesting, but you should check against the following list for more detailed comments.

0-5 This is an exceedingly interesting result and one which, if it had been achieved under the rigid conditions normally introduced into a scientific parapsychology experiment, would lead the experimenters to consider that you were a potentially prize subject, showing unusual evidence of ESP. But there is a strange twist to this. You may think because you got so few right that this must mean that you are a complete dud at ESP. On the contrary, the fact is that you may be showing evidence of a kind of ESP which parapsychologists have termed "psi-missing" or "negative ESP" – a tendency to do *significantly less well* than one would by chance. The number that one would expect to get right simply by guessing (with no ESP present) is 20, and the achieving of any large score in excess of chance would seem to imply that the individual was getting information from somewhere about the distribution of the cards. But to do significantly *less* well than chance could also be interpreted as implying that he was *rejecting* information!

Parapsychologists claim to have identified a substantial minority of subjects who show negative ESP, and most interestingly they claim that is often associated with the "goatish" (high skeptical) type of personality. To be frank, if you have conducted the experiment honestly, you should certainly try to arrange for yourself to be tested by an expert in the field. It may be of course that this was just a fluke in your case and a few simple tests will serve to clarify this. Parapsychologists will be particularly interested in this low score if it has appeared on both tests.

6-10 This an unusually low score which many parapsychologists would consider was possible evidence for the fact that you are demonstrating "psi-missing" or "negative ESP" (see explanation given above in the 0-5 score). It would certainly be worthwhile, if you were genuinely interested in this topic and have conducted the experiments properly, getting yourself tested again by some competent authority. This will be particularly worthwhile if you have scored a low figure on both the clairvoyance and the telepathy tests. With this low score you should, according to one parapsychological theory, have come up with a skeptical or "goatish" score in Part I.

11-15 This low score is typical of the kind of result which parapsychologists know as "psi-missing" or "negative ESP" (see explanation under 0-5). In your case on these simple experiments the result is suggestive only, and you might try repeating the experiment to see whether you get the same kind of result again. A score of this kind is likely to be associated with a skeptical frame of mind about ESP, which would place you as a "black" or "gray goat" on Part I of the questionnaire. If you are interested in this topic it would be worth your while getting yourself tested again, by someone familiar with experimental parapsychology.

16-25 The only thing that can be said about your score is that it is average and, on the face of it, it would not seem as though you are showing any evidence of extrasensory perception. But this test is a pilot experiment only and if you still believe strongly that you have ESP you can always arrange to be tested by an expert. On the other hand, if you score in this range on one of the tests, but with an exceedingly high or low score on the other, then there may be something more to go on. Whatever happens remember that this is a simple pilot study only and to establish for certain whether one has or has not any ESP is a complicated scientific procedure. It is most likely, incidentally, that your score in Part I of the ESP questionnaire will place you as a "gray goat" or a "gray sheep."

26-30 This is an encouraging result, particularly if you have fallen into this range on both the clairvoyance and the telepathy tests. In a limited experiment of this kind, one can say no more than that it would be worth your while being retested if you can arrange it by someone with experience in parapsychological methods. If you have had a hunch for some time that you have psychic powers, then you could consider this score to provide some slight extra ammunition for your belief. The score is particularly interesting if it is associated with a "sheepish" personality as determined by Part I of the questionnaire.

31-40 A score in this range, particularly if it is above 35, is really a remarkably interesting one and is even more remarkable if you have achieved it on both the telepathy and clairvoyance tests. Are you sure that you conducted the experiment carefully and did not cheat or glance at the results beforehand? It would certainly be worthwhile trying to arrange to be tested independently by a parapsychologist who could then establish whether this was a lucky break in your case or whether you are showing any real evidence of extrasensory powers. Parapsychologists would expect you to be a "sheep," and probably a "white sheep" on Part I of the questionnaire.

Over 40 Anything above 40 is an abnormal and, for someone who believes he has ESP, a tremendously encouraging score. The odds against your scoring even in the low 40s by chance are literally thousands to one against and anything in the 50s, provided that you have conducted the experiment honestly, is truly sensational. Even with such a high score however you should not treat this as firm evidence of ESP until you have been tested in a parapsychology laboratory. If you have hit these high scores on both the telepathy and the clairvoyance tests, however, you should certainly do your best to contact a university department specializing in these experiments.

NOTE Anyone scoring below 10 on the first test and above 35 on the other would appear to be showing evidence of both negative and positive ESP. This would be an exceedingly interesting finding, and anyone who scores less than 5 on one test and over 40 on the other should make a point of being retested under experimental conditions.

EXPERIMENTAL SHEET

1	2	3	4	5	6	7	8	9	10		
11	12	13	14	15	16	17	18	19	20		
21	22	23	24	25	26	27	28	29	30		
31	32	33	34	35	36	37	38	39	40		
41	42	43	44	45	46	47	48	49	50		
51	52	53	54	55	56	57	58	59	60		
61	62	63	64	65	66	67	68	69	70		
71	72	73	74	75	76	77	78	79	80		
81	82	83	84	85	86	87	88	89	90		
91	92	93	94	95	96	97	98	99	100		
101	102	103	104	105	106	107	108	109	110		
111	112	113	114	115	116	117	118	119	120		

Are You a True Leader?

Ron Embleton

"All men are born free and equal" is an old and revered saying but one which does not stand too searching an investigation. The truth of the matter is that in our present society there are many tremendous differences in the genetic and environmental forces which play on human beings and mold them into clearly separate individuals and personalities. Some day perhaps these inequalities will be ironed out, though what the consequences will be for society is hard to determine. At the moment it is these personality differences which govern the relationships between human beings in society and upon which our whole political and economical system and the majority of our social customs are based.

This questionnaire deals with one of the most important facets of human difference – that strange capacity which some people seem to have to persuade and lead others and, to some extent, to control their ideas and behavior. Fill it in on your own with complete honesty and without attempting to work out the "hidden meaning" of any of the questions. If you devote too much time to a critical analysis of the material in the test you may end up with a seriously misleading picture of your own qualities in respect of this important factor – leadership. In our present society qualities of leadership tend to be associated with the male sex, but the questionnaire has been designed so that it also reflects leadership in women.

Mark your answers on a separate sheet.
1. Which of the following personality types would you feel was closest to yourself? (You may find it difficult to get an exact match, but pick the one which seems to you, on balance, to be closest.)
- **a.** An aggressive, pushy person determined to get things done at all costs – and generally manages to!
- **b.** An aggressive and generally pushy person who likes to get things done, but is rather less successful doing so than he might have hoped.
- **c.** A slightly aggressive and not overpushy type who enjoys getting things done but doesn't believe in letting them get him down.
- **d.** An average, not particularly pushy type who still likes to make sure that work is done and done properly.
- **e.** A quiet, withdrawn type who nevertheless knows what he wants and tends to get it.
- **f.** A quiet, withdrawn type who couldn't care less whether work is done or not.

2. (All men and women who are employed full-time answer this question.)
You are told that you are to be promoted in your job. It will involve considerable extra responsibility with a larger number of people under your supervision. Which of the following most closely corresponds to your reaction to the sudden news?
- **a.** Absolutely delighted to get the promotion.
- **b.** Pleased to get the promotion.
- **c.** Pleased, but rather surprised to get it.
- **d.** Surprised and not as happy as you might be.

3. (All men and women who are employed full-time answer this question.)
Which of the following most closely corresponds to your feelings about how you will handle the responsibilities of looking after this larger team?
- **a.** Completely confident about your ability because you have never found the slightest difficulty in handling people before.
- **b.** Confident and stimulated, but aware that there may be many complicated personality and social problems to face.
- **c.** Prepared to have a go as you feel it will teach you to handle people.
- **d.** Definitely uneasy about the problems of coping with so many subordinates.

4. (For housewives and those not employed.)
You have been given the opportunity of organizing a new social group in your neighborhood which will involve running a large committee and supervising voluntary workers. Which of the following most closely corresponds to your reaction to the news?
  a. Absolutely delighted at the opportunity.
  b. Pleased to get the opportunity.
  c. Pleased, but rather surprised to get it.
  d. Surprised, and not as happy as you might be.

5. (For housewives and those not employed.)
Which of the following most closely corresponds to your feelings about how you will handle the responsibilities of looking after this large committee?
  a. Completely confident about your ability because you have never found the slightest difficulty in handling people before.
  b. Confident and stimulated, but aware that there may be many complicated personality and social problems to face.
  c. Prepared to have a go as you feel it will teach you to handle people.
  d. Definitely uneasy about the problems of coping with so many workers.

6. Imagine you could observe yourself at a party or social gathering, in which of the following roles would you most likely be seen?
  a. The center of a largish conversational group, with you doing the majority of talking.
  b. Participating in a conversational group, not necessarily doing much talking, but steering it your way in accordance with your interests.
  c. Drifting around from group to group picking up the conversation when it suits you.
  d. Generally hanging around waiting for someone to engage you in conversation.

7. Imagine that you have to tell a subordinate in his twenties that he is to be dismissed. Which of the following tactics would you be *most* likely to adopt?
  a. Invite him into your office and give him the news without drama but straight between the eyes.
  b. Take him out to lunch, buy him a few drinks and then tell him.
  c. Write him a personal letter giving him the facts and ask him to see you if he wants to discuss it.
  d. Break the news as gently as you can, making up an excuse which you feel will help to preserve his ego as much as possible.

8. Indicate whether you strongly agree, tend to agree, tend to disagree, or strongly disagree with each of the following statements.
  a. Manners maketh the man.
  b. A firm handshake denotes a strong personality.
  c. It is difficult to lead people if one is short in stature.
  d. One should beware of exceedingly talkative people.
  e. Firmness is the most important quality in leadership.

  f. One cannot get through to people on the telephone.
  g. A good speaking voice is essential if one is to command respect.
  h. Before making any decision one should weigh up the pros and cons most carefully.
  i. The best way of arriving at a solution to a complicated problem is to form a committee.
  j. You gain nothing by raising your voice in argument.

9. You are invited to give an after-dinner speech to an important group. Which of the following most closely approximates your response?
  a. Accept willingly and plan an impromptu off-the-cuff speech which you know your audience will enjoy.
  b. Accept willingly and plan to use the opportunity to put over some new ideas that you are eager to talk about.
  c. Accept with reservation and decide to read a carefully prepared "formula" speech.
  d. Refuse as the idea makes you quake.

10. In a working or social situation you badly want something done a particular way. Do you
  a. Fight to get what you want done and press on until you get it, come what may?
  b. Work hard on getting what you want done, compromising where necessary, but generally on minor points only?
  c. Go for what you can get, but give way whenever you meet serious opposition?

11. Answer the following questions with "yes" or "no".
  a. When you are making a point or presenting an argument, do people listen respectfully and intently?
  b. Do you tend to interrupt people when they are in conversation with you?
  c. Do you keep a careful diary of your future work and appointments?
  d. Do you frequently seem to be able to get your way without really trying?
  e. Do you make a practice of looking intently in people's eyes when you speak to them?
  f. Do people tend to stand aside for you or let you go through doors ahead of them? (Men only answer)
  g. In a social situation do you tend to find yourself "running things"? (Women only answer)
  h. Would you say that people tend to be afraid of you?
  i. Would you say that most people tend to respect you?
  j. Would you say that most people tend to like you?
  k. When you speak do you tend to emphasize your points with vigorous hand gestures?
  l. Do you feel that, given luck and the right people to work with, you could solve almost any problem?

12. The dictators Hitler and Mussolini both had huge offices with a single desk situated on the opposite side of the room from the door. Do you think that this was a good strategy on their part?

13. If "yes" to 12, was this because
  a. The large room was symbolic of power?

Popperfoto

The magnetic personality of the true leader is a powerful social tool. Churchill made personal visits to the front to boost the morale of the troops of World War II.

b. The long walk across the room was guaranteed to make their visitors feel small?

c. They were probably men who hated to be confined?

14. By hypnosis it is claimed that one person can influence another in a highly unusual way. Which of the following do you think is the most likely explanation of this?

a. Hypnotism is probably a supernatural power.

b. The ritual in hypnotism is designed to make an already dominating person even more dominating.

c. Hypnosis is probably more a matter of applied psychology than anything else.

d. Hypnosis is a lot of bunk which is mainly play acting.

15. Someone has asked you for advice on how to improve their ability as a leader. Which of the following would you be most likely to recommend him to do?

a. Cultivate some self-confidence by learning about his own strong points.

b. Take a "Dale Carnegie"-type self-improvement course.

c. Learn to listen to other people carefully and become aware of social relationships.

d. Take a good course in elocution and public speaking.

16. Here are a number of attributes or qualities which a person could possess and which may contribute to his capacity to exercise effective leadership qualities. Check in each case whether you consider these to be highly important, quite important, relatively unimportant or totally unimportant to his success as a leader.

a. Commanding speaking voice.

b. Impeccable manners.

c. Good quality clothes, just right in fashion.

d. Efficient administrative back-up – secretaries, juniors, and so on.

e. Ability to take control of committees.

f. Limitless energy and capacity for hard work.

g. Knowing the right people.

h. Determination to succeed at all costs.

i. Refusal to take "no" for an answer.

j. Striking or dominating physical appearance.

k. Good sense of humor.

l. Cultured, educated background.

m. Expensive, but tasteful office furnishings.

n. Understanding of psychology and human nature.

o. Ability to make people work hard whether they like it or not.

p. Reputation as a good host and social entertainer.

q. Determination not to hurt others' feelings.

Now turn to page 60 to check your scores.

Scores

(Total your score to find your analysis.)

1. a. 2B b. 1B c. 0 d. 1L e. 2L f. 0
2. a. 1B b. 1L c. 0 d. 0
3. a. 2B b. 2L c. 0 d. 0
4. a. 1B b. 1L c. 0 c. 0
5. a. 2B b. 2L c. 0 d. 0
6. a. 2B b. 2L c. 0 d. 0
7. a. 2B b. 0 c. 0 d. 1L

	Strongly agree	Tend to agree	Tend to disagree	Strongly disagree
8. a.	0	1L	0	2B
b.	0	1B	0	1L
c.	0	0	1L	1B
d.	0	1L	1B	2B
e.	2B	1L	0	0
f.	0	0	1L	2B
g.	0	0	1L	0
h.	0	0	1L	1B
i.	0	0	1L	1B
j.	0	1L	1B	2B

9. a. 2B b. 2L c. 0 d. 0
10. a. 2B b. 2L c. 0

11.	Yes	No			Yes	No
a.	1B	0		g.	1B	0
b.	1B	0		h.	1B	0
c.	1L	0		i.	1L	0
d.	1L	0		j.	0	1B
e.	1B	0		k.	1B	0
f.	1B	0		l.	1L	0

12. yes 1B no 0
13. a 1B b. 1L c. 0
14. a. 0 b. 2B c. 2L d. 0
15. a. 1L b. 0 c. 1L d. 1B

	Highly important	Quite important	Relatively unimportant	Totally unimportant
16. a.	0	1B	1L	0
b.	0	0	0	1B
c.	0	0	1L	1B
d.	0	1L	1B	0
e.	1B	1L	0	0
f.	1B	1L	0	0
g.	0	1B	1L	0
h.	2B	1B	0	0
i.	2B	1B	1L	0
j.	1B	1L	1L	0
k.	0	1L	0	1B
l.	0	0	1L	1B
m.	0	0	1L	0
n	0	1L	0	1B
o.	2B	1B	1L	0
p.	0	0	0	0
q.	0	0	0	1B

After scoring you will have a number of B scores and a number of L scores. On the whole, the higher your total scores (Bs and Ls together) the more likely it is that you are a good leader in at least one, possibly many, situations.

But there is more to it than this. The B scores denote a pushy, bossy kind of leadership, while the L scores denote more subtly, psychologically based qualities. On the whole, the former are more likely to be a part of your "nature," while the latter are more likely to have been learned or acquired as the result of experience, training and clever observation. Add B and L scores together and read on for a more detailed analysis.

Analysis

0-10 This is really a rather unlikely score which means, assuming that you have filled the questionnaire in properly, that you really have little to offer the world as a leader. In fact you are probably an exceedingly passive person who tends to get pushed around quite a bit. If your combined score really is as low as this, then you are almost certainly not doing yourself justice and life will be much happier for you if you try to identify and exercise your real talents.

11-20 This is not a very high score and the chances are that you are a relatively quiet person, not inclined to take the lead and content to let decision making and project direction fall into other people's hands. It is very possible that you are basically content with this, though if you have a very high B score and are low on Ls, the chances are that you would like to run things rather more effectively than you do. If this is the case, you should try to learn to be more observant and conscious of social relationships. Conversely, if you are high in Ls and low in Bs you are probably simply not being assertive enough.

21-30 You have the makings of a leader, though unless your score is touching on 30 you do not have the where-withall at the moment to succeed as one. This is particularly true if you are very high in Bs, which means that you are being bossy and self-assertive and yet lack the social graces and psychological knowledge to go with it. If you are high in Ls you may be a bit introverted and this will hold you back, at least as far as leadership is concerned.

31-40 This score denotes, without doubt, that you have many of the basic qualities which make up leaders in our society. This is particularly true if your score is balanced nicely between Ls and Bs. The chances are that you already have some measure of administrative responsibility and that people somehow seem to "like working for you." If your score is largely made up of Bs, however, then you may be a far less effective leader than you think – too dominating and yet tending to be insensitive to others. This may get you places, but not in the most satisfactory way. If your score is high in Ls, then you have lots of the natural understanding which makes up a leader, but your low B rating indicates that you are simply not dominating or aggressive enough to get very far. On the other hand, you may be able to achieve quite a bit in your own way, steering people who do not realize that you are steering them.

41-50 You have definite leadership qualities and probably already control and guide the destinies of a number of subordinates. Ideally, your score should be balanced so that you have a roughly equal number of Bs and Ls, but if you are high on Bs then you are getting your own way through the sheer force of your personality. No doubt this works, but it may not make you too well liked! If you have a high L and a low B score on the other hand you are achieving your goals by subtlety and psychology. Just a bit more pushiness and you could probably really go places.

Over 50 Congratulations, you are a real leader! This is particularly so if your Bs and Ls are balanced out pretty evenly. A very high B rate will be slightly alarming, however – this is the stuff that dictators are made of. A high L rating makes you more suited to diplomacy and a touch of intrigue. Either way, you really know how to move people around.

Spectrum

Are You a Hypochondriac?

The human body is a complex system which survives in a hostile world by virtue of its elaborate defense mechanisms, mainly aimed at preventing invasion from alien organisms which cause disease and tissue damage. But no living system is perfect and we all, at some time in our lives, suffer from illness of one kind or another. Furthermore there is a considerable difference in individual human resistance to disease, much of which is dependent upon our genetic inheritance. Our basic constitution can also be helped along (or hindered) by our attitude to health – how sensibly we look after our bodies, their nutritional and exercise requirements and how speedily and appropriately we treat them when an illness *does* strike.

A reasonable preoccupation with health is one thing – an obsessive interest in it, generally known as hypochrondria, is another. Doctors are now agreed that far from raising one's general level of health, a hypochondriacal tendency can do more harm than good. This questionnaire is designed to give an indication of whether you have a streak of hypochondria in your make-up and, if so, how deeply ingrained it is! As with all questionnaires, you should answer the questions completely honestly for the best results, and ideally fill out the questionnaire on your own.

Mark your answers on a separate sheet.

1. Which of the following most accurately describes your overall *physical* condition?
   a. More or less totally free of physical illnesses of any kind.
   b. Physically very fit, but subject to the occasional illness.
   c. Reasonably fit physically, but with a tendency to be troubled with minor illnesses of one kind or another.
   d. Rather prone to suffer physical illnesses and rarely fully fit.
   e. Generally in a poor and debilitated state of health.

2. Which of the following most closely approximates your overall *psychological* condition?
   a. Bursting with energy and optimism at all times.
   b. Generally pretty energetic and optimistic.
   c. Sometimes energetic, sometimes not.
   d. On the whole rather lacking in energy and tending to feel flat.
   e. Feeling flat and short of vitality pretty well all the time.

3. How likely do you feel you are to suffer from illnesses of one kind or another in comparison with other people of your age group?
   a. Much more likely
   b. Rather more likely
   c. About the same
   d. Rather less likely
   e. Much less likely

4. Have you ever suffered from mysterious flutterings or palpitations of the heart?

5. If yes to 4, have these worried you to the extent that you have consulted a doctor about them?

6. If yes to 5, did the doctor find anything physically wrong with your heart?

7. If no to 5, have you continued to be worried by the fluttering, palpitations, and so on?

8. If you find a magazine for doctors or the medical profession around, do you read it eagerly even if you do not fully understand it?

9. If yes to 8, have you ever found yourself worrying about some of the illnesses that you saw described in it?

10. Have you ever felt worried that you had some major illness such as TB or cancer?

11. If yes to 10, did you visit your doctor about this?

12. If yes to 11, when you visited him did the doctor give you a clean bill of health?

13. If no to 11, have you continued to be worried that you may have such an illness?

14. Do you have a really well stocked medicine chest?

15. If yes to 14, is it full of bottles, lotions and pills prescribed long ago which you cannot quite bring yourself to throw out?

16. How often do you take aspirin? (In women, other than for period pains.)
  a. Daily
  b. Once or twice a week
  c. Once or twice a month
  d. Once or twice a year
  e. Hardly ever

17. Is this aspirin prescribed to you by the doctor?

18. Do you find that one particular proprietary brand of aspirin is far more effective than any other?

19. Do you *really enjoy* TV hospital dramas – say more than Westerns or detective stories?

20. Do you tend to suffer frequently from breathlessness, giddiness, dizzy spells, and so on?

21. Assuming that you are in average health, how frequently do you seek a medical checkup either for routine or specific reasons?
  a. Less than once a year
  b. Once a year
  c. Twice a year
  d. Three or four times a year
  e. Monthly or more frequently

22. Do you take a daily dose of vitamin pills?

23. Do you sometimes take "extra" vitamins when you feel run down or out of sorts?

24. When eating out in restaurants does it put you off your food if you see even the slightest sign of uncleanliness in your surroundings?

25. If someone tells you that they have a particular illness can you almost immediately think of someone in your family (including yourself) who has also had it?

26. If yes to 25, are you then inclined to give the other person specific details of the treatment as it applied to you or your family?

27. When you get a common illness of the 'flu, sore throat or stomach variety, do you seem to be more affected by it than other people?

28. If yes, do you let it affect your work or social life?

29. When you have illnesses of this kind, do you have a "pet treatment" for them – other than those prescribed by the doctor?

30. If yes to 29, do you recommend these pet treatments urgently to friends when they have the illnesses?

31. Supposing that you had the opportunity to witness a major intestinal operation, which of the following would be closest to your reaction?
  a. Accept with eagerness as you have always wanted to see how something like this looks.
  b. Accept with curiosity because you feel it would be a mistake to turn down such an opportunity.
  c. Accept with trepidation and fear that you may faint when the time comes.
  d. Refuse on the grounds that you are afraid you might faint or be shocked.
  e. Refuse on the grounds that the less one knows about these things the better.
  f. Refuse because you are simply not interested.

32. Do you find yourself seriously upset at the sight of blood?

33. Tick which most closely mirrors your own attitude to "patent medicines."
  a. Never use them.
  b. Use them sometimes, more for fun than anything.
  c. Use them sometimes, when nothing else seems to work.

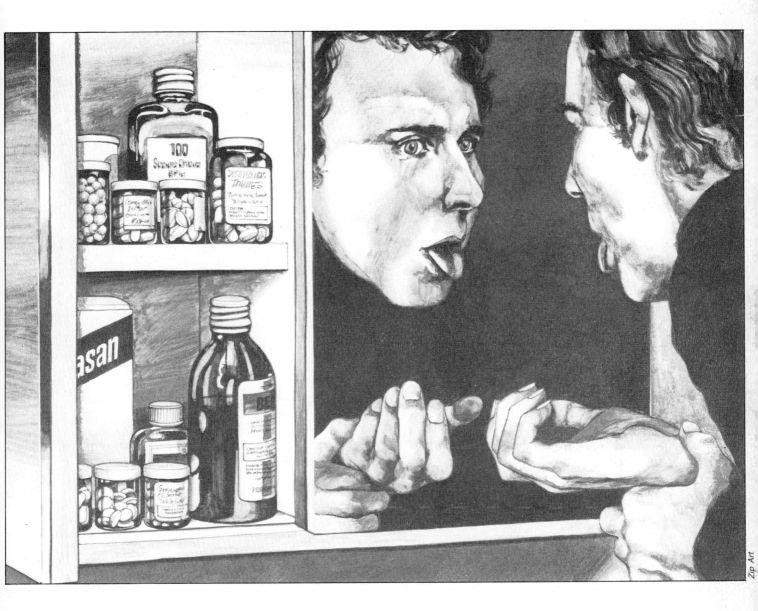

d. Use them sometimes, for certain things, because they do seem to work.

e. Use them regularly.

34. You meet a friend and he or she starts to tell you about his/her latest medical problem. Do you

a. Listen to it with patience and produce a few sympathetic remarks?

b. Listen with interest and offer advice where you can?

c. Listen impatiently and shut him/her up as soon as you can?

d. Wait until he/she has finished and then respond with your own medical anecdote?

35. How often do you take your own temperature to find out if you

are ill?

a. Never.

b. Only when you suspect you have the 'flu or some other illness.

c. Whenever you feel a bit run down.

d. Regularly.

36. How often do you take your own pulse?

a. Never.

b. When you feel seriously ill.

c. Whenever you feel flustered or agitated.

d. Regularly.

Now turn to page 64 to check your answers.

Scores

(Total your scores to find your analysis below.)

1.	a. 0	b. 0	c. 0	d. 1	e. 3	
2.	a. 0	b. 0	c. 0	d. 1	e. 3	
3.	a. 5	b. 1	c. 0	d. 0	e. 0	
4.	yes 1	no 0				
5.	yes 3	no 0				
6.	yes –4	no 2				
7.	yes 3	no 0				
8.	yes 1	no 0				
9.	yes 2	no 0				
10.	yes 1	no 0				
11.	yes 3	no 0				
12.	yes 2	no –4				
13.	yes 3	no 0				
14.	yes 1	no 0				
15.	yes 3	no 0				
16.	a. 5	b. 3	c. 1	d. 0	e. 0	
17.	yes: subtract any points scored in 16					
	no 0					
18.	yes 3	no 0				
19.	yes 3	no 0				
20.	yes 2	no 0				
21.	a. 0	b. 0	c. 1	d. 3	e. 5	
22.	yes 1	no 0				
23.	yes 3	no 0				
24.	yes 2	no 0				
25.	yes 2	no 0				

26.	yes 2	no 0				
27.	yes 1	no 0				
28.	yes 2	no 0				
29.	yes 2	no 0				
30.	yes 2	no 0				
31.	a. 3	b. 0	c. 3	d. 0	e. 1	f. 0
32.	yes 1	no 0				
33.	a. 0	b. 1	c. 2	d. 3	e. 5	
34.	a. 0	b. 2	c. 0	d. 3		
35.	a. 0	b. 0	c. 1	d. 3		
36.	a. 0	b. 1	c. 3	d. 5		

NOTE

This questionnaire is likely to be extremely unreliable for people over the age of 70 and will not represent a true hypochondria factor for those who have suffered a severe physical illness. It is also necessary to introduce an age correction factor so that, to your score, you should add or subtract points according to your age on the following scale of years:

Over 70	subtract 5 points
50 – 70	subtract 3 points
40 – 60	score as is
30 – 40	add 3 points
Under 30	add 5 points

Analysis

0-10 This is a very low score which indicates that there is almost certainly no trace of hypochondria in your nature. In fact one might even go as far as to say that you are supremely indifferent to the changes that take place to your state of health in the course of your life. This could be because you really are exceedingly healthy or it might just denote a slight degree of insensitiveness. If so, be careful – do not take your health too much for granted and overstress your body or mind as a consequence.

11-20 This is probably closest to the normal or average person. Like most human beings you have occasional anxieties about your health but provided they do not preoccupy you, you are in no danger of being a hypochondriac. Judging by your low score there is no chance of this.

21-30 You have a touch of the hypochondriac about you, and while this is unlikely to be strong enough to upset your social or domestic life it does mean that you tend to fuss about minor illness rather more than is necessary. The chances are that you are also a bit inclined to self-medication, dosing yourself with things which probably don't do you any harm, but may not do you much good either. But as long as this does not worry you unduly or prevent you from going to a doctor for proper treatment *when necessary,* then no harm is likely to be done.

31-40 There is not much doubt that you are a bit of a hypochondriac. It is also possible that people recognize this in you and you may have had a few jokes told at your expense. The trouble is that you probably do not look upon your behavior as being hypochondriacal at all and, if you *do,* you may argue that dosing yourself or being over-solicitous about your health staves off deeper worries.

Even this level of hypochondria is not really harmful unless it definitely interferes with your happiness and makes you a nuisance to yourself and family. But if you have not been to see a physician recently (say within the last year), it could do no harm to see one. The chances are that you will get a perfectly clean bill of health, and if you take the test again in a month's time you might come out with quite a different rating!

41-60 Let's face it, you are a hypochondriac. You probably love pills, medicines, all medical paraphernalia and even very likely get a big thrill out of seeing your doctor. Fine, as long as it doesn't cripple your pocket or bore him to distraction. But seriously, try to relax a bit about your health – if you are not suffering from a serious illness and your physician has told you this, there is not much point in worrying about what *might* happen to you if you really did get ill. Psychological advice might help; sometimes chronic hypochondria masks anxiety about problems which could be sorted out by discussion with a qualified psychologist.

Over 60 This really is a very high score and if you have filled out the questionnaire honestly and accurately you really are a hypochondriac and no mistake. There are two things you can do if you have not already done so: first, go to a physician for a complete medical checkup, and if he tells you there is nothing physically the matter with you, then try to accept his statement as an expert; and second, if you still find yourself worried about your health, then seek the ear of a sympathetic and qualified psychologist who may be able to help you with your anxieties.

How Creative Are You?

Most people speak of creativity without knowing quite what it means. Is it just the capacity to paint an original picture or write a poem? Far from it. Creativity is a basic characteristic built into all human beings and almost completely absent in animals. It involves seeing novel relationships between things, and as such it is closely related to intelligence. It involves converting the random, the mediocre or the dull into something with form, style and originality. It is relatively easy to measure, and psychologists have recently devised tests to do this.

Interest in measuring creativity in an objective way only started in earnest after the launch of the first Sputnik. Staggered by the apparent lead which the USSR had gained in space technology, the US began to realize the great need for selecting the most creative scientists and technologists. The focus of interest shifted from what had once been considered to be the essence of creativity—artistic appreciation, skill and endeavor—towards the problem-solving nature of the creative process. Special psychological tests of great sophistication are now employed to study this and the following questionnaire should be taken as establishing a guideline only. Nevertheless, if you tackle it carefully, thoughtfully and honestly, it could help you to an appreciation of your own creative potential. The first section deals with creative thinking itself.

Section 1: Creativity tests

The first section is divided into eight "do-it-yourself" tests. You should allow yourself two minutes, and two minutes only, for each test, so have a watch with a second hand at your side. Do each test independently, and do *not* refer to the scoring code and analysis until you have completed all eight tests. Give yourself a break between the tests—the break can be as long as you like, but a quarter of an hour is perhaps the ideal. This means that to do this test properly you will have to set a few hours aside without interruption. You could, of course, spread it over a few evenings, but remember *do not refer* to the analysis and *do not start* the second section until you have completed all eight tests.

Mark your answers on a separate sheet.
It is important that you keep strictly to the time limit of *two minutes* for each question.

Test 1   Start off with any word, idea or image then write down the next thing that comes to mind, then the next associated with the second, and so on. Let your mind roam freely: it does not matter about making sense.

Test 2   How many things could this picture represent?

Test 3   Write down as many names of trees as you can.

Test 4   Look at the diagram steadily. How many times does your perspective change in the two minutes?

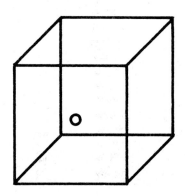

Test 5   Name as many objects as you can that are white, soft and edible.

Test 6   How many uses can you think of for a piece of brown paper?

Test 7   Write down as many words as you can beginning with the letter I.

Test 8   Take away two matches from the pattern and leave two complete squares and no spare matches.

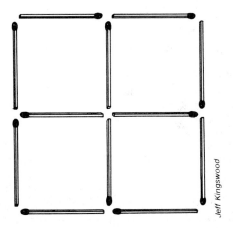

Jeff Kingswood

Section 2: Multiple choices

This is a more straightforward multiple choice questionnaire and it simply deals with creativity in everyday life. Complete the questionnaire and then refer to the end for the analysis of Sections 1 and 2.

1. If you get the chance to do something you have never done before, do you
   a. Turn it down?
   b. Hesitate between interest and apprehension?
   c. Take it eagerly?

2. You visit a friend's house and notice that the furniture is not arranged conveniently or comfortably. Would you
   a. Say nothing?
   b. Figure out roughly how you might change it?
   c. Make suggestions and draw up a plan?

3. Do you find you question things that most people seem to take for granted?
- **a.** Rarely
- **b.** Often
- **c.** Sometimes

4. When you see a competition for dreaming up slogans, do you
- **a.** Turn the page quickly?
- **b.** Consider it idly for a couple of minutes?
- **c.** Really try to work something out, and perhaps send it in?

5. When you read something interesting do you
- **a.** File it in your mind for future use?
- **b.** Forget it soon afterwards?
- **c.** Follow it up by trying to find out more about the topic?

6. You have to look after a child for an afternoon and he complains of being bored. Would you
- **a.** Think of some activities that you know will keep him happy and busy?
- **b.** Tell him to stop bothering you and to play by himself?
- **c.** Make suggestions for activities to him?

7. When you go in for "do-it-yourself" or when you cook, do you
- **a.** Improvise rather than follow the instructions or recipe exactly?
- **b.** Always stick to the instructions?
- **c.** Only try variations after you have followed the recipe or instructions a couple of times?

8. Do you have ideas about how improvements could be made at work?
- **a.** Often
- **b.** Occasionally
- **c.** Not really

9. If you answered a or b to question 8, do you
- **a.** Not bother to tell anyone else your ideas?
- **b.** Tell them to someone else, but not work out the details?
- **c.** Draw up a plan, get your facts and figures right, then present it to your boss?

10. How do you feel if you see a movie with a strange ending, leaving you uncertain about what actually happened?
- **a.** Uneasy, wanting it to be clear.
- **b.** Intrigued, and interested in thinking it out for yourself.
- **c.** Puzzled, but not worried.

11. When friends come to you with problems, do you
- **a.** Listen sympathetically?
- **b.** Think of what you would do in their situation, but say little?
- **c.** Make constructive suggestions?

12. Which is true for you?
- **a.** I like a peaceful life with a dependable routine.
- **b.** I like lots of change and excitement in my life.
- **c.** I like a certain amount of excitement in my life, but not too much.

13. When a change takes place in your life, like leaving home, taking a new job, getting married or getting divorced, do you
- **a.** Feel frightened about the unknown future?
- **b.** See the positive possibilities in the new situation?
- **c.** Alternate between fear and excitement?

14. If you inherited your parent's home, would you
- **a.** Keep it as they did, because it would feel somehow wrong to change it?
- **b.** Change it to suit your own personality and day-to-day convenience?
- **c.** Make some changes, but keep some things to remind you of them?

15. Do you find that unconventional sexual experimenting between two people who care for each other is
- **a.** Disgusting?
- **b.** Pleasurable?
- **c.** Possibly fun?

16. How would you choose to spend a birthday or special anniversary?
- **a.** Going out to a favorite restaurant.
- **b.** Quietly at home.
- **c.** Going somewhere new.

17. You get stuck on some practical task (making a dress or building a patio for example) and nothing seems to be going right. Would you be more likely to
- **a.** Give up in disgust?
- **b.** Keep doggedly on the same lines as before?
- **c.** Think of a new way round the problems?

18. When you read about the problems of world poverty, do you
- **a.** Feel that nothing can be done and that human beings have to put up with harsh conditions?
- **b.** Get angry and upset, but feel helpless?
- **c.** Make some effort, even if it is only sending a little money to a charity?

19. You are on the brink of a love affair that would bring you the disapproval of your friends and associates. Would you
- **a.** Go ahead joyfully?
- **b.** Go ahead, but take care to conceal your activities?
- **c.** Regretfully back out?

20. Which are you more afraid of?
- **a.** Boredom
- **b.** Loneliness
- **c.** Uncertainty

Now turn to page 67 and check your scores.

Scores

(Total your scores to find your analysis below. The scores here refer to Section 2 of the questionnaire only. For a discussion of your results on the tests in Section 1 refer to the analysis which follows.)

1. a. 0 b. 1 c. 2
2. a. 0 b. 1 c. 2
3. a. 0 b. 2 c. 1
4. a. 0 b. 1 c. 2
5. a. 1 b. 0 c. 2

6. a. 2 b. 0 c. 1
7. a. 2 b. 0 c. 1
8. a. 2 b. 1 c. 0
9. a. 0 b. 1 c. 2
10. a. 0 b. 2 c. 1

11. a. 0 b. 1 c. 2
12. a. 0 b. 2 c. 1
13. a. 0 b. 2 c. 1
14. a. 0 b. 2 c. 1
15. a. 0 b. 2 c. 1

16. a. 1 b. 0 c. 2
17. a. 0 b. 1 c. 2
18. a. 0 b. 1 c. 2
19. a. 2 b. 1 c. 0
20. a. 2 b. 1 c. 0

Analysis

Section 1: Creativity Tests

The essence of creativity is of course originality, and trying to find ways of scoring such an elusive concept has been a major problem confronting psychologists working in this area. After research, it was found that when people are faced with a problem situation, whether simple or complex, the number of possible responses or solutions to the problem they were able to come up with was a good indication of their creativity. In other words, the more ideas people produce relevant to a particular situation, the more original they tend to be.

Test 1

Score one point for every association you were able to come up with in the two minutes. If you score less than 10, generally low creativity; 11-20 average creativity; over 20 indicates high creativity.

Test 2

Count one for each answer you were able to come up with. 0-5 indicates low creativity; 6-10 average and over 10 high creativity.

Test 3

Count one for each answer you were able to come up with. 0-7 indicates low creativity; 8-15 average and above 15 is high.

Test 4

On the whole the more this Necker cube fluctuates the more flexible your perception. If it changed one, two or three times, this indicates low flexibility and hence creativity; four or five times average; more than five times shows high flexibility.

Test 5

Count one for each answer. 0-5 indicates low creativity; 6-10 average and above 10 high.

Test 6

Count one for each answer. In this case you should try to assess the originality of your answers by working out how many *types* of response you gave. Wrapping would be one type of response, and if you suggested wrapping several kinds of objects that is less original than suggesting one thing to be wrapped and then going on to other uses, such as making it into a blind, for example. Take two bonus points for each truly different use. 0-5 indicates low creativity, 6-10 is average and over 10 high.

Test 7

Count one for each answer. 0-5 indicates low creativity; 6-10 medium; above 10 high.

Test 8

The instructions did not say that the two squares had to be the same size! Did you get stuck on this one, or were you able to switch to a new way of seeing the problem? If you got it right you score in the high creativity group.

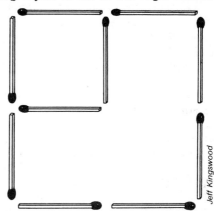

Jeff Kingswood

If you picked up between 2 and 4 high creativity scores in the eight tests this is a good average score. 4-6 indicates a high level of creativity, and 7 or 8 an especially high level.

Section 2

Here we are concerned with your potential for creativity in everyday life. The factors contributing to a high score can be summed up in the following seven questions:
1. How open are you to novel experience?
2. What kind of need do you feel to have stimulation from the environment?
3. How much are you prepared to tolerate uncertainty or ambiguity?
4. How adventurous are you?
5. How quick are you at perceiving the nature of problems?
6. How flexible are you in your thought processes?
7. How free are you from fear of authority?

You will have ended up with a score between 0 and 40. A score under 10 indicates a low level of creativity, between 11 and 20 an average level, 20-30 generally high level, and between 30 and 40 an exceedingly high level of creativity.

Could You Survive a Catastrophe?

For most people life is generally placid, untroubled and free from physical danger. But for all of us, sometime in our lives, there comes the moment of unexpected shock, danger and the risk of injury. Statistics show that the chances are exceedingly high that every motorist will be involved in at least one serious car accident and that as many as one in three motorists will receive at least one minor injury as a result. Car accidents are the mini-catastrophes of the twentieth century—but catastrophes occur on much wider and deeper levels. Each age worries about its own kind of global catastrophe—the ravages of famine, disease, war or revolution. Think for a moment and you will realize that all over the world people are fighting and surviving catastrophes every minute of the day.

How well would you survive if faced with a dramatic upset in your way of life? At a very personal level many of us can expect to be forced to change our way of living at a number of junction points in our lives. For some, these junction points will be catastrophic; for others—those psychologically geared to optimism—they need not necessarily be so. This questionnaire will test your capacity for survival at all levels of catastrophe from the major to the minor.

Mark your answers on a separate sheet.

1. A peaceful weekend at home is suddenly disrupted by the news of a close relative being rushed to hospital. You have to go to the hospital and look after the distraught wife of the sick man. Would you
- **a.** Feel completely unable to cope with the demands?
- **b.** Do your best, but long for everything quickly to get back to normal?
- **c.** Have a surge of energy to cope with the situation?

2. What would you do if you were suddenly made redundant?
- **a.** Get drunk.
- **b.** Feel quite pleased to have some time to yourself.
- **c.** Start immediately to make plans for another job.

3. Circumstances give you an evening on your own, with nothing pressing to do. Would you
- **a.** Relax and enjoy the solitude?
- **b.** Keep telephoning until you find someone to talk to?
- **c.** Create some busy work to keep yourself occupied?

4. Some younger friends ask you to join them on a camping holiday. Would you be more likely to
- **a.** Go if you had nothing better to do?
- **b.** Be keen enough to cancel any other arrangements in order to go?
- **c.** Refuse, because you prefer a more luxurious kind of holiday?

5. Imagine you were told that you had only six months to live. Would you
- **a.** Do as many of the things you had always wanted to do as you possibly could?
- **b.** Spend the time setting your affairs in order and preparing your family and friends?
- **c.** Go to every specialist you could find in an effort to regain your health?

6. When you have a mild headache, do you
- **a.** Take yourself to bed, or at least away from company?
- **b.** Ignore it and go on as usual?
- **c.** Take a painkiller and go on as usual?

7. You have decided to have an early night. An hour after you have fallen asleep, a friend telephones and invites you to what sounds like a good party. Would you
- **a.** Tell him that you want to sleep?
- **b.** Get up and join him?
- **c.** Decline politely?

8. You have the beginnings of toothache—not much, just an occasional twinge. Would you
- **a.** Make an appointment with your dentist?
- **b.** Think that you should see your dentist, but wait till it gets worse?
- **c.** Try to pretend that nothing is happening?

9. When you have been in trouble, have you ever thought that suicide would solve your problems?
- **a.** Never
- **b.** Fleetingly
- **c.** Often

10. You have saved up enough money to buy a house. A good buy comes up but you don't have enough money for furniture as well. Would you
- **a.** Move in and live in an empty house until you had more money?
- **b.** Make, or renovate, the essentials?
- **c.** Postpone buying until you could live in comfort?

11. How do you think you would react if you were a survivor of the collapse of society as we know it?
- **a.** By choosing death.
- **b.** By making the best of new conditions as you found them.
- **c.** You do not know.

12. Which statement is most true for you?
- **a.** The most important thing in my life is my work.
- **b.** My family is the most important thing in my life.
- **c.** Living every moment to the full is the most important thing in my life.

The 1972 Andes air disaster:
what began as a carefree trip
ended in calamity for the
passengers. Pictured (top) a few
minutes before the crash they were
reduced to eating the bodies of
dead companions. (Bottom) only the
fittest survived the
physical and mental ordeal.

13. Do you feel anxiety
   a. Only when there is something really bad happening to you?
   b. Often, for no apparent reason?
   c. Occasionally, when circumstances do not really warrant it?

14. If you saw someone being attacked in the street would you
   a. Try to help?
   b. Get out of the way quickly?
   c. Run for help?

15. Which statement is most true for you?
   a. I am a bit of a dreamer, and I put off taking action.
   b. When I have to make a decision, I hesitate a bit, then I plunge into action.
   c. I am more inclined to act than to sit around thinking.

16. If there was a serious accident outside your home, would you be more likely
   a. To help out, as you have a working knowledge of first aid?
   b. To help under direction, as you would not know what to do?
   c. At best, be able to help only by telephoning for an ambulance?

17. If your house was burgled, would you
   a. Feel shocked and upset?
   b. Call your insurance company with resignation?
   c. Feel really mad and want some kind of revenge on the burglars?

18. If your partner threatened to walk out, would you
   a. Offer to call a taxi?
   b. Try to talk reasonably?
   c. Beg him/her to stay?

19. Which would you find it easiest to go without?
   a. The telephone
   b. A car
   c. Convenience foods

20. Do you react to power cuts
   a. By using the candles and camping stove you keep for emergencies?
   b. By regretting your failure to make preparations?
   c. By going to bed until it is over?

21. How far could you walk before getting tired?
   a. Half a mile.
   b. Two miles.
   c. Six miles or more.

22. How far can you walk *after* you are tired?
   a. A couple of miles.
   b. Not a step.
   c. As far as you have to.

23. Which situation would frighten you most?
   a. Losing all your money, and your job.
   b. Losing your family and friends.
   c. Having a nervous breakdown.

24. Which of the following subjects do you know something about?
   a. Growing and preparation of food
   b. Medicine
   c. Building
   d. None of these

25. When you need money, do you
   a. Save it up as best you can?
   b. Figure out a way to make it?
   c. Borrow it if you can?

26 Which statement is true for you?
   a. I make flexible plans for my life, but I am certainly ready to change them if a good opportunity comes my way.
   b. I plan almost everything in my life and I always make sure I stick to it.
   c. I take life as it comes.

27. Which of these would you choose to be cast away with on a desert island?
   a. A box of tinned food
   b. A box of books
   c. A box of tools

28. If someone attacked you with intent to kill, would you be more likely to
   a. Give in, rather than kill your attacker?
   b. Kill your attacker if you got a chance?
   c. Run?

29. Do you need other people around you to give you a sense of purpose?
   a. Yes
   b. No
   c. Sometimes

30. Which of these unpleasant situations is most difficult for you to tolerate?
   a. Physical pain
   b. Social disapproval
   c. Depression

Now turn to page 71 and check your scores.

Scores

(Total your scores to find your analysis below.)

1.	a. 2	b. 4	c. 6	12.	a. 2	b. 4	c. 6	23.	a. 4	b. 6	c. 2
2.	a. 2	b. 4	c. 6	13.	a. 6	b. 2	c. 4	24.	a. yes 6	no 0	
3.	a. 6	b. 2	c. 4	14.	a. 6	b. 2	c. 4		b. yes 6	no 0	
4.	a. 4	b. 6	c. 2	15.	a. 2	b. 4	c. 6		c. yes 6	no 0	
5.	a. 6	b. 4	c. 2	16.	a. 6	b. 4	c. 2		d. yes 2	no 0	
6.	a. 2	b. 6	c. 4	17.	a. 2	b. 6	c. 4	25.	a. 4	b. 6	c. 2
7.	a. 2	b. 6	c. 4	18.	a. 6	b. 4	c. 2	26.	a. 6	b. 2	c. 4
8.	a. 6	b. 4	c. 2	19.	a. 2	b. 4	c. 6	27.	a. 2	b. 4	c. 6
9.	a. 6	b. 4	c. 2	20.	a. 6	b. 4	c. 2	28.	a. 2	b. 6	c. 4
10.	a. 4	b. 6	c. 2	21.	a. 2	b. 4	c. 6	29.	a. 2	b. 6	c. 4
11.	a. 2	b. 6	c. 4	22.	a. 4	b. 2	c. 6	30.	a. 4	b. 2	c. 6

Analysis

Check your score carefully and then count up your total number of points and refer to the analysis below. As a broad rule, the higher your score the greater your chance of surviving a catastrophe and handling it on both a short-term and long-term basis. But for more detailed comment on your individual score refer to the appropriate paragraph below.

Under 80: Exceedingly high risk
A score this low indicates frankly that you are amongst that section of humanity least likely to survive catastrophes in your life. The only advice one can give you is to stay out of trouble—avoid travel, do not go out at nights, and choose most carefully the company you keep! Life may be very dull for you, but you are too great a risk to be let out on your own! Are you sure you answered the questions honestly and added up your sums correctly?

80-100: Relatively high risk
This is a low score which suggests that on the whole you are not well-adapted to survive catastrophes in your life. You are probably overdependent, somewhat inflexible in your ideas and ways of behaving and a rather fearful individual. Actually a *real* catastrophe rather than the imaginary ones in this questionnaire would probably bring out a stronger urge for survival, and you may be better able to cope with situations of this kind than you think. Part of the problem is that you are rather hesitant in testing yourself and your abilities because of your "fear of failing." Be a little bolder!

101-135: Average survival factor
You, with the majority of other human beings, are reasonably competent to deal with catastrophic situations. There is a strong streak of caution in you, which would actually help your survival chances in a tight spot. This is tempered, however, by a certain amount of flexibility which would prevent you from being over-cautious. If the chips were really down you would stand a good chance of surviving, provided that a very great deal of initiative was not required of you. Built into your character is a definite inclination to follow rather than to lead. This works well and to your advantage in some situations, but not in all.

136-165: Good survival factor
This is a high score and it indicates pretty clearly that you would be one of life's winners in a really tough situation. Part of this is because you are a flexible individual which means that you see a number of possible escape routes out of any problem situation. You also have a basically courageous nature, which means that you will not be afraid to take chances in a risky situation. Very likely you are a vivacious person who enjoys problems rather than fears them. You can take your chance—and certainly survive—with the best in any part of the world.

Over 165: Very high survival factor
This is an exceedingly high score which suggests that you are one of those people who can get out of any kind of pickle. You would probably have survived the *Titanic* sinking, the San Francisco earthquake and the explosion of the Island of Krakatoa, even if you had been at all three of them! Seriously, if you really *are* scoring this high you are certainly a purposeful, energetic survivor. But perhaps you may even go so far as to court perilous situations: be careful, for recklessness could be a big danger factor in your life.

Are You a Happy Human? Part I

Anyone who studies the human condition knows that man passes through life in a fluctuating state of mind, sometimes deep in despondency and pessimism, at other times raised to the heights of happiness and elation. Few humans spend much time in the "balanced" state in between the two extremes, and most seem to have more than their fair share of joy or sadness.

One thing that everyone agrees on is that happiness is a truly desirable state – we all seek it out when we can, and escape from its opposite whenever possible. But despite the fact that happiness is so desirable, no human being has yet discovered a formula to achieve it with certainty. Some seek happiness through a quest for money and physical possessions; some through a hunt for power; some through the diversions of love and sex; some through drugs; some through intellectual pursuits; some through domestic happiness; some through vigorous interaction with others; and some again through total withdrawal from the world. But ask a happy man what it is that makes him happy and how he defines his happiness and he will be hard put to explain it to you. The truth of the matter is that whereas peaks of happiness – the joys of love, the rewards of physical fitness, the deep pleasures of satisfaction in seeing "a job well done," and so on – can be identified when they occur and are therefore useful goals in the quest for happiness, no single task or behavior pattern will in itself produce happiness for more than a brief period. True happiness arises out of a combination of different aspects of life, and in particular the achievement of a balance between these different aspects.

This questionnaire attempts to give you the opportunity to assess whether you have achieved such a balance and therefore how closely you approach the goal of being a "happy human." In the long run, of course, happiness is itself a state of mind and in most people's hearts lies the knowledge of whether they are truly happy or not. The chances are however that your scores in this detailed questionnaire, when plotted on the multifactorial chart at the end, will match pretty closely with your own intuitive feeling. What the final plot will do is to help you to identify those aspects of your life where the state of happiness is elusive and uncertain. Whether this will allow you to correct matters is largely up to you and your own essential personality.

Answer all the questions as honestly and truthfully as you can. In particular try not to score yourself as you feel you would *like to be,* or feel you ought to be. If you do that, you will come out with a score which may cheer you up for a moment, but won't tell you much about yourself!

Mark your answers on a separate sheet.

1. Do you sometimes wish that there were more than 24 hours in the day?

2. If you could move to another part of the country would you gladly do so?

3. Would you say that you actively enjoy the company of other people?

4. On the whole do you have deep refreshing sleep?

5. Do you suffer ever from any phobias or any other unnatural fears?

6. Would you say that you have made a contribution of some kind, however small it may be, towards other people's happiness?

7. Is you relationship with the person closest to you in life a really happy one?

8. Do you wish that you could have a bigger house or apartment than you have at present?

9. Which of the following most closely corresponds to what you feel about your general health, both physical and mental?

   a. Exceedingly fit at all times with no physical or mental problems whatsoever.
   b. Generally very fit with only the occasional and quite minor illness.
   c. Pretty fit on the whole, but occasionally prone to illness of one kind or another.
   d. Rather below the average in fitness, either physical, mental or both.
   e. Definitely rather a sick person with fairly serious mental or physical health problems.

10. Do you sometimes feel that life is just simply not worth living?

11. Do you like the neighborhood you live in?

12. Do you find yourself getting agitated and tense without good reason?

13. Is there anyone you come in frequent contact with that you actively dislike?

14. Do you have a job?

   a. If yes, do you get on pretty well with most of the people working with you?
   b. If no, do you honestly feel that you would be happy working with a group of people?

15. Do you find your life made less pleasant than it might be by noise from aircraft, traffic, neighbors, and so on?

16. When disappointed or let down by something, can you generally get over it by "looking on the bright side" or thinking of some treat to come?

17. Do you have a problem with your weight?

18. Where you live and the conditions in which you live are often important to your overall happiness. Which of the following most closely approximates the way you feel about your own home environment?
  a. Couldn't possibly be happier anywhere other than my present home.
  b. Generally very happy in my present home but could imagine that some places could be nicer.
  c. Pretty satisfied on the whole, but wouldn't mind moving somewhere better given the chance.
  d. Put up with my present home, but really would like to live somewhere else.
  e. Can't stand my present home and would do anything to leave it.

19. Do you feel that your own happiness and success in life has been hindered by your background or upbringing?

20. Do you have to take lots of aspirin or similar painkilling drugs?

21. Have you got a close friend, other than wife, husband or lover, with whom you can exchange confidences?

22. Do you really wish that you could afford better food for you and/or your family?

23. Do you generally have plenty of physical go and what is called "pep"?

24. Do you feel that man's great artistic and scientific achievements go some way to making up for his cruelty and selfishness?

25. Do you live alone?
  a. If yes, would you rather that you weren't living alone?
  b. If no, do you get on well with the person or people that you are living with?

26. Do you feel at ease with a crowd of strangers?

27. For most people life sometimes presents problems which seem insoluble and when these arise the thought of suicide sometimes comes into their minds. Which of the following is closest to your own attitude to suicide?
  a. I have never ever contemplated suicide and cannot imagine that I ever would.
  b. On very rare occasions the thought of suicide has flitted into my mind, but I have never given it any serious consideration.
  c. Once in a while I've thought of suicide but always dismissed it as being an unreasonable solution.
  d. I must confess that there are times when I've seriously wondered whether suicide might not be the best way out.
  e. I've often thought that I might be better off dead.

28. After a period away from your home, do you honestly look forward with pleasure to coming back to it?

29. Are you suffering from any kind of illness which is spoiling your pleasure in life?

30. Are you married?
  a. If yes, is your marriage a happy one?
  b. If no, are you quite happy that you are not married?

31. Are you deeply moved by music, poetry or other works of art?

32. Do you feel generally dissatisfied with the way in which you communicate with people?

33. In your home, do you have a place where you can get away from other people if you want to and do more or less as you please?

34. Have you had at least one deeply satisfying love affair in your life?

35. Do you seem to get more than your fair share of troublesome illness?

36. Indicate the statement that most closely matches your attitude to other people.
  a. I thoroughly enjoy other people's company and they enjoy mine.
  b. On the whole I get on very well with other people and mostly they get on well with me.
  c. I get on well with some people, others I simply don't hit it off with.
  d. There are few people that I really feel at ease with.
  e. I dislike other people and avoid contact with them whenever I can.

37. Is the place you live in furnished and decorated in a way that really pleases you?

38. Can you climb stairs or run short distances without getting puffed?

39. Do you often feel bursting with health and vitality?

40. Do you feel that, if you had the opportunity, you could be a good politician?

41. Are you having any type of treatment for psychological problems?

42. Would you describe yourself as being "difficult to get on with"?

43. Do you own a car?
  a. If no, do you really wish that you could own one?
  b. If yes, do you really wish that you could afford a much better one?

44. Has life become more challenging and rewarding for you since you became an adult?

Now turn to page 74 and check your scores.

Scores

1.	yes 1G	no 0				24.	yes 1G	no 0	
2.	yes 0	no 1D				25.a.	yes 0	no 1D	
3.	yes 1i	no 0				b.	yes 1D	no 0	
4.	yes 1H	no 0				26.	yes 1i	no 0	
5.	yes 0	no 1H				27.	a. 3G	b. 2G	c. 1G	d. 0	e. –1G
6.	yes 1G	no 0				28.	yes 1D	no 0	
7.	yes 1i	no 0				29.	yes 0	no 1H	
8.	yes 0	no 1D				30.a.	yes 1i	no 0	
9.	a. 3H	b. 2H	c. 1H	d. 0	e. –1H	b.	yes 1i	no 0	
10.	yes 0	no 1G				31.	yes 1G	no 0	
11.	yes 1D	no 0				32.	yes 0	no 1i	
12.	yes 0	no 1H				33.	yes 1D	no 0	
13.	yes 0	no 1i				34.	yes 1G	no 0	
14.a.	yes 1i	no 0				35.	yes 0	no 1H	
b.	yes 1i	no 0				36.	a. 3i	b. 2i	c. 1i	d. 0	e. –1i
15.	yes 0	no 1D				37.	yes 1D	no 0	
16.	yes 1G	no 0				38.	yes 1H	no 0	
17.	yes 0	no 1H				39.	yes 1G	no 0	
18.	a. 3D	b. 2D	c. 1D	d. 0	e. –1D	40.	yes 1i	no 0	
19.	yes 0	no 1G				41.	yes 0	no 1H	
20.	yes 0	no 1H				42.	yes 0	no 1i	
21.	yes 1i	no 0				43.a.	yes 0	no 1D	
22.	yes 0	no 1D				b.	yes 0	no 1D	
23.	yes 1H	no 0				44.	yes 1G	no 0	

As you score you will notice that you begin to accumulate four sets of values – D, i, H and G factors – in either plus or minus points. These refer in general to domestic, interpersonal, health and general factors and your maximum score in each case will be 13.

To interpret the significance of the scores you should plot them on the profile chart which appears at the end of Part II of this questionnaire. In the meanwhile, note down your scores for Part I so that they can be plotted on the chart *after* you have filled in the second part of the questionnaire. Do not, under any circumstances, read off your score at this stage against the analysis given at the end of Part II. If you do, this could affect the usefulness of the test.

Happiness Profile

When you have completed Part II of the questionnaire you will be able to plot your own Happiness Profile. As an example, we have shown on the right a hypothetical profile which includes all the personality factors from both parts of the test.

Each person's profile will be utterly individual, and the details of your own are likely to be quite different from the details shown here. Nor should you take them as any kind of norm: this imaginary man may seem to have some exalted areas of happiness, but his low scores on achievement and interpersonal relationships show that his cup of happiness is by no means full to the brim!

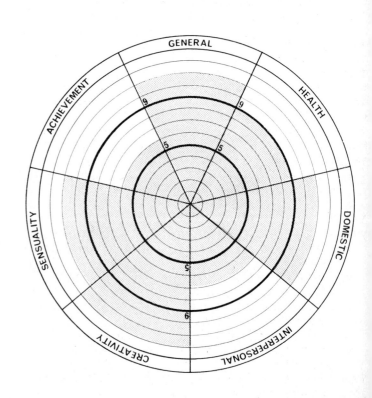

Are You a Happy Human? Part II

(Questions marked A should be answered by men: questions marked B should be answered by women.)

Mark your answers on a separate sheet.

1. Do you have any kind of hobby or creative pastime?
2. Do you really love good food?
3. (A) Have you been advancing in your job or profession as rapidly as you would like?
4. (B) Do you feel that you could get more out of life if you were a man?
5. Do you get real pleasure out of reading?
6. Do you feel that most people's success is largely due to their good luck?
7. Would you say that sexual enjoyment was one of the greatest pleasures in life?
8. (A) Do you feel that other people appreciate the contribution that make in your job?
9. How do you rate yourself as a sensualist?
   a. I enjoy the physical pleasures of life to the full and will continue to do so as long as I can.
   b. I very much appreciate life's physical pleasures and indulge them to some extent.
   c. Physical pleasures have their part to play, but they can be overrated.
   d. I don't get too much satisfaction from the "pleasures of the flesh."
   e. Physical pleasure of any kind leaves me cold.
10. (B) Do you have children?
    a. If yes, are you completely happy with the way they are developing or have developed?
    b. If no, do you very much wish that you had children?
11. Do you really enjoy setting off on holiday?
12. Do you like to indulge yourself in long hot baths?
13. Would you say that one of your greatest pleasures was facing up to a difficult task and succeeding in it?
14. Do you enjoy the feeling of well-being that follows vigorous exercise?
15. Are there some things which you would like to do right but which always turn out failures when you try them?
16. (B) Do you have a job at this time?
    a. If yes, do you feel that you have been able to make the most of it?
    b. If no, do you really wish that you could have one?
17. Which of the following is closest to your own view of yourself from the point of view of creativity and originality?
    a. I believe I am creative and in some respects a gifted individual.
    b. I have flashes of definite creativity and originality which please me greatly.
    c. I have a certain amount of creativity in me, but it is not my big thing.
    d. I am not a particularly creative person on the whole.
    e. I do not seem to have any sense of creativity or originality.
18. (A) Do you have problems with difficult or "unreasonable" superiors at work?
19. Could you sympathize, at least to some extent, with hedonists, who say that "Life was meant for pleasure"?
20. Do you ever seriously envy other people their capacity to "get things done"?
21. Do you get real pleasure out of interior decoration or fixing things round the house?
22. (B) Are you married or do you have a lover?
    a. If yes, do you feel that your husband/lover really appreciates you?
    b. If not, do you really wish that you could have a husband/lover?
23. Do you feel that the deliberate indulgence in sex for the sake of pleasure is somehow wrong or sinful?
24. If a friend of yours has done something different or bought something new, do you yourself get a great urge to do the same?
25. Have you ever, for the sheer pleasure of it, written a poem, short story or painted a picture?
26. (A) Are you paid less than you feel you are worth?
27. Do you feel that factors quite outside your control have prevented you from achieving what you want in life?
28. Do you get a definite sense of pleasure from touching or wearing fine clothes?
29. Which of the following seems closest to the way you feel about your own level of achievement in life?
    a. Have achieved a great deal in one way or another and expect to go on succeeding in the future.
    b. Have been pretty successful on the whole and with few disappointments.
    c. I have had my share of success and failure.
    d. I do not seem to have achieved too much, though I have had one or two successes.
    e. I have really achieved nothing at all in life so far as I can see.
30. Do you love soaking up the sun and then plunging into cool water?
31. Do you positively enjoy the occasional smoke or drink? (If you feel that you drink or smoke too much, tick "no" here.)
32. (A) When you come home at the end of the day do you often find yourself saying "That was a good day's work"?
33. Do you think that other people see you as an original and imaginative type?
34. Are there times when you find nothing nicer than curling up in a warm bed with a good book?
35. (B) Do you get genuine satisfaction out of housework and domestic activities?
36. In tackling a new problem, do you like to "go it alone" rather than rely on other people's advice?
37. On the whole, do you feel that people respect you for what you have achieved?
38. Do you often sit around wondering how to pass the time away?

Now turn to page 76 and check your scores.

Scores

(Total your scores to find your analysis below.)

1.	yes 1C	no 0						
2.	ycs 1S	no 0						
3.	yes 1A	no 0 (A)						
4.	yes 0	no 1A (B)						
5.	yes 1C	no 0						
6.	yes 0	no 1A						
7.	yes 1S	no 0						
8	yes 1A	no 0 (A)						
9.	a. 3S	b. 2S	c. 1S	d. 0	e. –1S			
10.a.	yes 1A	no 0 (B)						
b.	yes 0	no 1A						
11.	yes 1C	no 0						
12.	yes 1S	no 0						
13.	yes 1A	no 0						
14.	yes 1S	no 0						
15.	yes 0	no 1C						
16.a.	yes 1A	no 0 (B)						
b.	yes 0	no 1A						
17.	a. 3C	b. 2C	c. 1C	d. 0	e. –1C			
18.	yes 0	no 1A (A)						
19.	yes 1S	no 0						
20.	yes 0	no 1A						
21.	yes 1C	no 0						
22.a.	yes 1A	no 0 (B)						
b.	yes 0	no 1A						
23.	yes 0	no 1S						
24.	yes 0	no 1C						
25.	yes 1C	no 0						
26.	yes 0	no 1A (A)						
27.	yes 0	no 1A						
28.	yes 1S	no 0						
29.	a. 3A	b. 2A	c. 1A	d. 0	e. –1A			
30.	yes 1S	no 0						
31.	yes 1S	no 0						
32.	yes 1A	no 0 (A)						
33.	yes 1C	no 0						
34.	yes 1C	no 0						
35.	yes 1A	no 0 (B)						
36.	yes 1C	no 0						
37.	yes 1A	no 0						
38.	yes 0	no 1C						

As you score, you will find that you begin to accumulate three sets of values – C, S and A – with both plus and minus points. Your maximum score in each case will be 13. These refer in general to creativity, sensuality and achievement factors.

Now is the time to consider the significance of your scores in order for you to plot and interpret them on the "Happiness Profile" chart. To do this you will need your scores for the four factors, D, i, H, and G, from Part I of the questionnaire, and the three from Part II. You must have completed *both* parts of the questionnaire in full before the interpretation and plotting can take place.

Analysis

Happiness is a state of mind – but there is no doubt that numerous fairly well defined factors in life add together to contribute to it. This is particularly true as we pass into the adult world: the happiness that is so much a feature of childhood and adolescence (though it is by no means universal to these age groups) is often because young people are supported and cushioned from complicating and stressful factors by their parents.

For the purpose of this questionnaire we have isolated seven factors which, all in all, contribute strongly to happiness in life. The higher your score on all these factors, the happier you are likely to be. Of course there is no golden rule here – you might score high on all seven factors and yet consider yourself to be miserable! More to the point, your score as plotted on the Happiness Profile will indicate to you which aspects of your life are happier than others. On the whole you are more likely to feel generally happy and content if you have a very high profile – that is much the same score in all segments of the chart – rather than scoring high in some and low in others. The individual interpretation of the profile however is up to you in the end. Read the following breakdown of the seven factors for a more detailed discussion.

PART I

Domestic One of the most common causes of unhappiness is a disturbed or unsatisfactory home life. This may apply whether one is a young person anxious to break away from parental influence, a single person living in lonely or boring surroundings, a married individual engaged in conflict with wife or husband, or a happily married person who lives in drab or depressing surroundings. Your D factor will give some indication of how happy you are with your domestic situation and your score will lie somewhere between 0 and 13. On the whole, anything at 5 or below indicates that this is an area of dissatisfaction or unhappiness in your life. Scores between 6 and 9 can be counted as average, and those of 10 or above as indicating a level of satisfaction and general happiness.

Interpersonal The i factor relates to the very important facet of life involving your relationship with others. This not only includes your love life, but also your ability to interact with and relate to other people. We are all part of a complex society and society forces us to respond to it. The degree to which we can respond effectively and in turn make society respond to *us,* is a measure of our success and happiness in this sphere. A score of 5 or below implies some measure of unhappiness, 6-9 is average, and 10 or above suggests satisfaction and ultimately happiness in this sphere.

Health With the best will in the world and everything else going for you, it is hard to be totally happy unless you are healthy. Health of course involves body and mind and the questions in this section have been devoted to ascertaining your status in this respect. If you have scored 5 or under you certainly have health problems and there's no doubt they will be affecting your happiness adversely. Score between 6 and 9 and you are average to the extent that you are not much affected by ill health. If you score 10 or above, then you have health and the happiness that goes with it.

General In assessing human happiness there are one or two facets of experience which are not easily categorized under major headings, and questions dealing with the G (or general) factor try to take due account of these important variables. The best possible expression of their significance can be gauged by studying the questions themselves and you will see what we are getting at. On the whole, 5 and under denotes dissatisfaction in this category, 6-9 is average, and 10 and over is above average.

PART II

Creativity   The human brain is not only a marvelous device for responding rapidly to changes in the environment, avoiding danger and so on, but it is also a superb problem-solving mechanism which allows human beings to play an active dynamic role in manipulating and improving the environment in which they live. This dynamic, positive manipulation of the world is creativity – the generation of novel solutions to old problems. At one end of the continuum, creativity is exemplified by the work of great painters, artists and scientists; at the more common level, which most of us have to be content with, it merely involves sensing that feeling of satisfaction which comes when we catch hold of a problem and solve it, or turn something dull into something beautiful. If you score 5 or below you are probably rather low in creative ability and will certainly feel that you are missing out as the result. Between 6 and 9 is a reasonable average, and if you score 10 or above you have got a definite creative sense.

Sensuality   The human body is equipped with sense organs to allow it to relate itself to changes in the world outside and elaborate pleasure mechanisms to ensure that it does things vital to its survival which would otherwise seem pointless and purposeless. We can hardly imagine ourselves eating, drinking or making love, unless we felt a deep sense of pleasure or satisfaction from doing so! There is no doubt that the indulgence of the senses is a contributing factor to happiness, though of course, like all other factors, it is only part of the picture. If you score 5 or less you probably have a rather cold nature and may be missing a good deal of happiness. On the other hand, if you score 12 or 13, you may be paying too much attention to sensuality, and if you have rather low scores on the other segments of the profile then you may have found already that sensual pleasure provides only brief periods of happiness.

Achievement   Whether in the long term it is an illusion or not, most men and women like to feel that their lives have a purpose and that this purpose is somehow being achieved. Achievement can be spread over many levels – in your job, your domestic life, your relationship with other people, in your capacity to face up to a difficulty in life and continue facing up to it until it has been solved or overcome. On the whole, people with high achievement ratings stand a high chance of achieving overall happiness as well. If your score is 10 or above, then you are amongst the achievers. A score of between 6 and 9 is average, and a score of 5 or less means that you are disappointing yourself.

Plotting and Interpreting Your Scores

To get an overall view of how happy a human you are, use the example on the right to draw up your own Happiness Profile. On a separate sheet of paper, copy the graph using a pencil and compass if you have one. Then take your individual scores for the seven factors and plot them on the Happiness Profile chart, filling in the appropriate line for your score in each segment. For example if you scored 6 in the A factor, you fill in the line that represents number 6 in the A segment; if you have scored 9 for the H factor, you fill in the line that represents 9 in the H segment, and so on. When you have done this for each of the seven factors, your Happiness Profile will be plain to see. To make the relative balance of the various factors easy to recognize, we suggest that you shade in the interior sectors in pencil or colored ball pen.

The chart is divided into three distinct rings – 0-5, 6-9 and 10-13. On the whole, scores lying between 6 and 9 are average or normal for that factor, scores lying between 0 and 5 are below average, and those between 10 and 13 are above average. You should congratulate yourself therefore when your profile enters the outer segment.

While outer segment scores may be gratifying and spectacular in themselves, their effect is weakened if they are accompanied by an equivalent number of scores in the inner segment – suggesting an erratic profile, good in some factors and poor in others. On the whole the "best" type of profile is one in which the segments are all roughly equal – suggesting a more balanced general picture. The only exception to this of course is if all your scores fall within the inner ring, which, if the questions have been answered honestly, would be a disappointing and unsatisfactory picture.

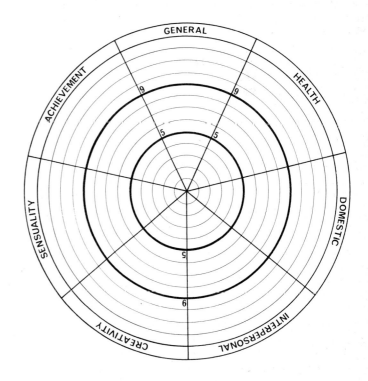

Happiness Profile

How Well Do You Cope?

Life is a jungle of complications and difficulties which face all human beings from the moment they are born. This may seem daunting and depressing, but that is the way it is and throughout life we all have to learn to adjust to surprises and adversity and accommodate our behavior appropriately. Fortunately brain and body are flexible and resilient – the perfect mechanism, in fact, for meeting the complications of life. But there is no doubt that some people are better at adjusting than others, and this questionnaire is designed to give you some idea of how well you yourself rate as a successful adjuster.

How well do *you* cope? The majority of situations where people are called on to cope require psychological rather than physical adjustment, though many are a mixture of both. But stressful situations which demand a thorough ability to cope or adjust are not always of the instant, "over and done with in a flash" variety. Of course we vary day-to-day in our ability to cope and adjust, and some factors – a painful illness, for example – can intervene and lower even the most self-sufficient individual's capacity to deal with other problems. Making allowances for these unpredictable variations, however, one can say that if you score well on the following test, the chances are that you are one of life's "copers" – which is pleasant for you and doubly gratifying for those who depend on you. As always, for this test to have any meaning it must be answered quite frankly and honestly.

Mark your answers on a separate sheet.

1. Imagine that you are on the scene of a severe and particularly bloody road accident in which you are not personally involved. A small crowd of onlookers has gathered. Which of the following patterns of behavior would be closest to the one you would adopt. (Please try to be absolutely honest.)
   a. Leave the scene as quickly as possible without looking, feeling nauseated and unable to tolerate all the carnage.
   b. Hang around amongst the spectators eyeing the accident with curiosity.
   c. Despite the fact that you have no first aid or medical training, get a grip on yourself and do everything that you can to move the injured from the scene of the accident.
   d. Because you have first aid or medical training, volunteer your services immediately and play whatever role is required of you.

e. Immediately check whether anyone has telephoned for the ambulance, fire brigade and police, and telephone them if necessary.

2. Indicate how upset—"extremely seriously," "seriously," "slightly" or "not at all"—you would be if you were faced with the following situations.
   a. Your old dog, a faithful companion, dies at the end of a long life.
   b. Three weeks before you are due to set out on your long-planned vacation you realize that it has to be postponed for three months.
   c. One of your parents dies unexpectedly.
   d. You hear that a major cholera epidemic has broken out in an African country and that many thousands are dying.
   e. The day before you and your family are due to go on a long airplane ride there is a major air disaster with hundreds dead.
   f. You have lent one of your favorite books to a friend and a few weeks later he tells you he has lost it through carelessness.
   g. You are driving into the city and are seriously held up by traffic jams. With at least an hour's driving ahead of you, you are already late for a very important appointment.
   h. You drop a container of a dozen eggs, all of which break.
   i. You hear that the cost of gasoline is soon to go up by 10 percent.
   j. The government announces their decision to crack down on income tax defaulters.

3. You have invited your boss (or your husband's boss) and his wife home for dinner. He agrees and asks if he can also bring an important and wealthy business associate. The day before the dinner you suddenly realize that the only room in your house in which you can hold the dinner party is in a terrible state of decoration. Which of the following is closest to your strategy?
   a. Ring up the boss, plead illness in the family and postpone the dinner.
   b. Stay up all night decorating the room and hold the dinner as planned.
   c. Hold the dinner as planned and apologize, saying that you are just about to decorate.
   d. Disguise the worst horrors, lower the lights and hope for the best.
   e. Book a table at a really nice local restaurant and hold the dinner there.

4. You are driving your car with a friend when you become involved in a serious collision with another vehicle. Which of the following is the first thing you should do?

a. Get out of the car to see how the occupants of the other car are.

b. Turn towards your passenger and release his or her seat belt.

c. Remain absolutely still for a moment to collect your thoughts.

d. Switch off the ignition.

e. Immediately look around to see if other vehicles are heading for you to prepare yourself in case of a multiple collision.

5. Indicate how upset—"extremely seriously," "seriously," "slightly" or "not at all"—you would be if you were faced with the following situations.

a. It is after midnight and you are anxious to sleep, but the neighbor's baby is crying incessantly.

b. You hear there is to be a major transport strike over a trifling dispute.

c. Your children's pet cat is killed by a car.

d. Your bank statement comes and you are much worse off than you thought you were.

e. Your holiday snaps come back all duds because you forgot to take the lens cap off.

f. You spend a lot of money decorating a room and then realize after you have finished that you do not like it after all.

g. You are set to watch an evening of favorite programs on TV when your set breaks down.

h. You hear that the latest space spectacular has failed with a loss of three astronauts' lives.

i. You normally receive a big birthday check from a relative and you have come to count on it; this year he writes saying times are hard and sending you a much smaller one instead.

j. One of your children is pulled up by the police for a minor theft offence.

6. Your nextdoor neighbors, who have been living there for a year, hold an anniversary housewarming party – the first party that they have held since they moved in. The noise is tremendous right into the small hours of the morning. Which of the following reactions is closest to the way you would behave?

a. Ring the police and complain about the noise.

b. Ring your neighbors and ask them politely if they could tone things down a bit.

c. Cover your head with the bedclothes and try to force yourself to sleep in spite of the noise.

d. Ring up in a rage and warn them that if they don't keep quiet you will inform the police.

e. Go round, knock on the door and ask if you can join the party.

f. Plan to hold a noisy party yourself in retaliation at the first opportunity.

7. Your new hi-fi set, bought at great expense, gives you nothing but trouble. Which of the following is closest to what you would do?

a. Write an indignant and sarcastic letter to the makers, telling them exactly what you think of their inferior merchandise.

b. Take it back to the suppliers and tell them you want your money back.

c. Make a determined effort to fix it yourself.

d. Never get round to actually doing anything but continually complain to yourself and others about its poor performance.

e. Trade it in for another make, getting whatever money you can for it.

f. Write a polite note to the manufacturers saying that for the money you paid you had expected a more reliable product.

8. Answer honestly yes or no to each of the following questions:

a. Have you ever come to blows with anybody in an argument?

b. Is there a certain type of family situation or "scene" which you have come to dread?

c. If someone wants to borrow money from you are you capable of handling the situation without embarrassment?

d. Do you find it very aggravating when the "other side" wins in elections?

e. Do you tend to get touchy if you are beaten in a sport or game?

f. Do you believe that some people are "born lucky"?

g. Do you sometimes dread the day because of the problems it is likely to bring you?

h. Do decisions over financial matters – bills, taxes or debts – get you down?

i. Do you find it difficult to do things if your ritual or usual way of doing them has to be altered?

j. Are you a good timekeeper?

Now turn to page 80 and check your scores.

Scores

(Total your score to find your analysis below.)

1. a. 1 b. 1 c. 2 d. 0 e. 0

2.	Extremely seriously	Seriously	Slightly	Not at all
a.	2	0	0	2
b.	1	1	0	0
c.	0	0	1	2
d.	0	0	0	0
e.	2	1	0	0
f.	2	1	0	0
g.	2	0	0	1
h.	2	1	0	0
i.	2	1	0	0
j.	0	0	0	0

3. a. 2 b. 2 c. 0 d. 0 e. 1

4. a. 2 b. 2 c. 2 d. 0 e. 2

5.	Extremely seriously	Seriously	Slightly	Not at all
a.	2	1	0	0
b.	0	0	0	0
c.	2	0	0	1
d.	2	0	0	1
e.	2	1	0	0
f.	1	0	0	1
g.	2	1	0	0
h.	0	0	0	0
i.	2	1	0	0
j.	0	0	1	2

6. a. 2 b. 0 c. 2 d. 2 e. 0 f. 2

7. a. 2 b. 0 c. 1 d. 2 e. 2 f. 0

8.	Yes	No		Yes	No
a.	2	0	f.	2	0
b.	2	0	g.	1	0
c.	0	1	h.	1	0
d.	0	0	i.	1	0
e.	1	0	j.	0	1

Analysis

All the questions you have answered dealt with situations which occur in life and which most people meet sooner or later and have to face up to as best they can. In almost every case the situations are such that the normal person would be disturbed to *some* degree when facing them, but the significant factor is the extent to which this disturbance is felt. Failure to cope really means failing to be able to make a *reasonable response* to circumstances, at one end of the scale by overreacting, and at the other end of the scale by underreacting. If difficulties in the world around you and the sufferings of others leave you completely unmoved, then you are not really coping with the world but are probably denying it.

Most people answering this questionnaire will pick up the bulk of their points – the fewer points you have, the better you are able to cope – in question 8, and the more you collect points in the earlier sections of the questionnaire the more likely it is that you are not adjusting satisfactorily to the crises of life. Now check your score.

0-5 You are probably almost too good to be true. If your score really is as low as this and you have answered all the questions really honestly, then you are indeed one of the most self-sufficient and well-adjusted of human beings. Of course the possibility is that you have not yet met a major crisis, in which case you are really scoring on how you feel you *would* behave in difficulties rather than what actually would take place. However, with this low score the chances are that you face most crises squarely and with resolution.

6-10 You cope with the problems of life pretty satisfactorily, taking situations as they come and never letting things get you down. If your score is as low as this and you have, in your life, faced at least one major crisis, then you are to be congratulated. In all probability you will have picked up most of your points in the last ten questions.

11-15 All in all you cope pretty well, but there are some things which get you down and definite areas in your life where you feel unable to handle crises as they arise. Perhaps at least one major crisis has really hit you and you found yourself unusually troubled by it. But in nine cases out of ten you will manage, and manage pretty well.

16-25 This relatively high score suggests that life's crises can hit you, and sometimes hit you hard. You probably have less confidence in yourself than you should, and maybe undervalue your capacity to cope and give up rather than persist when problems actually arise. Try to look back over the things which you really *have* achieved and you may surprise yourself at how much you actually can handle when you try.

26-35 You find life a handful and there are many occasions where you evidently let things get completely on top of you. The most likely explanation for this is that you are easily upset emotionally and that when a crisis situation arises you simply can't "keep your cool." This is unfortunate, but there are people whose emotions override them in this way. This is quite often a characteristic of youth, or sometimes emerges when the individual has been battered and felt defeated by some major crisis, such as the death of a very close relative or friend. In such cases recovery generally takes place and the individual in due course regains self-confidence and the capacity to handle the troubles of the world.

Over 35 If you have answered the questionnaire honestly and correctly and not misunderstood it (check over it again carefully) then there is no doubt that you are a person who finds the crises of life very difficult to bear. If this is so, then you should confide first in a trusted friend, and, particularly if you have *suddenly* been troubled with feelings of inadequacy, you might then consider seeking advice from your family doctor, who will probably be able to give you help and reassure you.

How Assertive Are You?

Aggression is one of the most basic animal drives and it is present to some degree in all of us. However, not everyone realizes this and because society considers aggressive behavior to be on the whole "antisocial," we tend to deny the presence of aggressive impulses within ourselves. This is not always a good thing for it leads to unfortunate conflicts, generally unconscious, between what a person *wants* to do and what he actually has to end up doing.

The problem here is that most of these unconscious drives are not related to language at all and are therefore not easy to identify in verbal terms. The difference between conscious and unconscious motivation is largely a matter of whether we have *words* to describe or define the behavior. To take a rather simple example: babies will instinctively suck at their mother's breast, and it is clear that at one level they "know" what they are doing. This "knowledge" is related to the instinctive behavior pattern, however, and not to words in any way. Similarly, when we are annoyed by someone sufficiently we may assault them physically.

Often the only way to detect the immense power of these unconscious drives is to look at aspects of your life and behavior which demonstrate a consistent pattern for which there is no obvious explanation—or at least no explanation that can be described in words.

The following questionnaire deals with just one of these unconscious drives—aggression. The following rules should be closely observed in order to achieve the most accurate result.

1. Mark your answers on a separate sheet so that you do not spoil the test for others, who might unconsciously be influenced by seeing your responses.

2. Fill out the questionnaire at what seems to you to be a "natural" rate. Do not linger too long on each question trying to work out the "hidden meaning" behind it. This will almost certainly upset your scores. On the other hand, do read the question and its alternative answers carefully.

3. Set aside a time when you can complete and score the questionnaire on your own. Do not look at the answers or their evaluation until you have finished, and do not discuss the results or conclusions with anyone else.

4. Do not attempt to administer the test to anyone else. It is not suitable for anything but self-administration.

5. Answer all questions as frankly and honestly as you can. You can fool the questionnaire (and yourself) by dishonest answers, but in that case there is no point in filling it out at all!

6. Treat the results as a guide only. There is a margin of uncertainty in all questionnaires of this kind.

1. Which of the following do you think *most closely* describes the type of person you are?
   a. Busy, always active, perhaps even a bit "pushy."
   b. Pretty active in bursts.
   c. Rather placid on the whole.
   d. Definitely subdued, perhaps even a bit withdrawn.
   e. Simply a normal person.

2. Here are some types of TV programs. None of them may be your ideal, but pick the two from the list that you would prefer if you had to watch them.
   a. An uninhibited comedy show.
   b. A live professional boxing match.
   c. A talk show in which a controversial figure is closely questioned about his activities.
   d. A play with a theme of strong domestic drama.
   e. An all-action Western.
   f. A detective thriller in which police relentlessly hunt down a criminal of some kind.

3. The following questions are about sexual behavior. Say whether on the whole you agree or disagree with each of the following statements.
   a. Men should always take the lead in love-making.
   b. All women like the "caveman" approach to sex.
   c. In most cases of rape, 50% of the blame lies with the woman.

4. Here are 17 statements. You may not agree or disagree with any of them *exactly* as they are put, but you should try to make up your mind which of the four attitudes is *closest* to your own. Do you strongly agree, agree on the whole, disagree on the whole, or strongly disagree with each statement?

a. Young people these days tend to be lazier, less responsible and less clean in their habits than they used to be.
b. Slow drivers are more of a menace on the roads than fast drivers.
c. Man is a dangerous and aggressive animal who is slowly becoming civilized.
d. There is a lot of truth in the old saying "Spare the rod and spoil the child."
e. No punishment is too severe for sexual criminals.
f. People who watch bullfights ought to be given a taste of the suffering the bull has to experience.
g. Most politicians are decent, ordinary folks simply doing the best job they can.
h. Nail biting is a disgusting habit which should be firmly stamped out in children.
i. An untidy house denotes an untidy mind.
j. Football is a more manly game than baseball.
k. The majority of unemployed people could get jobs if they really wanted to.
l. If stricter legislation was introduced to prevent drivers from drinking, road accidents would be reduced.
m. Homosexuality is a crime against nature and society.
n. People who fail to pay parking tickets are only making a legitimate protest against excessive government spending.
o. "When guns are outlawed only outlaws will have guns."
p. There are times when the best thing for a country is a dictatorship.
q. "Wars will cease when men refuse to fight."

5. Your local car dealer is advertising a sale of the very latest models from a number of different car manufacturers. You have no information as to their price, style, performance or economy, but you do know their names. Which one of the cars do you suspect that you will like the most?
   a. Florida
   b. Spider
   c. Viper
   d. Emerald
   e. Tomahawk
   f. Cheetah
   g. Rocket
   h. Hurricane

6. Do you own any of the following? If not, are there any which you would *like* to own?
   a. A replica of a pistol, rifle or other modern firearm.
   b. A Nazi badge, flag, dagger or insignia of any kind.
   c. A dog which some people might consider dangerous.

7. Do you ever feel so angry or annoyed at a person that you feel you could hit him?
   a. Often
   b. Sometimes
   c. Never

8. The following question concerns your sense of humor. Being as honest as you can, mark which of the following categories amuse you, even if only slightly.
   a. Good, clean slapstick fun.
   b. The sight of some pompous person being deflated in some way.
   c. "Blue" humor or sexy jokes.
   d. Dry, sarcastic wit.

9. Do you believe that there are certain crimes for which the state should exact the death penalty?

10. If you answered yes above, indicate to which crimes listed below you think the death penalty should apply.
   a. Murder for robbery
   b. Murder of a policeman on duty
   c. Rape
   d. Kidnapping
   e. Large-scale profiteering from the sales of illegal addictive drugs
   f. Sexual offenses against children

11. How do newsreel shots of students engaged in peaceful sitdown demonstrations make you feel?
   a. Very annoyed
   b. A bit annoyed
   c. Neutral on the whole
   d. Pleased to see them protesting

12. On the whole do you believe that our society is too soft in the way it treats convicted criminals?

Now turn to page 84 and check your scores.

Analysis

A certain amount of aggression, conscious or unconscious, is really a necessary part of the make-up of any animal, human beings included. In the case of human beings, much aggression can be channeled healthily into external activities, such as sport and competitive life situations. The remaining component is generally unconscious, and this questionnaire has been geared heavily to detect *unconscious* patterns of aggression.

0-10 This really represents a very low score on the aggression scale. If you have scored less than 10 you are certainly not an aggressive person by any standards. Of course it is possible that you are channeling all your quota of aggression into leading an exceedingly dynamic life, but the combination of a high output of

aggression and such a low score on this questionnaire would be unusual to say the least. To be quite frank you have either not filled out the questionnaire with sufficient care and accuracy, or you are a very placid person indeed—perhaps even so placid that people find you somewhat characterless.

11-25 This denotes a normal and, so far as anyone can categorize these things, balanced proportion of aggression in your personality. You probably lead a life which allows you a reasonable outlet for your quite normal aggressive impulses and even those that you have to bottle up find expression in socially acceptable and psychologically satisfactory channels.

26-50 You are naturally a somewhat aggressive person. If your score is in the range 26-35 you probably strike a reasonable balance, channeling a certain amount of this aggression into "natural activities" in your daily life, but there is a hidden side to you which features an aggressive *persona* of which neither you nor your friends are probably aware. If you have scored between 36 and 50, however, the aggressive side of your nature, which to you is "unconscious," may well have shown its face to your friends and those close to you, and they will see you as more aggressive than you believe yourself to be! Try to look closely at things which would "make you angry if you would only let them." If they are unimportant things, then maybe you should let off some steam from time to time. No one will really mind this and you will feel all the better for it.

Can you tell the assertive characters from the rest? And are you one of them?

51-75 This score denotes a very high level of aggression in your total psychological make-up. It may be that you are a person with tremendous drive and energy which is not finding an outlet in the external world through a really challenging job or some similar task. If you are a woman and score in this range, you *will* almost certainly be finding domestic life to be an exceptional strain. This is probably not because domestic life is too *much* for you, but because it is too *little* for you. So take up an outside interest of some kind and channel this dynamic aggression into something useful. If you are in business or a profession, and whether you are male or female, you may achieve a high score like this when you are faced with a particularly difficult hurdle or set of hurdles in your working life. Your "aggression quotient" would probably slide dramatically once the hurdles were overcome. Other people who can score so highly on a "temporary" basis are adolescents or young people.

Over 75 This is a very high score and denotes an unusually high level of aggression—probably largely unconscious. If you are scoring in this range and you do not honestly believe yourself to be aggressive, then you have either not filled in the questionnaire correctly, or the aggression is so deeply repressed that you may be aware of neurotic complications of some kind in your daily life. You may find it helpful to talk to a friend or someone you trust about these problems.

Mary Evans

Scores

(Total your scores to find your analysis on page 82.)

1. a. 1   b. 0   c. 0   d. 0   e. 3

2. a. 0   b. 1   c. 3   d. 1   e. 0   f. 3

3. a. Agree 2   b. Agree 1   c. Agree 5

4.

	Strongly agree	Agree on the whole	Disagree on the whole	Strongly disagree
a.	3	1	0	1
b.	5	2	0	0
c.	0	0	0	1
d.	3	1	0	0
e.	5	2	0	0
f.	3	1	0	2
g.	0	0	0	1
h.	3	1	0	0
i.	2	1	0	0
j.	1	0	0	0
k.	3	1	0	0
l.	0	0	1	3
m.	3	1	0	0
n.	4	1	0	0
o.	3	1	0	0
p.	3	1	0	0
q.	0	0	0	1

5. a. 0   b. 3   c. 3   d. 0   e. 4   f. 4   g. 1   h. 1

6.

	Own	Would like to own
a.	3	3
b.	3	3
c.	3	3

7. a. 1   b. 0   c. 3

8.

	Amused	Not Amused
a.	0	2
b.	0	2
c.	0	2
d.	2	0

9. Yes 3   No 0

10. a. 1   b. 0   c. 5   d. 1   e. 3   f. 5

11. a. 3   b. 1   c. 0   d. 3

12. Yes 3   No 0

Grigori Rasputin came to dominate Imperial Russia by asserting his power over the Czar.

How Permissive Are You?

Carol Binch

This questionnaire is designed to assess your attitude to sex and current sexual practices and behavior. There are no "right" or "wrong" answers to questions, and the score you end up with does not class you as correct or incorrect in your views. It merely reflects how your own attitudes to the subject compare with other people's. There are a number of golden rules which need to be obeyed if the questionnaire is to provide you with meaningful answers. The first is that all questions should be answered with absolute honesty. This is less easy to do than you might imagine, particularly where emotions, prejudices, moral values and various taboos can make one basically unsure of what one really *does* feel about a particular issue. Secondly, make sure that you answer the questions *on your own*—don't discuss them or your answers with anyone else. Thirdly, don't spend too much time trying to work out any "hidden meanings" in the questions—if you think that you detect a trap or trick, then you're on the wrong track anyway!

Mark your answers on a separate sheet.

1. Read the following opinions and indicate whether you definitely agree, tend to agree, tend to disagree or definitely disagree with each of them.
  a. A girl's most treasured possession is her virginity.
  b. Masturbation is an unhealthy practice.
  c. It is offensive to see someone "petting" in public.
  d. Children should be given clear sex education.
  e. It's unwise to experiment with sex before marriage.
  f. The pill should be freely and universally available.
  g. For some people homosexuality is normal.
  h. Prostitution should be legally permitted.
  i. Films should not be censored on sexual grounds.
  j. Absolute faithfulness to one partner throughout life is not really a worthwhile ideal.

2. A close friend of the same sex offers to show you a book of pornographic pictures. Which of the following is *closest* to your response to this invitation?
  a. Look at the book with unashamed interest.
  b. Accept, feeling a bit uncertain and bashful.
  c. Accept because you don't want to be thought a prude, skim through the book without comment.
  d. Decline, politely, commenting "that's not my line."

  e. Refuse flatly and make it clear that you won't welcome any further invitations of the kind.

3. Your lover, wife or husband has been invited to go along to a "wife-swapping" party and urges you to go along. Which of these is closest to your reaction?
  a. Agree to go along eagerly.
  b. Agree to go along mainly to please him/her.
  c. Agree, but plan to duck out at the last moment.
  d. Turn it down flatly.
  e. Turn it down flatly and tell your partner that you are disappointed that he/she should consider it.

4. Show if you definitely agree, tend to agree, tend to disagree or definitely disagree with the following.
  a. On the whole it is better not to have sexual intercourse with someone before you are married.
  b. Sex play among children is normal and harmless.
  c. Even though you are having regular intercourse, masturbation is normal if you feel like it.
  d. A decline in sexual morals is a sure sign that society is collapsing.
  e. If couples like to look at pornographic pictures before making love there's nothing wrong with it.
  f. There's something abnormal about people who like to look at strip shows.
  g. Contraception is morally wrong because it implies that sex is for enjoyment rather than procreation.
  h. If newspapers, magazines, movies and TV weren't so preoccupied with sex, people would be less interested in it too.
  i. Sexual behavior reflects the "animal" side of man's nature, but the spiritual side is more important.
  j. People who break the laws on sexual behavior should be more severely punished than at present.

5. Your daughter, who has just turned 16, is invited to go away on vacation with a mixed group of her own age. You know that there are going to be some uninhibited characters in the group and no adult supervision. Which of the following most closely matches your reaction?
  a. Accept that the time has come for her to move into adult life, and after making sure she's clued up on sexual matters and equipped with contraceptives, send her off without misgivings.

85

b. Give her a straight talking to about the dangers of pregnancy and venereal disease, but let her go on the trip after exacting a solemn promise that she won't sleep with anyone.

c. Tell her frankly that she's too young for a vacation of this kind and promise her that you'll reconsider next year.

d. Say that you'll think about it, but meanwhile make plans for an alternative family treat to take her mind off the invitation.

e. Make it clear that she can't go and that there's no question of this kind of thing until she's over 21. Also resolve to make sure that she changes the company she's keeping.

6. You receive an invitation to attend the charity premiere of a new movie which you have heard contains long sequences of quite explicit and uninhibited sexual intercourse. Which of the following is closest to your response?

a. Return the ticket and write to the charity concerned saying that you are surprised they will accept money from such a film.

b. Throw the ticket in the wastepaper basket.

c. Hand the ticket to a friend who may be interested in the movie.

d. Go along with some misgivings and more out of curiosity than anything else.

e. Go along and take your family.

7. Here are some statements which may or may not reflect your attitude to sex. Indicate whether you agree or disagree, and only if you really find it impossible to make up your mind should you indicate "not sure."

a. There is no reason why children shouldn't see their parents making love.

b. Some forms of love making are disgusting to me.

c I object to four-letter swear words being used in mixed company.

d. I wouldn't at all mind admitting that I have sometimes masturbated.

e. I wouldn't mind my usual partner having sexual intercourse with someone else.

f. There are too many immoral films and plays on TV.

g. I prefer to make love in the dark.

h. If someone wanted to watch me making love I shouldn't mind.

i. I very much enjoy "oral sex."

j. I believe that as soon as mankind is free of all sexual taboos the world will be a better place.

Now turn to page 87 and check your scores.

Scores

(Total your score to find your analysis below.)

	Definitely agree	Tend to agree	Tend to disagree	Definitely disagree
1. a.	5C	2C	1P	2P
b.	5C	2C	1P	2P
c.	3C	1C	1P	2P
d.	2P	1P	2C	5C
e.	5C	2C	1P	2P
f.	2P	1P	1C	3C
g.	2P	1P	2C	5C
h.	2P	1P	2C	5C
i.	2P	1P	2C	5C
j.	2P	1P	1C	3C

2. a. 5P   b. 2P   c. 0   d. 1C   e. 3C
3. a. 5P   b. 4P   c. 1P   d. 1C   e. 3C

	Definitely agree	Tend to agree	Tend to disagree	Definitely disagree
4. a.	5C	2C	1P	2P
b.	2P	1P	2C	5C
c.	2P	1P	2C	5C
d.	3C	1C	1P	3P
e.	2P	1P	2C	5C
f.	5C	2C	1P	2P
g.	3C	1C	1P	3P
h.	3C	1C	1P	3P
i.	3C	1C	1P	3P
j.	3C	1C	1P	3P

5. a. 5P   b. 2P   c. 2P   d. 1C   e. 3C
6. a. 3C   b. 1C   c. 1P   d. 2P   e. 5P

	Agree	Not sure	Disagree
7. a.	5P	1C	2C
b.	2C	1C	5P
c.	2C	1C	2P
d.	3P	1C	2C
e.	5P	1C	2C
f.	3C	1C	1P
g.	2C	1C	0P
h.	5P	1C	2C
i.	3P	1C	2C
j.	2P	1C	2C

After you have totted up your score you will find that you have a C rating—this denotes the conservative side to your nature—and a P rating—which denotes the permissive side to your nature. Now, having arrived at this figure you make a correction for age. To do this, you award yourself 1P score for each five years of your life after the age of 25. (For example, if you are 28 years old you award yourself 1P; if 31, 2P; if 49, 5P and so on.) Now subtract your total P score from your C score—or the other way round if the P score is higher than the C. You will end up with a final score which will give you a trend to conservativism or permissiveness. To give an example, suppose that you have a C score of 31, a P score of 11 and, at the age of 42, you add 4P points for age. Now you deduct 15 from 31, which leaves you with 16C points. Now refer to the code below.

Analysis

Over 90C   A score this high is very extreme indeed and suggests an error in filling out or scoring the questionnaire, or such a conservative frame of mind that the world at the moment must seem a very objectionable place indeed. It may be very difficult for anyone to change your mind for you, but you might do well to reflect that you are probably expecting from people a degree of tolerance which you will not allow them.

76C-90C   This score suggests an extremely conservative frame of mind. Your conservatism on sexual matters is such that there is no doubt that you are offended, upset and perhaps even enraged by many aspects of today's so-called permissive society. It is unlikely that you will ever change your attitudes much, nor is there any real reason why you should force yourself to do so. The chances are, however, that there are many aspects of human behavior which you yourself would like to change for what you believe to be "the better." The best advice would be for you to remember that moral values are hard to define and what one person sincerely considers bad, another might sincerely believe good.

51C-75C   This denotes a strong streak of conservativism regarding sexual matters—possibly many aspects of today's permissive society may offend you for religious or moral reasons. Before judging people too strongly, remember that beliefs and attitudes do change imperceptibly with time and that there are probably aspects of your behavior which *you* believe to be normal which other people, in another time or place, might well have condemned as shocking!

36C-50C   On sexual matters you are undoubtedly conservative. However your attitude is not extreme in any way, and is probably supported by many millions of other people the world over. Nor is conservative frame of mind wrong in itself—it merely sometimes leads to unfortunate conflicts, most commonly of a domestic or family nature. If you are a parent of a teenager or adolescent, then you may have already come up against these conflicts, or will do so in the near future. It is at this point that other facets of your personality—patience and good sense particularly—must be brought into play.

21C-35C   Your score reveals that you have a conservative streak to your nature. But it is not excessive and puts you very much in the same camp as many millions of educated and intelligent adults. It also suggests that you have probably adjusted satisfactorily to the rather dramatic change in moral values and attitudes to human sexual behavior which have taken place in the last ten years. In fact, many of your friends may even think of you as being rather "permissive." However, you are still shocked occasionally by some of the strange flavors of the modern world, and if the trend continues upon present lines you might well have to be prepared for more shocks yet to come.

20C-10P On the whole this represents a rather balanced score and it would be hard to define you as being either of a conservative or a permissive nature. The only exception to this will be if you reached your present score by subtracting a high P score from an even higher C score, or vice versa—say of over 30 in each case. Such a case would reveal a rather strong personality conflict suggesting that part of you is strongly conservative, another part strongly permissive. The two poles don't get on together and this could cause trouble in your social and family life. With this exception your score is best described as "average." No doubt there are aspects of the permissive society which surprise you but nothing shocks you enough to trouble you.

11P-30P There is a permissive streak and a measurable dose of tolerance in your attitude to sexual behavior in general, and many of your friends will be aware of this. Unfortunately (or fortunately?) you are the kind of person who is likely to have friends in both camps, and you may find that many of your acquaintances even consider you to be a bit conservative. There probably is a bit of truth in both points of view and if you arrived at your present score by taking a rather high C rating (say over 30) from an even higher P rating (say over 50) you may be suffering from conflicts in this field.

31P-50P In the eyes of many people—perhaps the majority of people—you would be considered to be definitely tolerant and permissive on sexual matters. You no doubt see yourself as adopting only a balanced and "sensible" approach, and this could be. Even so there will be aspects of today's so-called permissive society which you find somewhat offensive, and it's fairly clear that you have at least hidden feelings that there should be moral constraints on some aspects of sexual life. On the whole you are probably a flexible person also—which is just as well for changes take place in society with considerable speed, and whether the "per-missive society" gets stronger or weaker, you are the kind of person who will adjust easily to its new status.

51P-75P You are exceptionally permissive and open-minded on sexual matters, and the current move to sexual freedom which is coursing through our society isn't moving any too quickly for you. Fair enough—but make sure that you do not occasionally offend friends or family by your (to them) outspoken views. Also remember that the history of social change reminds one that there is a limit to the swing of the pendulum, and if the permissive society begins to wane you may find yourself in danger of being classed as "antisocial." In permissive societies being antisocial is allowed but in conservative societies, tolerance is not so great.

Over 75P This represents permissiveness on a grand—perhaps almost eccentric—scale (unless of course you have made some error in filling out or scoring the questionnaire). With a score this high you will probably be so openminded on sexual matters that you have come round full circle into narrowmindedness. In this case you are in danger of assuming you know the "rules" for human sexual behavior and relationships—a trap which the most conservative also fall into.

Special note Some people filling out this questionnaire may have ended up with a relatively low P or C score which was achieved as the result of subtracting two rather high C or P scores from each other. Anyone scoring initial C and P scores higher than 30 in *each* case is showing evidence of uncertainty and even perhaps conflict in terms of their attitude to present day sexual matters and morals. Even higher extremes of *both* C and P—say over 40 of each score—are indicative of definite conflict and people achieving such scores might find it interesting to do the questionnaire again and reconsider which answers they really *believe,* and which they merely feel they *ought to believe.*

How Good is Your Self-Image?

Deep down inside who do you really think you are? From the moment of birth we all devote tremendous energy and thought – much of it unconscious – towards assembling an image of ourselves which we find personally acceptable and which we also believe is acceptable to the outside world. This self-image, as it is called, tends to be rather idealized and often fails to match with reality. At its simplest level – physical characteristics such as handsomeness and beauty, age and youth – our self-image is frequently shattered when we look at ourselves in the mirror, or more dramatically when we are caught unsuspectingly by the cruel eye of the camera. Many a woman has found herself rushing into a crash diet after being shocked at the sight of a portly figure in a photograph, which she has grudgingly identified as herself. The expression "Can that really be me?" which all of us have at some time uttered, is a classic example of how personal and objective images of oneself can often be wildly different.

But there are no cameras which allow us to capture that more elusive psychic self-image. However, psychologists have found ways of allowing people to inspect the reality or plausibility of their own self-image, and this questionnaire, specially devised by psychologists, sets out to allow you to check your personal image against the "facts." The questionnaire should be used as a guide only, but you should nevertheless be prepared for some surprises. You *could* be carrying round outdated notions of your own powers and personal capabilities!

Answer the following questions as honestly and as carefully as you can.

Mark your answers on a separate sheet.

1. How did you react the last time someone of the opposite sex found you attractive?
  a. Without surprise, because you saw it coming.
  b. Glad, because you suspected it but weren't completely certain.
  c. With pleased astonishment.

2. Do you call your parents by their first names?
  a. Yes, since you became an adult.
  b. Yes, only because they suggested it.
  c. No, you don't like the idea somehow.

3. Do you think about what job you might have had if circumstances had been different?
  a. Rarely
  b. Sometimes
  c. Often

4. If b or c to question 3: Are the jobs you feel that you might have done
  a. Of much the same status as your present job?
  b. Of higher status than your present job?

5. You are on the point of undertaking an important assignment, something you have not done before. One of your friends says casually, "I wish I had your confidence." Would you
  a. Accept the compliment?
  b. Acknowledge that you don't feel completely confident, but that you are fairly optimistic?
  c. Think, "If only you knew how nervous I feel"?

6. You have managed to take an afternoon off work, or away from home. Do you feel
  a. Great – you can really enjoy yourself?
  b. Pretty good – but with twinges of guilt?
  c. So guilty that the fun disappears?

7. Do you feel that other people don't appreciate your good qualities?
  a. Not really
  b. Sometimes
  c. Often

8. When you feel angry, do you usually
  a. Keep it to yourself?
  b. Express it directly?

9. If a to 8: Do you find that other people perceive you as calm when you are inwardly furious?
  a. Rarely
  b. Sometimes
  c. Often

10. If b to 8: Do you find that you are perceived as strong when you feel insecure?
  a. Rarely
  b. Sometimes
  c. Often

11. Do you ever get the feeling that you are only *playing* at being a worker or a parent?
  a. Rarely
  b. Sometimes
  c. Often

12. Which of the following statements do you feel is most true for you?
  a. I have a pretty good idea of my talents and I am using them pretty well.
  b. Sometimes I think that I could do better at some things, but on the whole I am generally quite satisfied with my efforts.
  c. I could do almost anything if I put my mind to it, but I don't get the chances I deserve.

13. When you have told someone who knows you well about your actions or feelings on a particular occasion, has

he or she said, "I'd never have thought it of you"?
a. Never
b. Rarely
c. Sometimes

14. When you have a piece of work that you want to do, with no one pushing you to achievement, do you
a. Get on with it immediately?
b. Have mild feelings of distraction, but get into the task fairly easily?
c. Experience reluctance to settle down, or find your concentration seriously distracted?

15. When someone appears to dislike you, do you
a. Accept philosophically that you can't win them all?
b. Wonder if you did something to offend him?
c. Think he must be jealous of you?

16. Do you fear that you will let others down, and disappoint their expectations of you?
a. Rarely
b. Sometimes
c. Often

17. Going through customs you are stopped and your bags are thoroughly searched. You have nothing contraband. Do you
a. Feel a bit annoyed about the delay?
b. Think "Thank goodness I'm clean"?
c. Feel tense and guilty as if you were in the wrong?

18. Do you daydream?
a. Not much
b. Occasionally
c. Often

19. If b or c to 18: Are your daydreams
a. Pretty close to possible situations?
b. Fantasies of great power, where everyone looks up to you and you always get your own way?

20. In the last two years, have several people said something about your personality (complimentary or otherwise) that surprised you?
a. Not really
b. Not several people, but one or two
c. Yes

21. When you have made a mistake at work, or ruined dinner at home, do you
a. Shrug it off and reckon that no one's perfect?
b. Need reassurance that it doesn't matter too much?
c. Feel really anxious and defensive?

22. When someone has annoyed you do you

a. Feel angry for a while, then forget it?
b. Find it hard to shake off hurt and resentment?
c. Feel vengeful and take pleasure in imagining terrible punishments for him?

23. You have to take an interview or test of some kind, for which you are reasonably well prepared. Do you
a. Feel a bit nervous, but ready to do your best?
b. Feel sometimes confident, sometimes nervous?
c. Have severe doubts of your competence?

24. If you are unhappy in your job or in your neighborhood, do you
a. Simply decide to go elsewhere and do it as soon as you can?
b. Keep changing your mind about what to do, but make a move eventually?
c. Feel trapped and unable to take action?

25. If you have put time and money into a venture which has gone badly, would you
a. Figure out what went wrong in order to learn from it?
b. Determine to play safe in future?
c. Think that it's just a bit of bad luck and things are bound to go better next time?

26. Show which adjectives you feel apply to you. Then, without revealing your answers, get two people who know you well to tell you—independently—their choice of words which best apply to you.
a. Even-tempered   *or* Anxious
b. Shy   *or* Outgoing
c. Incautious   *or* Cautious

27. A friend quarrels with you on what you consider unreasonable grounds. Do you
a. Tell him straight out how you see things?
b. Try to meet him halfway?
c. Feel hurt and angry, but do everything you can to avoid a confrontation?

28. Do you feel that, whatever you do, someone will take care of you?
a. No – you have to rely on your own efforts.
b. Only up to a point, you can't push people too far.
c. Yes, they generally do.

29. Do you feel that other people control your life, leaving you no say in what you do?
a. No
b. Sometimes
c. Often

Now turn to page 91 and check your scores.

Scores
(Total your scores to find your analysis below.)

1. a. 0	b. 1D	c. 2D	**11.** a. 0	b. 1G	c. 1G	**21.** a. 0	b. 1G	c. 2G		
2. a. 0	b. 1G	c. 2G	**12.** a. 0	b. 1P	c. 2P	**22.** a. 0	b. 1P	c. 2P		
3. a. 0	b. 1P	c. 2P	**13.** a. 0	b. 1D	c. 2D	**23.** a. 0	b. 1D	c. 2D		
4. a. 1P	b. 2P		**14.** a. 0	b. 1G	c. 2G	**24.** a. 0	b. 1G	c. 2G		
5. a. 0	b. 1D	c. 2D	**15.** a. 0	b. 1P	c. 2P	**25.** a. 0	b. 1P	c. 2P		
6. a. 0	b. 1G	c. 2G	**16.** a. 0	b. 1D	c. 2D	**26.** a, b & c: Each time you differ				
7. a. 0	b. 1P	c. 2P	**17.** a. 0	b. 1G	c. 2G	from your friends, add 1D.				
8. a. 0	b. 0		**18.** a. 0	b. 1P	c. 2P	**27.** a. 0	b. 1G	c. 2G		
9. a. 0	b. 1D	c. 2D	**19.** a. 1P	b. 2P		**28.** a. 0	b. 1P	c. 2P		
10. a. 0	b. 1D	c. 2D	**20.** a. 0	b. 1D	c. 2D	**29.** a. 0	b. 1G	c. 2G		

In the course of answering this questionnaire you will have picked up three types of scores, D, G and P. Psychologists have found that the validity of an individual's self-image is a function of three basic factors, and it is these three factors that the D, G and P scores reflect.

The D score

This relates to a basic discrepancy between what is known as "self" and "other" perception. At its simplest level this is merely the distinction between the view that you have of yourself and the view that other people have of you. Psychologists have also found that people with *severely* distorted self-images – in other words who would barely recognize the image that other people have formed of them – are almost always people who down-value themselves. Most people tend to up-value themselves slightly on a number of points and may get small shocks from time to time. People with exaggeratedly good images of themselves can rarely hold these images for very long because the world instantly disputes them, forcing the person to persistent reappraisal. For example, anyone with an average IQ who fancies himself as a genius will soon find unshakable evidence contradicting his self-image when he matches his intellectual skills against an objectively high IQ scale. On the other hand, a person with a poor self-image generally withdraws from the world, refusing to test out the image and therefore reinforcing his feelings of inadequacy. The higher your D score the greater the discrepancy between your "self" and "other" images, and the more likely it is that you undervalue yourself.

As a rough guide, you could say that 0-4D indicates a reasonable match between "self" and "other" perception. With a score between 5-10D, there is clearly some degree of mismatch and you are probably undervaluing yourself. A score of 11-17D indicates a serious mismatch, almost certainly due to the fact that you have a poor opinion of yourself. This is a pity because people probably appreciate you much more than you think! Take a chance on it!

The G score

This relates to persistence of childish feelings of guilt, powerlessness and punishment. As we grow older and personality matures ideally we should shed childish thought, habit and behavior patterns. The extent to which we can rid ourselves of the self-images of childhood is a measure of how mature we are as adults. Conversely, if we retain a childish self-image, then there must clearly be a major discrepancy between our "self" and "other" perceptions. During childhood we alternate between feelings of total dependence and powerlessness, and feelings of omnipotence and super-confidence. The G score deals with the former dimension – feelings of powerlessness, guilt and punishment, which become embedded in our minds as the result of parental prohibitions and disciplines. The higher your G score the more closely you are strapped to the past on this dimension.

As a rough guide, 0-4G means that you are almost entirely free of irrational guilt hanging over from your childhood, and the chances are that your "self" and "other" images are not seriously apart. Between 5-10G there are clear indications that your self-image is partly controlled by memories of your childhood with the result that, particularly in times of crisis, you often do yourself less than justice. A score of over 10G implies a high degree of irrational links with childhood and this is almost certainly handicapping you. Try to be less harsh on yourself, to feel less guilty when you make simple errors and give yourself more pats on the back when you have successes.

The P score

This relates to the persistence of childish feelings of total power and unrealistic fantasy. Because children need to be supported more or less completely in the early years of life they unconsciously acquire the feeling that the world is totally at their beck and call. This can lead to delusions of power and to the belief that whatever their fantasy or wish it will be immediately granted. The coming of adolescence and adulthood generally leads to a shattering of these delusions, but all of us retain ties with the past and perhaps cling to memories of the time when we had total power. The stronger these ties the less objective our self-image. The higher your P score the more you are a slave to your past.

As a rough guide, 0-4P indicates that you are more or less totally free of such ties. 5-10P implies that you are still trapped, though not severely, in beliefs more appropriate to childhood. If you score over 10P you still believe, irrationally, that the world is at your beck and call, or at least ought to be. Such delusions have little practical value and you should take stock of the situation and "come down to earth."

Overall score

Total your score for all three sections, and read off your general analysis below.

0-15 The match between your self-image and other peoples' image of yourself is a close one.

16-30 You have a reasonably realistic appraisal of yourself, though the chances are that in one of the three dimensions above the match is not as good as it might be.

31-40 This denotes a rather unrealistic self-image. Try to identify what are the roots of the disagreement. Can you gain helpful information from studying which of the three dimensions is most seriously out of balance?

Over 40 If you have scored correctly and answered the questionnaire honestly you probably have a highly unrealistic view of yourself, and the chances are, candidly, that there is not much you can do about it!

What Are Your Social Attitudes?

This is a test of your attitudes to society, to the world in which you live, to your friends, neighbors, to religion and to politics. There are no right or wrong answers, and all that is necessary is for you to be absolutely honest with yourself when you answer the questions that are put to you.

Because of the nature of the test itself, it is not possible to give too much introductory explanation to it and its aims, and it is doubly important this time that you *don't look* at the final analysis on page 96 until you have completed both sections of the questionnaire. If you do, the results will definitely be invalidated and you will lose the opportunity of gaining a valuable insight into two important aspects of your personality – aspects which will certainly influence your relationships with other people and your level of interaction with society. As you come to answer the questions some will seem to you to be obvious, others less easy to answer, and some may seem to you to be absurd or perhaps even offensive. Try to disregard any emotional reaction to these questions and answer them as honestly as you possibly can. Under no circumstances answer them in a way that you feel *other people would expect you to answer them!* This is a test for you, and you alone.

Part I

Answer each of the following questions by indicating whether you "strongly agree," "agree on the whole," "disagree on the whole" or "strongly disagree" with each.

Mark your answers on a separate sheet.

1. Most men just get a wage out of the company they are working for; they should also be entitled to a fair share in its ownership.

2. A man who runs an expensive car and doesn't keep a good home for his family is a fool.

3. In the long run, science makes a greater contribution to human happiness than art.

4. Premarital sexual intercourse is perfectly harmless, and it is astonishing that there are still taboos against it.

5. People who complain about aircraft noise should move away from airports.

6. The Women's Liberation Movement may have had some successes, but sooner or later women will realize that they were better off before it came along.

7. The education system will greatly benefit when computers do more of the teaching.

8. Rape and sexual offences against children deserve flogging as a punishment as well as imprisonment.

9. International organizations like the United Nations are good in their way, but we should make sure that they don't interfere with our country's prestige and power.

10. The abolition of private property and the introduction of a socialist state would greatly benefit this country.

11. It is a pity that more effort has not been put into developing international languages like Esperanto.

12. Sterilization is justifiable when it prevents someone passing on a serious hereditary condition.

13. I would sooner have my country occupied by a foreign power than see millions of lives lost in defending it.

14. If politicians spent more time in politics and less in feathering their nests, we should all be better off.

15. If muggers were given a dose of their own medicine we would soon see a reduction in street crime.

16. Nationalization of many big industries makes good sense, particularly if they have already been receiving government aid.

17. If more help were given to the underdeveloped countries, the world would be a better place.

18. People with phobias are suffering from weak wills more than anything else.

19. Canned and frozen foods cannot be as nutritious as fresh garden produce.

20. Too many people fail to appreciate public services, such as libraries, swimming baths and social centers.

21. Human beings would be physically and mentally improved if they had fewer hangups on sexual matters.

22. Girls should be given complete sex education and advice on birth control in their early teens.

23. Antipollution laws should be considerably toughened up – and quickly.

24.   It is a pity that we spend so much time punishing criminals instead of trying to cure them.

25.   There is a lot to be said for racial segregation; racial conflicts have only developed since segregation between the races broke down.

26.   Cigarette smoking is an antisocial habit and should be banned in public places.

27.   One of the many symptoms of our society's decline is its increasing acceptance of homosexuality.

28.   It is important that every child should be given clear religious guidance and education.

29.   Traitors are just about the lowest form of human life.

30.   If the world population isn't reduced sharply we shall exhaust our food supplies.

31.   Whoever said "The love of money is the root of all evil" knew what he was talking about.

32.   It was a great mistake to soften up abortion laws.

33.   People nowadays are very much less courteous than they used to be.

34.   If there was less public welfare some of the "unemployed" might decide to look for work.

35.   Genuine patriotism is one of the noblest ideals.

36.   There is a great deal too much nonsense spoken about vitamins these days.

37.   Most accidents are caused by inadequate roads and not by bad driving.

38.   The less governments interfere with industry and business life the better.

39.   It is terrible that there should be well-fed pets around while elsewhere children starve.

40.   It stands to reason that the death penalty must have a deterrent effect.

Now turn to page 94 and check your scores.

Washington Star News

Scores

(Total your scores to find your analysis below.)

	Strongly agree	Agree on the whole	Disagree on the whole	Strongly disagree
1.	0	0	1C	1C
2.	1X	0	0	1X
3.	1X	0	0	1X
4.	0	0	1C	1C
5.	1X	0	0	1X
6.	1C	1C	0	0
7.	1X	0	0	1X
8.	1C	1C	0	0
9.	1C	1C	0	0
10.	0	0	1C	1C
11.	1X	0	0	1X
12.	1X	0	0	1X
13.	0	0	1C	1C
14.	1X	0	0	1X
15.	1C	1C	0	0
16.	0	0	1C	1C
17.	1X	0	0	1X
18.	1X	0	0	1X
19.	1X	0	0	1X
20.	1X	0	0	1X
21.	0	0	1C	1C
22.	0	0	1C	1C
23.	1X	0	0	1X
24.	0	0	1C	1C
25.	1C	1C	0	0
26.	1X	0	0	1X
27.	1C	1C	0	0
28.	1C	1C	0	0
29.	1C	1C	0	0
30.	1X	0	0	1X
31.	1X	0	0	1X
32.	1C	1C	0	0
33.	1X	0	0	1X
34.	1X	0	0	1X
35.	1C	1C	0	0
36.	1X	0	0	1X
37.	1X	0	0	1X
38.	1C	1C	0	0
39.	1X	0	0	1X
40.	1C	1C	0	0

The first Labor Day parade in New York, 1882.

Interpreting Your Score

This part of the questionnaire relates, in particular, to a dimension of personality which, for the want of a better phrase, is generally described as radicalism/conservatism. On the whole, the conservative personality is the individual who likes to maintain the status quo, resisting innovation wherever possible. He sees the world's successes as having been achieved as the result of the stability of ideas, and feels that future plans should be based wherever possible on the solid achievements of the past. In contrast, a personality with a strong tendency to radicalism is often anxious for change, and even tends to the view that when change comes it should be widespread and far-reaching. He believes that "new brooms" are always preferable to old ones, and that the more vigorously they sweep, the cleaner everything will become.

Everyone has a trace of radicalism in them, and everyone a trace of conservatism, but most people tend, on balance, towards one direction or another. You will have emerged with two sets of scores: C points and X points. You should tot these up separately, note them down, and when you have completed the second part of this questionnaire, *and not before,* plot them on the special graph where their significance will be explained. Your C score is an index of the extent to which conservatism dominates your personality and the higher the score the more conservative you are. The X score will be explained later.

What Are Your Social Attitudes? Part II

This is the second part of the questionnaire, "What Are Your Social Attitudes?" In this part, as in the first, an important dimension of your personality will be measured. And, as in Part I, because of the nature of this aspect of personality, we will not be discussing it in detail before you take the test. You will have to wait until you come to plot your scores at the end for an interpretation.

Answer all the questions as truthfully and honestly as you can, indicating whether you "strongly agree," "agree on the whole," "disagree on the whole" or "strongly disagree" with each.

Mark your answers on a separate sheet.

1. It is clearly unfair that some children should be privately educated while others do not have that option.

2. Far too many people expose their bodies in public these days.

3. The average person can lead a perfectly good life without having any involvement in organized religion.

4. If one has a police force, the tougher it is the better.

5. The use of nuclear weapons against Japan was a crime against humanity.

6. It is vital to ensure the freedom of the press at all times.

7. "Mercy killing" for the aged or the seriously sick should be available to those who request it.

8. Fines for throwing trash and litter in public places should be increased.

9. Speed limits on roads are beneficial on the whole.

10. There is nothing wrong with people living together before they get married.

11. There are too many busybodies around these days.

12. Everyone tries "fare dodging" once in a while and there is really no harm in it.

13. The world oil crisis will benefit people's health by making them turn to bicycles, to walking and so on.

14. It is a good thing that the law has been changed to make divorce easier to obtain.

15. The so-called "underprivileged" are often people who could improve their lot if they worked a bit harder.

16. Most people buy cameras and other gadgets as status symbols rather than because they are useful.

17. If people have much more time off work they won't know what to do with themselves.

18. The idea that a society can perform ritual killing in the name of "capital punishment" is horrible.

19. The majority of people in this country are overfed.

20. The idea of "life after death" is just a superstition.

21. Birth control may be convenient, but it is morally wrong.

22. It is a good thing sport is compulsory in most schools.

23. If people wish to kill themselves then they should be allowed to do so.

24. Sometimes it is better to lie than tell the truth.

25. It is more important to maintain law and order within a society than to ensure complete freedom for all.

26. International sport is one of the first steps towards true international understanding.

27. Children should not be exposed to horror stories.

28. Life is short and one should enjoy it as one can.

29. In the long run it is a good thing that the weak perish and the strong survive.

30. Man probably has latent psychic powers which he could develop if he knew how.

31. Blood sports are cruel and should be abolished.

32. You can make out quite a convincing case for the fact that earth has been visited by flying saucers.

33. We may feel sorry for refugees, but on the whole they should be left to fend for themselves.

34. The collapse of the old Victorian attitudes to sex will lead to increased human happiness in the long run.

35. Taking it all in all, Jewish people are very similar in their personality and looks.

36. Man has invented God for his own peace of mind.

37. Most young men would benefit from a period of compulsory military service in peace time.

38. Honesty is the best policy.

39. Increasing foreign travel exposes people to unhealthy ideas from other countries.

40. A good, old-fashioned religious revival is long overdue and would greatly benefit the country.

Now turn to page 96 and check your scores.

Scores

(Total your scores to find your analysis below.)

		Strongly agree	Agree on the whole	Disagree on the whole	Strongly disagree		Strongly agree	Agree on the whole	Disagree on the whole	Strongly disagree
1.		1Y	0	0	1Y	21.	1T	1T	0	0
2.		1Y	0	0	1Y	22.	1Y	0	0	1Y
3.		0	0	1T	1T	23.	0	0	1T	1T
4.		1T	1T	0	0	24.	0	0	1T	1T
5.		0	0	1T	1T	25.	1T	1T	0	0
6.		1Y	0	0	1Y	26.	1Y	0	0	1Y
7.		0	0	1T	1T	27.	1Y	0	0	1Y
8.		1Y	0	0	1Y	28.	0	0	1T	1T
9.		1Y	0	0	1Y	29.	1T	1T	0	0
10.		0	0	1T	1T	30.	0	0	1T	1T
11.		1T	1T	0	0	31.	0	0	1T	1T
12.		0	0	1T	1T	32.	1Y	0	0	1Y
13.		1Y	0	0	1Y	33.	1T	1T	0	0
14.		0	0	1T	1T	34.	0	0	1T	1T
15.		1T	1T	0	0	35.	1T	1T	0	0
16.		1Y	0	0	1Y	36.	0	0	1T	1T
17.		1Y	0	0	1Y	37.	1T	1T	0	0
18.		0	0	1T	1T	38.	1Y	0	0	1Y
19.		1Y	0	0	1Y	39.	1Y	0	0	1Y
20.		0	0	1T	1T	40.	1T	1T	0	0

Interpreting Your Score

After you have completed Part II of the questionnaire you should total your scores ready for plotting on the two-factor graph on the next page.

The dimension of personality being examined in the second part of the questionnaire is rather an elusive one, but has been best summarized as "tough/tenderminded." The precise qualities making up a toughminded individual are a little hard to formalize, but broadly speaking they involve a certain amount of rigidity in thinking, a tendency to believe that all problems can be solved if enough effort is put to them, a slightly sluggish outlook on life, an inability to empathize or respond to other people's misfortunes. This is toughmindedness at the more extreme end of the scale. The tenderminded person, conversely, tends to be more fluid, less troubled by rules and regulations and more sympathetic to others' misfortunes. Your T score represents this tough/tenderminded dimension in your nature – the Y score we will explain later.

The first part of the questionnaire dealt with the personality continuum of conservatism and its opposite, which might best be described as radicalism. Although the two dimensions measured in Parts I and II are different in the main, there is a certain amount of overlap and for this reason the results can be plotted instructively on the same Personality Graph.

In questionnaires of this sort, if people are aware that their conservatism, tendermindedness or whatever is being investigated, they significantly change their answers, and it is for this reason that the questionnaire came in disguised form as a "social attitude" survey.

YOUR X AND Y SCORES
It is also important in self-scoring questionnaires on subjects of this kind that people do not realize which are the most "significant" questions and for this reason the key questions need to be embedded in a series of "dummy" or non-scoring questions. Your X and Y scores in fact refer to these dummy questions and you should disregard them. Do not attempt to plot them on the graph as they have no significance in this context.

THE C SCALE
The higher your C score the more conservative you are.
Over 15C If you score over 15C you would appear to be ultraconservative. The chances are that you are probably into or past middle age, in which case your personality reflects attitudes which were more fashionable a few decades ago. It is rather unlikely if you have this high score that you will ever change your views much. However, try to be a little more flexible and openminded, particularly as far as younger people and their ideas are concerned.

11C-15C This represents a high degree of conservatism, though it is not exceptional and your position might best be summed up by saying that you are "a bit of a traditionalist."

5C-10C The dominating theme in this strand of your personality is certainly not conservatism: in fact you are decidely liberal and almost radical in your views. You are probably openminded and politically flexible.

Under 5C You have a strong tendency to radicalism and are probably contemptuous of all people and institutions that resist change "for its own sake." The chances are that you are young and have the natural impetuousity of youth. Of course you are right that the world needs changing, but remember that those people who prefer not to change it have as much right to their say as you do!

THE T SCALE
The higher your T score the more toughminded you are. If you score over 15 you are very toughminded indeed and may be hard to get on with. A score of between 11 and 15T indicates a tendency to toughmindedness, while a score between 5 and 10, an inclination towards tendermindedness. If you score under 5T, you are tenderminded in the extreme. You may be a nice person to know, but you are probably also a sucker for a soft touch. This dimension of personality tends to be permanent through life so one cannot offer much in the way of advice to those individuals located in the extreme ends of this scale – if you are "tough" then you are likely to remain so, and the same applies if you are "tender."

Personality Graph

Make your own graph by drawing 2 lines (T and C, as in the example below) to cross in the middle, and by calibrating them with numbers as shown.

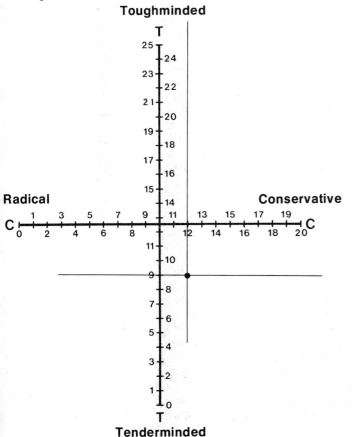

You will note that the Personality Graph has two axes: the vertical tough/tenderminded scale and the horizontal conservative/radical scale. To find your location on your own graph, take your T score and locate where you are on the T scale. Now take your C score and mark that on the C scale. Now draw a horizontal line through your T point and a vertical line through your C point. The spot where these intersect is where you are located on this personality profile. Your friends can find their positions in the same way.

In interpreting your position on the graph, as a simple rule you could say that the closer you are to the center point where the two axes cross, the more "normal" or average you are.

If you find yourself high in the top left-hand corner of the graph, the chances are that you have socialist or leftwing inclinations. If you find yourself high in the top right-hand corner, then you are more likely to be extremely rightwing, with a very strong authoritarian streak. The followers of most European and American political parties will tend to find themselves grouped much closer to the center cross.

If you have plotted your position in the bottom left-hand corner, you are showing strong liberal tendencies, but not much inclination to force your beliefs onto other people. People who find themselves in the bottom right-hand corner will probably agree that they are traditionalist in the extreme, though they are not intolerant of other people's opposing beliefs.

A graph of this kind becomes particularly instructive when you see yourself plotted with a group of other people that you know. You may find the comparison of all your positions – the unexpected similarities and differences – very revealing!

Jeff Kingswood

How Imaginative Are You?

The word imagination refers literally to our ability to form images—pictures in the mind. Actually, by a peculiarity which few psychologists understand, not everybody has the ability to form mental images—about three out of ten of the people reading these words will not even be sure what is meant by the phrase "mental imagery." Just test yourself briefly: close your eyes and try to conjure up a picture of a boat with red sails on a blue sea. Seven out of ten readers will be able to do this—the other three will simply not know how to set about it. But visual imagery is only part of imagination. It also involves the capacity to anticipate situations before they occur, the ability to feel for other people in difficult or pleasant situations and, of course, it lies at the root of most artistic endeavor.

Imagination is one of the most basic features of mental life. Having a vivid imagination can be helpful and allow you the full range of artistic expression, but equally if you are *too* imaginative this can lead to problems. This questionnaire is designed to assess how imaginative you are. Complete it carefully, check your answers and read the analysis at the end.

Mark your answers on a separate sheet.

1. When you have to invent a white lie, do you
   a. Blunder hopelessly and give yourself away?
   b. Invent too many details and complications and so invite suspicion?
   c. Say just enough to be convincing?

2. Do you believe your own white lies?
   a. Yes
   b. No
   c. Almost

3. When you come into a group of people who then fall silent, do you think
   a. That they must have been talking about you?
   b. That they have reached a natural break in the conversation?
   c. That they are acknowledging your arrival?

4. Do you tend to react to other people's hard luck stories with
   a. Tears?
   b. Some feeling of sympathy?
   c. Boredom?

5. When you are criticized, do you
   a. Reject the criticism totally?
   b. Figure out how justified the comments are?
   c. Feel as if nothing you do is ever right?

6. When you go out for an evening, do you
   a. Always stick to places you know you like?
   b. Try something different every time?
   c. Sometimes try somewhere new?

7. When you are expecting someone and he is rather late, do you
   a. Feel worried about accidents?
   b. Assume that something perfectly ordinary has happened to delay him?
   c. Refuse to feel worried for at least an hour?

8. Have you cried at the theater or cinema?
   a. Yes
   b. No
   c. Not for years

9. If you are alone at night do you
   a. Feel frightened?
   b. Feel quite unworried?
   c. Feel slight fear, but dismiss it?

10. Do ghost stories
    a. Make you laugh?
    b. Give you a creepy feeling?
    c. Interest you in a detached way?

11. When you gaze at a patterned wallpaper, do you
    a. See pictures in it if you look long enough?
    b. Pay little attention to it?
    c. Simply follow the design?

12. You are asleep in an unfamiliar place when you are awakened by strange sounds. Would you
    a. Think of ghosts?
    b. Think of burglars?
    c. Think of the hot water pipes?

13. When you fall in love do you
    a. Think that your lover is perfect, if only for a short time?
    b. Idealize your lover just a bit?
    c. See your lover pretty realistically?

14. When you see a movie of a book that you have read do you
   a. Usually enjoy it more with the visual presentation?
   b. Usually find it disappointing?
   c. Find that it varies with the quality of the film?

15. If you have time to spare can you
   a. Amuse yourself with your own thoughts?
   b. Amuse yourself if you find something to do?
   c. Amuse yourself only if you have something particularly interesting to think about?

16. Do you think you have a good idea for a book or film
   a. Often?
   b. Sometimes?
   c. Practically never?

17. If you were told that someone had committed suicide in a house that you wanted to buy, would you
   a. Go ahead if the place suited you?
   b. Halt your negotiations instantly?
   c. Think out whether it made any difference to you?

18. Do you rewrite, mentally, the ending of movies or books?
   a. Only if you were particularly impressed by the story.
   b. Often
   c. Never

19. When you retell an experience, do you
   a. Exaggerate to make a better story?
   b. Tell it straight?
   c. Modify a few details?

20. Do you daydream?
   a. Often
   b. Sometimes
   c. Rarely

21. When you daydream do you
   a. Invent a wealth of detail and intricacy?
   b. Think very vaguely about desirable situations?
   c. Put in the detail only occasionally?

22. When your Sunday newspaper carries yet another story about the starving Third World, do you
   a. Turn the pages quickly?
   b. Find that your appetite is spoiled?

c. Tell yourself that you really must do something about it?

23. Do you have imaginary conversations?
   a. Only after an argument.
   b. No
   c. Often

24. Is your thinking accompanied by strong visual imagery?
   a. Usually
   b. Rarely
   c. Sometimes

25. Would you rate yourself
   a. Very experimental in sex?
   b. Uninterested in experiment in sex?
   c. Interested, but not always confident, in experiment in sex?

26. Do sexy books or movies
   a. Disgust you?
   b. Leave you unmoved?
   c. Turn you on?

27. If a child told you about an imaginary playmate would you
   a. Enter into his fantasy?
   b. Tell him that lying is wrong?
   c. Smile indulgently?

28. Think of a song that you like. Do you
   a. Hear it clearly and completely?
   b. Hear only snatches?
   c. Have to sing under your breath to recall it?

29. Your neighbors have been burgled. Do you
   a. Make sure that your locks are secure?
   b. Buy a watch dog?
   c. Buy a gun?

30. Can you imagine that you could ever get into real trouble, like perhaps going to prison?
   a. No
   b. Yes, if circumstances were a bit different.
   c. Only with difficulty, as it seems so unlikely.

Now turn to page 101 and check your scores.

Scores

(Total your scores to find your analysis below.)

1. a. 1 b. 3 c. 5
2. a. 5 b. 1 c. 3
3. a. 5 b. 1 c. 3
4. a. 5 b. 3 c. 1
5. a. 1 b. 3 c. 5
6. a. 1 b. 5 c. 3
7. a. 5 b. 1 c. 3
8. a. 5 b. 1 c. 3
9. a. 5 b. 1 c. 3
10. a. 1 b. 5 c. 3
11. a. 5 b. 1 c. 3
12. a. 5 b. 3 c. 1
13. a. 5 b. 3 c. 1
14. a. 1 b. 5 c. 3
15. a. 5 b. 1 c. 3
16. a. 5 b. 3 c. 1
17. a. 1 b. 5 c. 3
18. a. 3 b. 5 c. 1
19. a. 5 b. 1 c. 3
20. a. 5 b. 3 c. 1
21. a. 5 b. 1 c. 3
22. a. 1 b. 5 c. 3
23. a. 3 b. 1 c. 5
24. a. 5 b. 1 c. 3
25. a. 5 b. 1 c. 3
26. a. 3 b. 1 c. 5
27. a. 5 b. 1 c. 3
28. a. 5 b. 3 c. 1
29. a. 1 b. 3 c. 5
30. a. 1 b. 5 c. 3

Imagination—quite literally—is the forming of mental images. How versatile is yours? In this picture there are two portraits, one of an old woman, one of a girl. Can you see both?

Analysis

If you have completed the questionnaire accurately you will end up with a score between 30 and 150. The general rule in interpreting this is that the higher your score the more imaginative you are. For greater detail, however, compare your score with the five categories below.

30-50 It is a great pity, but you are desperately low on the scale of imagination. You just do not seem to be able to invoke the world of fantasy at all to help you. You may be very practical and down-to-earth but even here your poor imagination is likely to let you down.

51-74 You do not let your imagination ride. You are not basically *un*imaginative but you tend to clamp down on your imagination wherever you can. Probably people respect you for your hardheadedness. All well and good, but do you miss out on some of the benefits of fantasy? Maybe you should let your fun and playfulness filter through more often.

75-109 You certainly have imagination and what is more you can use it to put yourself in someone else's place, which is often the most useful and productive thing you can do with it. On the other hand, you do not often let your imagination get the better of your common sense, with the result that you are spared the ups and downs of the highly imaginative person.

110-129 You are sometimes too imaginative for your own comfort. Sometimes your fears are unrealistically based and you are oversensitive to blame and pain. On the other hand you may be highly artistic and, whenever you can find a constructive use for your imaginative powers, you have a lot to offer.

130-150 You have a vivid and, to be quite honest, probably excessive imagination. This means that you will have an elaborate internal life but possibly at the expense of facing up to the problems of the real world.

How Strong is Your Unconscious?

The earliest theories of psychology assumed that man was a being composed of two distinct units—a body including a brain, which was purely physical, and a mind, soul or spirit, which was non-physical. The two interacted in some vague way with the conscious mind controlling the physical body in much the same way as a man controls a puppet. All human behavior could be explained in terms of the conscious personality of the individual and any mistakes that he made were his own fault, any sins that he committed were because he had deliberately diverged from the straight and narrow path. If someone drank too much, neglected his family or committed murder there was no real excuse because, with sufficient will-power, he would have been able to prevent himself from committing any such social crime.

Little wonder, then, that when Freud sprung the notion of the unconscious mind upon the world in the latter part of the 19th century public opinion was outraged. What Freud had done was to undermine thousands of years of simpleminded belief that the conscious personality was the dominant force in human behavior. Instead he drew attention to the fact that the mind is a multistructured organism with only part of this structure related to consciousness and a large segment—perhaps even the greater part—below consciousness, not subject to conscious control. Often our worst behavior is determined by the unconscious, and most of our neurotic conditions can be explained in terms of battles between the conscious and the unconscious forces of the mind. But the unconscious is not totally malevolent; from its depths spring not only aggression and selfishness but also creativity, artistic ability and intuition. This questionnaire probes the degree to which your unconscious intrudes into your everyday life. The unconscious resists inspection but there are benefits from being in touch with it. For example, by knowing something of this territory of the mind you can get a clearer idea of who you really are and what you really want. Ignored, the unconscious can assert itself in surprising and sometimes unpleasant ways.

Mark your answers on a separate sheet.

1. Do you always fall for the same type of person?
  a. Yes
  b. No

2. Which statement is most true for you?
  a. I remember clearly all the places I have seen.
  b. I sometimes get the feeling when I visit a new place that I've been there before.
  c. I only remember places well if I have a good or a specific reason to.

3. Have you ever mistaken a stranger for someone you very much wanted to see?
  a. Yes, frequently
  b. Never
  c. Only occasionally

4. Are you ever afraid in crowds?
  a. Yes
  b. No

5. Do you have any rituals, like putting things in exactly the right place or doing things in exactly the right order?
  a. Yes
  b. No
  c. Occasionally, if I am in a new place.

6. Have you ever misheard something that has been said to you?
  a. Never

  b. Sometimes
  c. Several times

7. Do you form strong dislikes for people without any apparent reason?
  a. Yes
  b. No
  c. Only rarely

8. Would you rate yourself as
  a. Highly superstitious?
  b. Not at all superstitious?
  c. Mildly superstitious?

9. Do you ever accidentally call someone close to you by the wrong name?
  a. Sometimes
  b. Never

10. If you were asked to join an encounter group of some sort would you
  a. Go out of curiosity?
  b. Feel afraid of what might happen there and not want to go?
  c. Feel a mixture of fear and curiosity, but probably decide to go anyway?

11. If someone says that your child (or young relative) has the same faults as you, would you
  a. Feel surprised?
  b. Acknowledge it indulgently?
  c. Feel worried?

12. If you have to avoid an embarrassing subject like death in conversation when you visit a friend in hospital, are you
   a. Constantly aware of the taboo subject?
   b. Likely to blurt out just exactly the wrong thing accidentally?
   c. Successful in avoiding any thought and mention of dangerous topics?

13. On waking up in the morning, do you
   a. Remember nothing of your dreams?
   b. Remember momentarily your dreams?
   c. Remember only vivid fragments?

14. Do you think that fairy tales are
   a. For children only?
   b. For adults as well as children?
   c. Nonsense?

15. Do the people you dislike resemble authority or parent figures?
   a. Yes
   b. No

16. Which statement is most true for you?
   a. I sometimes do things I don't want to do for not very strong reasons.
   b. I only do things I don't want to do for very pressing reasons.
   c. I often feel compelled to do things I don't want to do, even when I seem to have a choice.

17. When you do something that you were strictly told *not* to do as a child, do you
   a. Feel guilty?
   b. Feel slightly uncomfortable?
   c. Feel fine, if it doesn't conflict with your adult standards?

18. Do you find
   a. That you dream very little?
   b. That you dream a lot?
   c. That you often have powerful, pervasive and explicit dreams?

19. If your excuse for being late for an appointment is that you had some important things to do before you left home, would you
   a. Be making up a story to cover up the fact that you overslept?
   b. Be telling the truth?
   c. Be talking about rituals that would not seem important to anyone else?

20. Is the imagery of your dreams
   a. Related to everyday life, pretty realistic?
   b. Strange and fantastic?
   c. Too confused to be classified?

21. Do you find that you sometimes lose your confidence and self possession
   a. Under stress?
   b. For no good reason that you can see?
   c. Only where it makes sense not to feel confident?

22. When you go shopping do you
   a. Occasionally buy on impulse?
   b. Often buy things for no apparent reason?
   c. Stick closely to what you intended to buy?

23. Have you ever found yourself walking or driving in a direction different to the one you meant to take?
   a. Yes
   b. No

24. Have you ever tried to interpret your dreams?
   a. No, they don't make any sense.
   b. Yes, you can sometimes see a pattern.

25. When you dislike someone, do you
   a. Try to find out why?
   b. Stay away from him?
   c. Not think much about it?

26. Have you ever forgotten to sign your Tax Return?
   a. Yes
   b. No

27. Do you tend to dislike the same type of person?
   a. Yes
   b. No

28. Before a journey you suddenly feel uneasy about going. Would you
   a. Pull yourself together and go as planned?
   b. Act on your instinct and just not go?
   c. Find a convincing reason for not going?

29. Do you forget the dates of dental appointments?
   a. Yes
   b. No

30. Have you ever put the wrong date on a check?
   a. Yes
   b. No

Now turn to page 104 and check your scores.

Scores

(Total your scores to find your analysis below.)

1. a. 5Y	b. 0		**11.** a. 5Z	b. 1Z	c. 3Z		**21.** a. 3X	b. 5X	c. 1X
2. a. 3X	b. 5X	c. 1X	**12.** a. 5X	b. 3X	c. 1X		**22.** a. 3Z	b. 5Z	c. 1Z
3. a. 5X	b. 1X	c. 3X	**13.** a. 1X	b. 5X	c. 3X		**23.** a. 5Y	b. 0	
4. a. 5Y	b. 0		**14.** a. 3Z	b. 5Z	c. 1Z		**24.** a. 5Y	b. 0	
5. a. 5Z	b. 1Z	c. 3Z	**15.** a. 5Y	b. 0			**25.** a. 3X	b. 5X	c. 1X
6. a. 1Z	b. 3Z	c. 5Z	**16.** a. 3Z	b. 1Z	c. 5Z		**26.** a. 5Y	b. 0	
7. a. 5X	b. 1X	c. 3X	**17.** a. 5Z	b. 3Z	c. 1Z		**27.** a. 5Y	b. 0	
8. a. 5Z	b. 1Z	c. 3Z	**18.** a. 1X	b. 3X	c. 5X		**28.** a. 1X	b. 5X	c. 3X
9. a. 5Y	b. 0		**19.** a. 3Z	b. 1Z	c. 5Z		**29.** a. 5Y	b. 0	
10. a. 3Z	b. 5Z	c. 1Z	**20.** a. 1X	b. 5X	c. 3X		**30.** a. 5Y	b. 0	

Analysis

In scoring this questionnaire you will have achieved totals of X, Y and Z scores. These reflect different aspects of your personality in terms of the general activity of your unconscious mind. The boundaries between consciousness and unconsciousness are not easy to define and thus there is a certain inevitable overlap between the three factors. On the whole, they can be summarized as follows:

The X factor
Basically this relates to your *awareness* of the existence of your unconscious. How much do you accept it and how much do you deny it? Read off your own score in the discussion below.

10X-25X A low score in this range suggests that in your case there is little sign of unconsciously motivated action. Superficially this would seem to imply that your conscious mind is very strongly developed and keeps the unconscious pretty well at bay. It may also mean that your conscious mind has set up strong and vigorous defences against intrusions from the hidden layer of your mind.

26X-40X You probably have a rather active unconscious with the inevitable result that you will at times find yourself doing things and making decisions which seem to contradict what you really *ought* to do under the circumstances. If you find yourself in situations of this kind try to step back from the scene and identify what your real reasons and motivations are.

41X-50X Your unconscious is probably very active and the chances are that you have never been really aware of its existence. The outcome of this is likely to be that you often find yourself in conflict situations, doing just the kind of thing that you know you ought not to. This could lead to some uncomfortable results.

The Y factor
This relates to the extent to which your unconscious reveals itself to you by slipping past any guards your conscious mind sets up against it. Freud became very interested in slips of the tongue which he believed were instances when unconscious wishes burst to the surface—almost waving a flag to the conscious mind, drawing attention to its existence. There are other forms of "Freudian slip" of course—conveniently forgetting unpleasant appointments is the best example. It is difficult to be categorical about this factor but, as a

guide to how prone you are to these "giveaways," read the following analysis of your score.

0-25Y Your unconscious does not reveal itself to you readily. You are probably rather meticulous and careful and you may be one of those people who is always anxious to be right. Ask yourself whether this meticulousness really is natural to you. If it is not, then try to relax a little and you may find your unconscious popping through from time to time. It is better to have good communication between conscious and unconscious minds whenever you can.

30Y-50Y You are certainly prone to "Freudian slips" of one kind or another. This could be a clear indication that your unconscious pops easily to the surface. Consider yourself lucky! Look at the nature of your "slip" and learn to read the clear message that it is trying to convey to you.

The Z factor
This relates to how much your unconscious *dominates* your behavior and thus the extent to which it controls your destiny.

10Z-25Z With a score in this range it is fairly clear that your unconscious does not seem to control your life very noticeably. You—or to be more precise your conscious self—seem to be pretty much in control. The result of this is that you do not surprise yourself very much; you seldom find yourself doing things "against your will." The question is, have you managed to achieve a genuine harmony between the forces within your personality, or are you stamping out the unconscious by ruthless overcontrol? If the latter, you may find that it pops up someday and gives you a real surprise.

26Z-40Z The unconscious is exerting some power in your life. Some of your actions could be explained in terms of imperfectly understood unconscious motives, but they are rarely strong enough to worry you. You may be aware of tension between heart and head—perhaps acknowledging your feelings would help minimize anxiety.

41Z-50Z In many facets of your life the unconscious plays a strong and possibly dominant role. The result of this is that it is quite likely that you are often upset by conflicts within yourself. Try to understand the theory of the unconscious mind, even if you have to read a little Freud to do so! Does the theory of the unconscious seem to make sense to you?

Are You in the Right Job?

Ron Embleton

A hundred years ago people had literally no say in what their life's work was going to be. For most of the population, education was so scanty and illiteracy so widespread that the only jobs open to them were manual or unskilled laboring. Geographic factors also dictated how people should work—if you lived in the country you worked on the land; if you lived by the sea you probably had something to do with fishing; if you lived in a town you took whatever pickings there were from industry. This picture has been transformed in the twentieth century, with greater personal mobility and educational opportunities for all, ensuring that an increasing percentage of the population has some choice in how they spend their life and how they earn their daily bread.

Psychologists have long realized, however, that people vary not only in intelligence but also in their *aptitude* for particular jobs. With this in mind they have devised batteries of tests designed to sort out square pegs in round holes and make sure that people go to the job that fits them. Tests of this kind, for obvious reasons, are restricted in their use and must only be administered by properly trained experts, and for this reason are not suitable for inclusion in self-testing questionnaires. But there are factors other than simple aptitude which determine whether a person is in the right job or not. The following questionnaire has been developed to allow you to check this for yourself.

Mark your answers on a separate sheet.

1. Do you watch the clock when you are working?
 a. Constantly
 b. At slack times
 c. Never

2. When Monday morning comes, do you
 a. Feel ready to go back to work?
 b. Think longingly of being able to lie in hospital with a broken leg?
 c. Feel reluctant to start with, but fit into the work routine quite happily after an hour or so?

3. How do you feel at the end of a working day?
 a. Dead tired and fit for nothing.
 b. Glad that you can start living.
 c. Sometimes tired, but usually pretty satisfied.

4. Do you worry about your work?
 a. Occasionally
 b. Never
 c. Often

5. Would you say that your job
 a. Underuses your ability?
 b. Overstrains your abilities?
 c. Makes you do things you never thought you could do before?

6. Which statement is true for you?
 a. I am rarely bored with my work.
 b. I am usually interested in my work, but there are patches of boredom.
 c. I am bored most of the time I am working.

7. How much of your worktime is spent making personal telephone calls, or with other matters not connected with the job?
 a. Very little.
 b. Some, especially at crisis times in my personal life.
 c. Quite a lot.

8. Do you daydream about having a different job?
 a. Very little.
 b. Not a different job, but a better position in the same kind of job.
 c. Yes

9. Would you say that you feel
 a. Pretty capable most of the time?
 b. Sometimes capable?
 c. Panicky and incapable most of the time?

10. Do you find that
 a. You like and respect your colleagues?
 b. You dislike your colleagues?
 c. You are indifferent to your colleagues?

11. Which statement is most true for you?
 a. I do not want to learn more about my work.
 b. I quite enjoyed learning my work when I first started.

c. I like to go on learning as much as possible about my work.

12. Indicate the qualities you think are your best points:
   a. Sympathy
   b. Clear-thinking
   c. Calmness
   d. Good memory
   e. Concentration
   f. Physical stamina
   g. Inventiveness
   h. Expertise
   i. Charm
   j. Humor

13. Now indicate the above qualities that are demanded by your job.

14. Which statement do you most agree with?
   a. A job is only a way to make enough money to keep yourself alive.
   b. A job is mainly a way of making money, but should be satisfying if possible.
   c. A job is a whole way of life.

15. Do you work overtime?
   a. Only when it is paid
   b. Never
   c. Often, even without pay

16. Have you been absent from work (other than for normal vacations or illness) in the last year?
   a. Not at all
   b. For a few days only
   c. Frequently

17. Would you rate yourself as
   a. Very ambitious?
   b. Unambitious?
   c. Mildly ambitious?

18. Do you think that your colleagues
   a. Like you, enjoy your company and get on well with you in general?
   b. Dislike you?
   c. Do not dislike you, but are not particularly friendly?

19. Do you talk about work
   a. Only with your colleagues?
   b. With friends and family?
   c. Not if you can avoid it?

20. Do you suffer from minor or unexplained illnesses and vague pains?
   a. Seldom
   b. Not too often
   c. Frequently

21. How did you choose your present job
   a. Your parents or teachers decided for you?
   b. It was all you could find?
   c. It seemed the right thing for you?

22. In a conflict between job and home, like an illness of a member of the family, which would win?
   a. The family every time.

b. The job every time.
c. The family in a real emergency, but otherwise probably the job.

23. Would you be happy to do the same job if it paid one-third less?
    a. Yes
    b. You would like to, but could not afford to.
    c. No

24. If you were made redundant, which of these would you miss most?
    a. The money
    b. The work itself
    c. The company of your colleagues.

25. Would you ever take a day off from work just to have fun?
    a. Yes
    b. No
    c. Possibly, if there was nothing too urgent for you to do at work.

26. Do you feel unappreciated at work?
    a. Occasionally
    b. Often
    c. Rarely

27. What do you most dislike about your job?
    a. That your time is not your own.
    b. The boredom
    c. That you cannot always do things the way you want.

28. Do you keep your personal life separate from work? (Check with your partner on this one.)
    a. Pretty strictly
    b. Most of the time, but there is some overlap.
    c. Not at all

29. Would you advise a child of yours to take up the same kind of work as you do?
    a. Yes, if he had the ability and temperament.
    b. No, you would warn him off.
    c. You would not press it, but you would not discourage him either.

30. If you won or suddenly inherited a large sum of money, would you
    a. Stop work for the rest of your life?
    b. Take up some kind of work that you have always wanted to do?
    c. Decide to continue with the same work you do now.

Now turn to page 108 and check your scores.

Scores

(Total your scores to find your analysis below.)

1. a. 1	b. 3	c. 5	**11.** a. 1	b. 3	c. 5	**21.** a. 3	b. 1	c. 5
2. a. 5	b. 1	c. 3	**12. and 13.:** Score 5 each time			**22.** a. 1	b. 5	c. 3
3. a. 3	b. 1	c. 5	the qualities match			**23.** a. 5	b. *3*	c. 1
4. a. 5	b. 3	c. 1	**14.** a. 1	b. 3	c. 5	**24.** a. 1	b. 5	c. 3
5. a. 1	b. 3	c. 5	**15.** a. 3	b. 1	c. 5	**25.** a. 1	b. 5	c. 3
6. a. 5	b. 3	c. 1	**16.** a. 5	b. 3	c. 1	**26.** a. 3	b. 1	c. 5
7. a. 5	b. 3	c. 1	**17.** a. 5	b. 1	c. 3	**27.** a. 3	b. 1	c. 5
8. a. 5	b. 3	c. 1	**18.** a. 5	b. 1	c. 3	**28.** a. 1	b. 3	c. 5
9. a. 5	b. 3	c. 1	**19.** a. 3	b. 5	c. 1	**29.** a. 5	b. 1	c. 3
10. a. 5	b. 3	c. 1	**20.** a. 5	b. 3	c. 1	**30.** a. 1	b. 3	c. 5

Analysis

You will have finished with a score between 30 and 195—a very considerable range. As a basic rule the higher your score the more contented you are in your job, but check the sub-sections below for a more detailed analysis.

30-50: Very low job satisfaction

A score in this range is low indeed and there is no doubt that as far as your present job is concerned you really are a square peg in a round hole. If you are over 50 years it may mean that you are disheartened about the job because you have not achieved the promotion you had hoped for. The only thing one can say here is to wish you well when the joyous day comes when you can retire. If you are a younger person then the best thing you can possibly do is to face up to the reality of your dissatisfaction, take your courage in both hands and look for a more enjoyable job elsewhere.

51-84: Low job satisfaction

You do not seem to be very happy in your present job. This may be because you are actually in the wrong job for you. On the other hand it could be that it is jobs *in general* that you do not like. Perhaps you value your freedom so highly that you would resent the demands that most jobs put on you. Another possibility—perhaps your true abilities are not really being used. Think carefully about this and see if it would not be possible for you to find something that suits you better. If it is simply that you dislike your present boss or colleagues a change in the *place* rather than the *kind* of work could restore your satisfaction in your work. Perhaps new surroundings would give you a new start and cut down the misery of finding every day seeming like Monday.

85-144: Average job satisfaction

This is the good, solid, middle-of-the-road average. Like most people in modern society you have probably found work that suits you fairly well, though it is a safe bet that you do not feel that you are paid enough and it is also on the cards that you could do somewhat better in another kind of job. On the other hand the social aspects of work almost certainly appeal to you, so staying in a job where you like the people is as important to you as to the use of your talents. You strike a balance between your job and your personal life, and probably enjoy both. You could well be successful in your present work, though you are not driven to success in the same way as the higher scorer. If you *are* talented and move quickly to promotion, you may dislike the pressure of a top job, but wait and see and give it a try if it happens.

145-175: High job satisfaction

Work is very important to you and you show a high degree of job involvement and satisfaction. In fact you probably gain much of your personal identity from your work. This attitude suggests that you would also do well in another job and should circumstances change your present career pattern it is pretty clear that you will respond to the challenge and be successful. Monday mornings are very likely your happiest time.

Over 175: Abnormal job satisfaction

Candidly this score is too high for comfort. It could imply that work has become your god. Pause a while and think—has it become *too* important to you? Are you neglecting everything else because of it? Might not your job be more genuinely satisfying if you were not so deeply immersed?

Are You a Slave to Money?

The world as we know it is preoccupied with money. All human societies are bound together by a number of forces of which economics is one of the most powerful. The exchange of goods and services between human beings, nations and even continents contributes to social stability and assists in the development of political systems. Money is a bet on the future – an assumption that it is worth doing something today in exchange for a guaranteed return tomorrow. Some people take money as being the most important factor for human happiness or misery: others believe it has little relevance to either. But however you yourself stand on this scale of values, there is no getting away from the fact that an enormous amount of your life is bound up with the earning, the management and the distribution of money, and while money will not guarantee happiness, you can find yourself in a pretty uncomfortable mess if you do not learn to master it to some degree. No one has quite worked out the rules for mastery, but there is a twist of irony in the undeniable fact that many people who set out to achieve total mastery end up in slavery instead.

This questionnaire has little to say about the rules, but it does have something to say about the pitfalls, and if you answer it honestly and treat the results as a guide rather than as gospel truth you should be some way to establishing how much of you is master of money and how much is slave.

Mark your answers on a separate sheet.

1. Which of the following is closest to your attitude to your work and the money it earns you? (If you are retired, a housewife or not currently employed, look at the list and try to imagine what answer you would probably give if you *were* working.)
   a. I work only because of the money it earns me and if I did not have to earn money I would not work at all.
   b. Money is perhaps the most important reason for my working but, even if I had all the money I needed, I would do work of some kind.
   c. There are a number of reasons which motivate me to work and money is one of them, but is probably not the most important.
   d. I am pleased to get money but I take it as a bonus that goes with working – my main reason for work is the work itself.
   e. I love my work and I could not care how little I was paid to do it.

2. Mark whether you "strongly agree," "tend to agree," "tend to disagree" or "strongly disagree" with each of the following statements.
   a. Love of money is the root of all evil.
   b. In this world there is nothing that money can't buy.
   c. A stable financial basis is the best foundation for domestic happiness.
   d. There is nothing more irritating than a person who is mean with his money.
   e. There is no doubt that some people are naturally lucky when it comes to gambling.
   f. It is pointless to die with money in the bank.
   g. One should never under any circumstances lend money to friends.
   h. It is a great mistake to buy things on credit.
   i. The law is much too lenient in prosecuting and punishing shoplifters.
   j. People who do not pay their debts should be punished far more severely than they are at present.

3. Imagine that you have had a busy year and really feel the need for a vacation abroad. The money that you have been counting on to pay for the vacation is suddenly taken in taxes. You have little in the way of cash reserve and no likelihood of any windfalls in the near future. Which of the following courses of action do you think you would be most likely to take?
   a. Cancel the vacation and continue working to earn extra money.
   b. Give up all thoughts of an overseas vacation and enjoy a few weeks' rest and quiet in your own home.
   c. Take a more modest vacation than you had planned, even if it means that you have to borrow a small sum of money to do so.
   d. Take the vacation as planned, spend as freely as you had intended and face the music when it is all over.

4. A very close friend of yours comes to you in urgent need of money – equivalent to about twice your monthly salary – to help pay a family medical bill. He has never asked you for money before and you know him to be honest, but you also realize it will be a struggle for him to pay it back. You yourself would have no difficulty in finding the money to lend him. Do you
   a. Refuse point-blank, saying that you never lend money to friends because you really believe that it spoils friendships?
   b. Tell him that you would have lent it to him if you could, but that your own financial affairs do not permit you to do so?
   c. Agree to lend him the money but insist that the terms of repayment are drawn up by lawyers and a reasonable interest rate charged?
   d. Lend him the money, tell him to pay it back when he can?
   e. Let him have the money, tell him it is a gift and say "maybe sometime you will be able do the same thing for me"?

5. Indicate whether "always," "sometimes" or "never" is the most appropriate answer in your case to each of the following questions.
   a. Do you leave small sums of money around the house and forget about them?
   b. Do you know exactly what is the state of your bank balance?
   c. When you go shopping at a supermarket or big store are you surprised at how much it tots up to?
   d. Do you check your bill *carefully* in restaurants?
   e. If you find that you have been given more change than you should have been, do you hang on to it without saying anything?

f. Does the sight of someone spending money freely upset or annoy you?

g. When you meet someone for the first time do you find yourself working out how much he or she is earning or worth?

h. Do you actively dislike board games, such as monopoly, which involve "money dealings"?

i. Do you dislike opening the mail in the morning because of the bills that you might find?

j. Do you find shopping particularly stressful when you are in a hurry or rushed?

6. A friend whom you know and trust tells you confidentially that he has heard from an unimpeachable source that a horse cannot fail to win in a major race. The odds are 50 to 1, and your friend is so confident that he has placed a large sum of money on it. Do you

a. Tell him that he is silly to take a chance like that and say that you would not dream of betting?

b. Ponder for a moment whether there might not be something in what he says, but decide in due course that you will not bet?

c. Wish him good luck and ask him to put a small sum on for you for the fun of it?

d. Question him closely about the source of his information and, if you feel satisfied, place a biggish bet?

7. Answer yes or no to each of the following questions.

a. Have you ever had a check returned from the bank because your account was overdrawn?

b. Do you own and use a lot of credit cards?

c. Would you describe yourself as a generous tipper?

d. As a general rule do you believe that you "get what you pay for"?

e. Do you generally spend a good deal of time and effort shopping around for bargains?

f. Have you ever been told that you are careless or spendthrift with money?

g. Have you ever been told, or had it suggested to you, that you are mean or tightfisted?

h. Do you always find yourself in a muddle when it comes to filling in tax forms?

i. Are you inclined to drive some distance out of your way in order to save a few pennies on gas?

j. Do you fall an easy prey to "free samples," "special offers," and so on?

8. It is frequently said that people who come into large sums of money when they have not been particularly well off are made less happy in the long run. Assuming this is so, which of these reasons is most likely to be the cause?

a. Because they had no experience with money they did not know what to do with it, invested it badly and probably lost most of it.

b. They thought that buying things would make them happy in itself, and then found out that it didn't.

c. Their life was made a misery by begging letters, cadging friends, and so on?

d. They overindulged themselves physically and affected their health.

e. They simply had no imagination as to what fun you can get out of money well spent.

Now turn to page 111 and check your scores.

Scores

(Total your score to find your analysis below.)

1. a. 5P b. 2P c. 0 d. 0 e. 2R

2.		Strongly agree	Tend to agree	Tend to disagree	Strongly disagree
	a.	3C	0	0	3P
	b.	3P	0	0	1C
	c.	1P	0	1R	5R
	d.	3R	1R	0	3P
	e.	5R	1R	0	2C
	f.	3R	1R	0	3P
	g.	5C	1C	0	3R
	h.	3C	0	0	3R
	i.	3C	1P	0	2R
	j.	5P	1P	0	3R

3. a. 3P b. 0 c. 1R d. 4R

4. a. 5C b. 2C c. 2P d. 3R e. 1R

5.		Always	Sometimes	Never
	a.	3R	1R	1P
	b.	3P	0	3R
	c.	3R	0	2P

d.	2P	0	2R
e.	2C	0	2C
f.	3C	1C	0
g.	3C	1C	0
h.	3C	0	2R
i.	3R	0	1P
j.	2C	0	2R

6. a. 2C b. 0 c. 1R d. 5R

7.		Yes	No
	a.	2R	0
	b.	2R	0
	c.	2R	0
	d.	0	2C
	e.	2C	0
	f.	2R	0
	g.	2P	0
	h.	0	2C
	i.	2C	0
	j.	0	2P

8. a. 3P b. 0 c. 3P d. 3C e. 3R

Analysis

Many people assume that to be a slave to money is to be so destitute that you cannot pay your bills. Earning enough money to free you from all debt would therefore be considered to be the only way to turn from slave into master. In fact, the possession of money itself is no guarantee that you know how to control it – some of the world's wealthiest men, for example, have prostituted themselves completely to gold. The real question is to what extent your life is affected by your relationship with money – the man who is penny-pinching is no more or less a slave than the man who is spendthrift and ultimately has to face the consequences. The questions in this test explore three dimensions of economic slavery which, for the sake of generalization, can be called the dimensions of Risk, Compulsion and Possessiveness.

The risk factor is highlighted by a cavalier attitude to money, a frame of mind which on the one hand seems to treat money as nothing and yet on the other hand is only too conscious of the rewards it can bring. The dimension of compulsion is highlighted by eccentric attitudes to money which reveal a cranky, rather than a practical interest in it and whose roots may be traced back to childhood and compulsive parental preoccupation with money matters. The third dimension – possessiveness – deals with the stereotyped image of the miser, the man who knows precisely what money can and cannot do, and whose life is devoted to possessing it and making it work for him – not for physical rewards but merely to earn the satisfaction of getting even more. To some extent, traces of these three traits are present in all of us, and most of us are probably dominated by one (but rarely more than one) of these three factors. As you score you will notice yourself building up R,

C and P values and these give you some indication of the degrees to which the dimensions of risk, compulsion and possession are present in you as far as money is concerned. The higher your score on each and all of these factors, the more you are a slave to money.

First check your individual dimension scores against the evaluation below. Then to get a final evaluation divide your R score in half (rounding off to the highest number), add this number to your C and P scores and check the "final score."

Risk dimension
0-15R A score in this category indicates nothing more than the normal interest in risk-taking and it is clearly not a dominant feature of your personality.

16R-30R You like to take a risk and there is an element of incaution in your handling of money, but not enough to do you much harm.

31R-50R You are a risk-taker there is not much doubt; sometimes this pays off but sometimes it does not. A little more caution will do you no harm.

Over 50R As far as money matters are concerned you are a reckless and careless personality. People like you tend to be millionaires or paupers.

Compulsion dimension
0-5C Little trace of compulsiveness or crankiness about your attitude to money.

6C-15C In your dealings with money there is a streak of prejudice and compulsiveness. Try to be a bit more rational if you can.

16C-30C You have some funny ideas about money and about the way people handle it. If by some chance you are married to a person with a low C rating, and particularly someone with a high R or P rating, then you may find yourself in conflict situations.

Over 30C This is an unusually high rating and suggests that you are irrational, almost to the point of being cranky, about some aspects of money. With a high score like this there is probably not much you can do about it!

Possessiveness dimension

0-5P This is a normal score which suggests no trace of possessiveness in your personality with regard to money matters.

6P-15P There is a streak of possessiveness about you, though it is nothing approaching miserliness. You just like to count your pennies and make sure that you know where they are at all times.

16P-30P You are possessive all right; some people would call you tight. You may feel it is part of your nature, but in the long run you could make life happier for yourself and other people if you loosened up a bit.

Over 30P You are very close and probably mean with money. You may be very successful in terms of saving money and making it work for you, but it is really doubtful if it is making you happy.

Final score

Your final score should be the sum of your C and P scores, plus half your R score. You will find your score somewhere on a scale from 0 to 90. The lower your score, the more you are a master of money; the higher your score the more you are its slave.

0-10 This score implies that you are genuinely untroubled by economic problems. This does not mean that you "forget them" or push them out of sight, nor that you are necessarily wealthy. In no way are you money's slave.

11-30 This is a reasonable and healthy average. You have problems with money but not great ones and you have never, and probably never will, become its slave.

31-50 You are in a danger area. Money means too much to you, whether you are short of it or have too much of it. Try not to let it extend its stranglehold or you may find problems maturing into miseries.

Over 50 To one degree or another it is unfortunate, but you are a money slave. You may have a bulging wallet and bank balance, but you are none the happier for that.

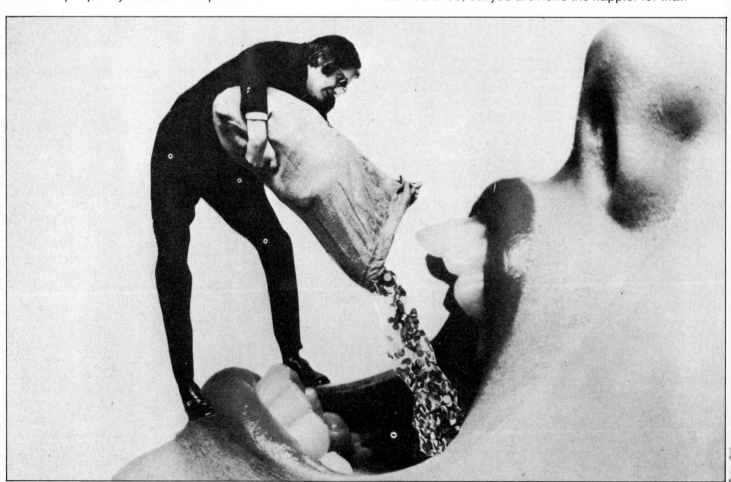

Check Your Artistic IQ

Most people are aware of the physical pleasures of life – the indulgence of the basic animal drives for food, sex and so on which ensure the survival of the human species. And some people argue that the principal purpose of life should be to indulge these physical pleasures. Unfortunately *over-*indulgence brings penalties of various kinds, of which the most obvious is the obesity which almost inevitably afflicts anyone who luxuriates too much in the delights of food and drink. In the words of the party joke, such a man would probably admit that: "Everything I like is either illegal, immoral or fattening."

There is however, a major dimension of life, a dimension of sheer pleasure which offers no penalty – either social or physical – and this is the cultivation and indulgence of the arts. The world of the arts is open to every human being though a very small percentage of mankind actively exploits it. Perhaps this is because, unlike physical pleasure, artistic appreciation has to be learnt through an apprenticeship which often seems dull at the outset. In a series of three separate questionnaires you will have the opportunity to explore to what extent you have accepted the challenge of the arts, and how far along the road you have progressed. The questionnaires cover music, the visual arts and literature, including drama. Each is scored independently, but if you complete the three you will have a rounded picture of your "Artistic IQ."

Part I : How Musical Are You?

This questionnaire – "How Musical Are You?" – explores the topic of music in three basic sections. Section 1 assesses the role which music plays in your life and everyday existence, Section 2 attempts to assess your musical skills, and Section 3 is best summed up by the self-explanatory title "Music and your body."

Answer each question as carefully and honestly as you can, but do not assess your scores on any section until you have completed the whole of the music questionnaire.

Mark your answers on a separate sheet.

Section 1: Music in your life

1. Are you very sensitive to sound?
   a. It depends on what the sound is.
   b. Yes, you cannot shut out unpleasant sounds, or ignore pleasant ones.
   c. Not really.

2. When you watch a movie do you
   a. Find that the music builds up the mood of the film?
   b. Not really notice the music at the time?
   c. Feel aware of the music and sometimes critical of it?

3. Do you remember pieces of music because they remind you of certain times in your life?
   a. Often
   b. Sometimes
   c. Rarely

4. Do you pick out a particular record to play because it expresses the way you are feeling?
   a. Often
   b. Only when you feel particularly emotional.
   c. Rarely

5. When you turn on your radio do you
   a. Listen to whatever you find?
   b. Tune into music for preference?
   c. Tune into "phone-in" programs, drama or news broadcasts for preference?

6. When you go to a party do you
   a. Like to dance most of the evening to cheerful music?
   b. Sink into a corner with one or two people?
   c. Get annoyed if music and dancing seem to dominate the party?

7. Do you go to concerts?
   a. Not if you can help it.
   b. Only if there is something you specially want to hear.
   c. As often as you can.

8. When you hear music on radio or television (classical or pop) can you usually
   a. Identify the music, artist and composer?
   b. Identify the music, and sometimes either composer or performer?
   c. Rarely identify any of them?

9. Do you ever get together with people to make or listen to music informally?
   a. Rarely
   b. Often
   c. Sometimes

10. Which of the following do you think is most important for children to learn at school?
    a. Crafts, like pottery, weaving and woodwork.
    b. Playing musical instruments and listening to music.
    c. Photography and film making.

Section 2: Musical skills

11. Can you play any musical instrument?

12. Can you sing in tune?

13. Can you tell if someone else is singing in tune?

14. If someone is singing out of time, could you be sure of putting them right?

15. Does it bother you to hear someone sing, or an instrument played, out of tune?

16. Can you pick out a recognizable tune on the piano or any other instrument that you have not already been taught how to play?

(For questions 17, 18, 19 and 20, you may have to listen to a record before answering.)

17. Can you remember tunes accurately after only one or two hearings?

18. Can you beat time accurately when you are listening to a piece of music?

19. When listening to a piece of music, can you pick out and sing at least one harmony that is being played alongside the main melody (or invent one of your own)?

20. Can you pick out and identify one or more musical instruments when you listen to music?

Section 3: Music and your body

21. Have you ever made love to music?

22. Can you beat out two different rhythms, one with your hand and one with your foot?

23. Do you go to a movement or keep-fit class?

24. If yes to 23, do you prefer to move or exercise to background music?

25. If you were at a pop or folk concert, or in the theater, and you were asked to clap and sing along with the performer, would you do it?

26. When you dance do you
   a. Use your whole body?
   b. Restrict your movement to your feet and hips, while your arms and head hardly move?
   c. Move as little as possible, feeling uncomfortable and hoping not to make too big a fool of yourself?

27. Would you dance
   a. Occasionally, with your partner when you are spending a romantic evening alone together?
   b. Anytime, even on your own if you feel like it?
   c. Only at a party, if you absolutely cannot avoid it?

28. When you hear music with a strong beat coming from someone else's record player, do you
   a. Feel an impulse to move in time to it?
   b. Tell them to turn down the sound?
   c. Listen happily without any inclination to move?

29. Do you consider music to be
   a. A private source of enjoyment?
   b. Something you enjoy more in the company of others?
   c. A useful background sound for socializing?

30. If you could listen to only one kind of music, which would you choose?
   a. Hard rock or pop
   b. Light, romantic music
   c. Strictly classical

Now turn to page 115 and check your scores.

Musical Profile Graph

The Musical Profile Graph will give you a clear visual guide to your musical abilities, but you must first read the analysis on the next page. Only then should you draw up your own personal graph.
So that you do not spoil the test for others who might want to do it in the future, make your own graph using a pencil, and a compass if you have one, and fill it in according to your own score. Draw in the line which matches your own score in each segment, and then shade the central area so that you can see your good and not-so-good facets at a glance.

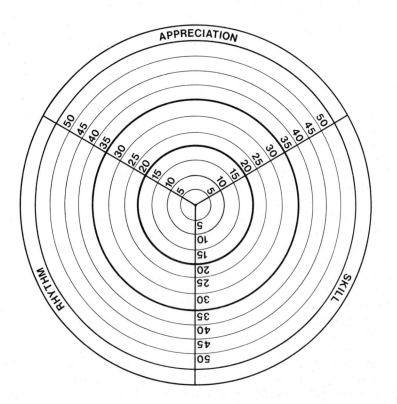

Scores

(Total your scores to find your analysis below.)

Section 1 Music in your life
1. a. 3A   b. 5A   c. 1A
2. a. 3A   b. 1A   c. 5A
3. a. 5A   b. 3A   c. 1A
4. a. 5A   b. 3A   c. 1A
5. a. 3A   b. 5A   c. 1A
6. a. 5A   b. 3A   c. 1A
7. a. 1A   b. 3A   c. 5A
8. a. 5A   b. 3A   c. 1A
9. a. 1A   b. 5A   c. 3A
10. a. 1A   b. 5A   c. 3A

Section 2 Musical skills
11. Yes 5S   No 0
12. Yes 5S   No 0
13. Yes 5S   No 0
14. Yes 5S   No 0
15. Yes 5S   No 0
16. Yes 5S   No 0
17. Yes 5S   No 0
18. Yes 5S   No 0
19. Yes 5S   No 0
20. Yes 5S   No 0

Section 3 Music and your body
21. Yes 2R   No 0
22. Yes 2R   No 0
23. Yes 2R   No 0
24. Yes 2R   No 0
25. Yes 2R   No 0
26. a. 5R   b. 3R   c. 1R
27. a. 3R   b. 5R   c. 1R
28. a. 5R   b. 1R   c. 3R
29. a. 3R   b. 5R   c. 1R
30. a. 5R   b. 3R   c. 3R

Having completed the three sections you will end up with an A score, an S score and an R score. Your A and S scores will lie between 0 and 50, and your R score between 0 and 35. Check the significance of your individual scores below.

Your A score

This basically refers to your sense of musical appreciation and the role which music plays in your life. On the whole this is a cultural rather than an inherited factor – in other words we *learn* musical appreciation of this kind and are not actually born with it. This means that even if you come out with a low score in this section, there is still hope for you to improve on it.

0-20A   This denotes rather a low level of musical appreciation and there is not much use pretending that music plays a big role in your life. You will probably be aware however that you are missing out on something. But have you ever seriously attempted to acquire a taste for music? For example, do you own a record player? Good equipment is not expensive these days and a fine choice of records is available for you to experiment with.

21-35A   This is a good average score. You have a definite sense of musical appreciation and you get a good deal of pleasure from music in general. But don't let things stop here – the deeper you go into the study of music the richer are the rewards and happiness of this aspect of art.

Over 36A   You are a real musical connoisseur – and you certainly did not need to do this questionnaire to find that out. Congratulations!

Your S score

This reflects your basic musical skills. This dimension is largely self-explanatory.

0-20S   This represents a low level of musical skill, probably due to the fact that you were brought up in an environment where music played little, if any, part. Skills can always be acquired, though if you have passed middle age acquiring a skill – such as learning the piano – will require an enormous amount of persistence. The rewards, however, are equally enormous.

21-35S   There are definite signs of real musical skill in your case, very probably in one area only. Achieving a score in this range however does suggest that it would really be worth your while taking further training or more intensive practice.

36-50S   If you have a score in this range then you are possessed with musical skill indeed. You are probably a talented pianist or instrumentalist and very likely come from a deeply musical family. Perhaps you will be able to spare some time to pass on your skill to others by example and perhaps by teaching!

Your R score

Before you read off your R score, the total you gathered must be corrected. Rules for correction are as follows:
  if you scored 0-11R, add 5;
  if you scored 12-23R, add 10;
  if you scored over 23R, add 15.

Your R score is an index of what might, in the absence of a more precise definition, be described as your sense of rhythm. Even in the womb infants respond to the rhythm of their mother's heartbeat, and there is good evidence that all human beings are equipped with a sense of responsiveness to the beat of music and other sounds. But whereas some people seem to be "naturally" at ease with the sound of music and respond readily to beat, others seem more inhibited and less on a rhythmic wavelength.

0-20R   If your score lies in this range, then to be quite honest your body feeling is probably somewhat repressed. Very likely this could show in other areas. Perhaps you are a somewhat anxious person, and too uneasy to let yourself slide into real contact with music. Tension could be relieved and enjoyment enhanced by relaxing a bit and going *with* the rhythm more completely.

21-35R   You have a good sense of rhythm, but also some inhibitions. You are probably a moderate dancer and may well enjoy it. Practice "feeling" music with your body, balancing emotional and intellectual responses.

36-50R   This is a high score and suggests that in your case there is a close integration of music and body awareness. Your coordination is probably good and you are capable of full-blooded enjoyment of rhythm.

Total Profile Graphs

Your own personal Musical Profile Graph—like that on page 114—will be divided into three segments. In each you should plot your score for each factor—your *corrected* score for the R factor. For example, if you have scored 25 in the skill factor, fill in the line joining the two figures 25 in that segment, and color the segment with a crayon or ball-point pen. If you were to score 32, for example, in the appreciation factor, you should approximate the points between 30 and 35 at each side of the A segment, trace your own arc between them, and color it in. You will end up with a very clear picture of your overall "Musical IQ."

It is impossible to give a detailed analysis of every personal graph, but if all scores lie within the inner segment then your musical life is indeed a restricted one. The "best" type of graph is one in which the scores are roughly equal: a very high score on one segment and a very low score on others suggests that you are putting all your musical eggs into one basket.

Check Your Artistic IQ
Part II: How Visual Are You?

The sense organs are the links every animal has with its outside environment. Their principal function is to enable the creature to detect danger in advance and locate the necessities of life—food, drink, a mating partner and so on. Man, in common with many higher animals, is dominated most by his visual sense: evolution has equipped him with magnificently sensitive visual receptors, capable not only of resolving supremely fine detail, but also of detecting a wide range of colors which provide vivid and important information to the brain. The brain in turn accepts this information and converts it into a moving panorama of some of the most important aspects of the world around us.

It is because the information provided by the visual senses is so rich that man can make aesthetic as well as purely practical use of visual perception, and it is no surprise that the visual arts—painting, architecture, drawing, graphic design—have played a tremendous role in our cultural heritage.

This questionnaire, if answered honestly and accurately, will give you an interesting glimpse of how strongly the visual arts figure in your life. It is divided into three basic parts. The first attempts to identify, in rather general terms, which type of visual imagery you prefer. The second deals with the important factors of observation and discrimination—how much do you notice about your visual environment. The third section is concerned with artistic skills and general appreciation. There are no right or wrong answers so respond to this questionnaire as spontaneously as you can.

Mark your answers on a separate sheet.

Section 1: Aesthetic appreciation
Here are a number of photographs of works of art —some more famous than others. Indicate which painting you prefer—a or b—from each pair of pictures. Please remember there is no *right* answer! You should make your decision on which *you* would rather look at. Put another way—which picture does more for you? A brief discussion of your choice is given in the analysis at the end of the questionnaire. Do not look at the analysis until you have completed all the questions in the remaining two sections.

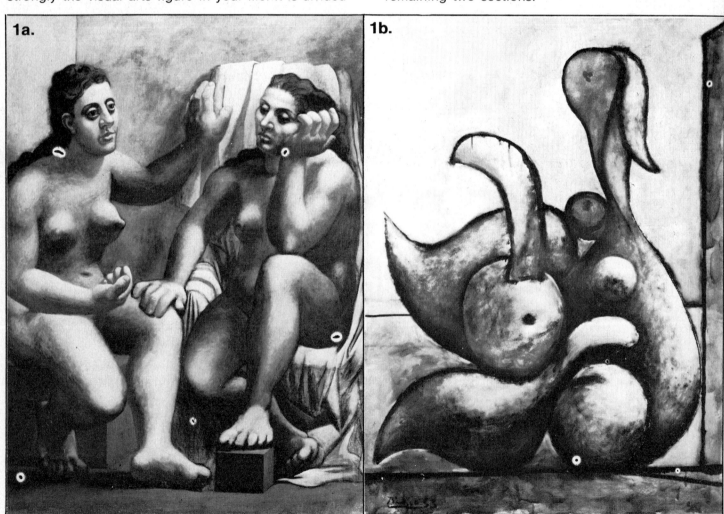

1a.

1b.

2a.

2b.

3a.

3b.

Section 2: Discrimination and observation

Answer the following questions honestly and to the best of your ability.

4. When you are walking along the street, do you normally

   a. Head straight for your goal, and notice very little of what is around you?

   b. Keep your eyes down, so that you can think of other things?

   c. Look around you and take in the whole scene, the effect of light on buildings, the changing picture?

5. When you have to buy something small for the house, like a can opener, do you

   a. Look for the sturdiest and best value for money?

   b. Choose the one that looks best, or fits in with your color scheme?

   c. Grab the first one that comes to hand?

6. If you lived with someone who had strong ideas about pictures and decorations about the house, would you

   a. Go along with his/her choice for the sake of peace?

   b. Push for your own choice?

   c. Go along unless he/she chose something you really could not stand?

7. Do you notice the cut of other people's clothes?

   a. Not unless they are specially good or bad.

   b. Always

   c. Never

8. You have won, in a competition, a couch and matching easy chairs, very expensive pieces but in a color you dislike. Would you

   a. Use them anyway?

   b. Change the rest of your decor so that they will fit in?

   c. Sell or exchange them?

117

9. Can you tell, by the feel, the difference between natural and man-made fibers?
   a. Immediately
   b. No
   c. Only if you really think about it.

10. Supposing that someone came and sat in your office or a room in your home while you were out. On returning would you
    a. Notice that someone had been there only if something was missing or there was obvious and considerable disarrangement?
    b. Notice that someone had been there immediately because things were not exactly as you know you left them?
    c. Not notice at all, even if the visitor had altered your arrangements?

11. When you take photographs on vacation, do they tend to be usually
    a. Of family or friends?
    b. Of the places you visit?
    c. Very few in number—postcards will remind you just as well?

12. Are you drawn to good-looking people?
    a. No, not particularly.
    b. Sometimes, at first, but you consider personality more important.
    c. Yes, you are impressed by physical appearances.

13. Do you buy reproductions of paintings that you particularly like?
    a. Yes
    b. It depends on the quality of the reproduction.
    c. No, you prefer to search for original works that you really like.

Section 3: Skills and appreciation
In the following questions, indicate which answer best matches your own.

14. Do you go to galleries and art exhibitions?
    a. Sometimes
    b. Often
    c. Not if you can get out of it.

15. Are you able to recognize the work and style of different artists?
    a. Usually
    b. Only of the better known artists.
    c. No

16. What is, or would be, most important to you in buying a painting?
    a. Impressing your friends or business associates.

b. Choosing something that will continue to give you pleasure day after day.
c. Matching it with your wall-colors and furnishing.

17. When you go shopping do you
    a. Find that you are very influenced by attractive packaging?
    b. Buy something new just for the novelty?
    c. Choose your purchase according to what you need, regardless of packaging?

18. Can you name the architect of
    a. One of the buildings in your nearest major city?
    b. Two or more buildings in your nearest major city?
    c. No building at all?

19. When you are looking for a place to live, what counts most with you?
    a. A fashionable neighborhood.
    b. Convenience for work, schools and so on.
    c. The look of the place, as you'll have to see a lot of it.

20. Do you ever have the urge to express what you feel by drawing or photography?
    a. Yes, and you sometimes carry it out.
    b. You would like to, but you never get round to it.
    c. No, it never occurs to you.

21. When you doodle, do you
    a. Try to draw things or people?
    b. Just enjoy playing with the pen or pencil?
    c. Make impatient marks?

22. Do you build things for your home, or make your own clothes?
    a. No, not at all.
    b. Yes, if they are simple enough.
    c. Yes, because it gives you great satisfaction.

23. If you bring back a piece of pottery from your vacation, which you thought was very attractive, and your best friend hates it, do you
    a. Find that your opinion begins to change?
    b. Go on protesting that you love it, but feel a sneaking doubt about your taste?
    c. Continue to enjoy it as before?

24. When you look at a piece of primitive, outlandish or very modern art which you strongly feel means nothing to you, do you
    a. Try to understand it?
    b. Say that it is meaningless?
    c. Keep quiet in case someone you are with thinks it is brilliant?

Now turn to page 119 and check your scores.

118

Scores

These scores refer to Sections 2 and 3 of the questionnaire only. For a discussion of the significance of your choice in Section 1, refer to the analysis which follows.

Section 2		
4. a. 1D	b. 3D	c. 5D
5. a. 3D	b. 5D	c. 1D
6. a. 1D	b. 5D	c. 3D
7. a. 3D	b. 5D	c. 1D
8. a. 1D	b. 3D	c. 5D
9. a. 5D	b. 1D	c. 3D
10. a. 3D	b. 5D	c. 1D
11. a. 3D	b. 5D	c. 1D
12. a. 1D	b. 3D	c. 5D
13. a. 1D	b. 3D	c. 5D

Section 3		
14. a. 3S	b. 5S	c. 1S
15. a. 5S	b. 3S	c. 1S
16. a. 1S	b. 5S	c. 3S
17. a. 5S	b. 1S	c. 1S
18. a. 3S	b. 5S	c. 1S
19. a. 1S	b. 1S	c. 5S
20. a. 5S	b. 3S	c. 1S
21. a. 5S	b. 5S	c. 1S
22. a. 1S	b. 3S	c. 5S
23. a. 3S	b. 1S	c. 5S
24. a. 5S	b. 3S	c. 1S

Analysis

Section 1: Aesthetic appreciation
First let us consider your choice of art forms.

1. You chose picture a: This painting *(Two Seated Nudes)* is by the great artist Picasso. It was painted in 1920, and is now in the Nordrhein Westfalen Collection, Dusseldorf. It is clear that you like pictures to be *about* something. That is fine, for art is essentially descriptive. However, finding out about more abstract forms of art could well increase the pleasure that you get from the visual arts. But this not to criticize your choice—the key to aesthetic enjoyment is to relax with what pleases you.

You chose picture b: This picture *(Seated Nude)* is, like the other one in this pair, by Picasso, and it also can be seen at Nordrhein Westfalen Collection in Dusseldorf. It was painted in 1933, almost a decade and a half after the other picture, and shows how dramatically the artist's style had evolved. Your choice indicates that *your* taste has evolved too, and that you have come to prefer abstract to representational art: you like something to think about as well as something to look at.

2. You chose picture a: This is a self-portrait by Erich Heckel painted in 1919, and now at the Kunstarchiv Arntz Haag. Simplicity of form and linear art appeal to you strongly. You very likely have an interest in modern architecture and your eye is probably drawn naturally to the balance of shape. A badly hung picture will jar with you while others might not notice it. Very likely modern furniture pleases you more than antique.

You chose picture b: Another self-portrait, this time by Max Liebermann, and lodged in the National Gallery, Berlin. By choosing the Liebermann portrait you indicate clearly that decoration and tone in painting are of real importance to you, and it is exceedingly likely that you chose picture a. in test one. You are probably put off by the functional shape of many modern buildings. Your choice of furniture may lean towards the antique.

3. You chose picture a: Rodin's famous sculpture *The Kiss* to be seen at the Paris Louvre. The erotic appeal of Rodin's naturalistic sculpture appeals to you. Do you tend to prefer representational works in painting as well? The highly finished surface, the easily-appreciated craft may also strike you as being "real art." You will find plenty to admire, even if you stick to this style alone.

You chose picture b: This sculpture, also entitled *The Kiss*, by Brancusi, can be found in the Museum of Art, Craiova, Rumania. What drew your attention to it? It may have been the clear geometric lines, or the intense closeness implied between the lovers: the impact is in the *idea*, not just in what appears to the eye. Your choice indicates that you prefer more abstract art.

Section 2: Discrimination and observation
10-15D You are basically not an observant person, which is a pity for it means you are missing a great deal. Try to train yourself to pay more attention to the world around you—the chances are that you will find it more pleasant and rewarding than you had ever imagined.

16-25D You are not really a very observant person and you may be aware that something is missing from your life in this general area. Perhaps other senses are simply more important to you than vision. If you are a real music lover then this may be the explanation. You might also tend to be wrapped up in yourself—try to open up a little.

26-40D You are a pretty observant person and you enjoy having pleasant objects and scenes around you. You are the kind of person who will value a carefully decorated house and most people will admire your choice in furnishings, wall coverings and so on. You also have a good sense of discrimination and have learnt to detect what is visually "right" from "wrong."

41-50D There is no doubt at all that you are a really sharp observer with a cultivated sense of visual discrimination. You are extremely sensitive to changes in your visual environment. In fact you may be almost oversensitive so that you find too many things jarring and unsatisfactory. You will not be happy unless your home and working environment are visually "just right."

Section 3: Skills and appreciation
12-15S This is a very low score, which, assuming you have answered the questionnaire properly, indicates that your sense of visual awareness is weak and seriously deprived. Try to cultivate some sense of appreciation: life will become much more rewarding.

16-25S Your visual awareness is undeveloped, and you do not give yourself the chance to put your possible artistic skills into practice. It could be that you are not independent enough about your own preferences and pay too much attention to what other people think is "good taste." Try making simple things for yourself —you need not show your efforts to anyone else.

26-44S A score in this range suggests that circumstances—it is not clear what they are—may have forced you to be practical rather than aesthetic in most of your judgments. However, you have far more of the artist in you than you might imagine. The trick here is not to close your mind to a deeper understanding of art.

45-60S This is a very high score and you can be congratulated because you probably have definite aesthetic skills going hand in hand with a vigorously developed artistic judgment. Beauty of shape and color play a large part in your life. Are you exploiting this ability in creative art yourself? If you are not already doing so, you should experiment with various art forms and see just how good you can be.

Part III: Your Literary IQ

Man has one unique and incomparable advantage over all other animals. It is an advantage which has allowed him to rise meteorically to a position of power in the animal kingdom, and detach himself from the mundane preoccupations of the vast majority of animal life. It is his acquisition of a written language. Animals employ sounds and visual signals to communicate to each other, but no animal other than man can store information in the form of symbols, such as writing or pictures, and distribute them universally so that his message can reach all his fellow animals. Even more important, the storing of information in written form allows events to persist *in time*. A great man with a great mind—whether he be scientist, poet, historian or philosopher—may die and yet his thoughts, his ideas and, to some extent, his personality can live on through the written word.

It is no wonder, then, that the written and spoken word plays such an enormous part in our lives—nor that poetry, literature and drama are of such significance in the world of the arts. Knowledge and ability in the visual and musical arts seem to come relatively instinctively, but developing a taste for drama and literature is a little less automatic. The "well-rounded" individual with a high artistic IQ is versed in the visual, musical *and* the literary aspects of art. This questionnaire sets out to explore your level of understanding and achievement in this realm. These questions probe various facets of your involvement in drama and literature: answer them honestly and straightforwardly.

Mark your answers on a separate sheet.

1. When you listen to a song, do you find that the words and their meaning are
   a. Just as important as the music?
   b. Not at all important?
   c. Sometimes more important than the music?

2. When you have a personal letter to write to someone you are close to, do you
   a. Groan, complain and find it an onerous task?
   b. Positively enjoy telling the latest news?
   c. Write very briefly, knowing that they will understand without too many words?

3. Do you go to the theater
   a. Whenever you can?
   b. Never of your own free will?
   c. Sometimes, but not nearly so often as you could?

4. Do you keep a diary?
   a. Regularly; it often helps to write down your day-to-day experiences.
   b. Never, or only for appointments.
   c. Off and on, when the urge comes over you.

5. Have you ever thought that your life story would make a good novel?
   a. Yes, but you would never get round to writing it.
   b. Yes, and you have actually written some notes.
   c. No, who would want to read it?

6. Have you ever taken part in a play?
   a. Yes, but only at school.
   b. Yes, since leaving school.
   c. Never in your life.

7. When you have a business letter to write, do you
   a. Leave it for someone else to do?
   b. Find it quite easy to write crisply exactly what you want to say?
   c. Struggle over expressions?

8. Do you read novels?
   a. Yes, for pleasure.
   b. Only if you cannot find anything else to do.
   c. Not at all, you prefer history and factual books.

9. Do you
   a. Prefer live performances to movies?
   b. Prefer movies any day?
   c. Feel little interest in either?

10. Have you ever gone on reading a novel that you found difficult at first?
    a. No—if it doesn't grab you immediately you lose interest.
    b. Yes, more than once.
    c. Only if you had to for an assignment at school.

11. Do you get excited watching a sporting event?
    a. Yes, very.
    b. Only if you are really interested in the players.
    c. Not at all.

12. Do you think that reading poetry is
    a. Strictly for the birds?
    b. An important part of your life?
    c. OK, but you can think of a dozen things you would rather do?

13. Can you remember any rhymes you learned when you were a child?
    a. Yes, and you have taught them, or will teach them, to your children.
    b. Now that you think of it, a few are coming back.
    c. No, you can't remember one.

14. Do you agree with the saying that the pen is mightier than the sword?
    a. Yes, books have changed the world.
    b. No, actions count for far more.
    c. It all depends on the books or the swords.

15. If you have to entertain a child before he goes to bed, would you
    a. Read him a story?
    b. Tell him a story?
    c. Play a game with him?

16. If you answered b to the last question: Would you
    a. Invent the story?
    b. Retell a story you knew?

17. If you answered c to question 15: Would you

a. Invent a game?
b. Play a well-known game?

18. Have you ever written any poetry?
a. Only Valentine verses, secretly, in adolescence.
b. From time to time.
c. No, you never have.

19. If you answered c to question 18: Have you ever
a. Adapted the words of a song to make it ruder?
b. Written your own dirty verses?
c. Still no.

20. When you get to the book review pages of your newspaper, do you
a. Turn over quickly?
b. Stop only if something catches your eye?
c. Nearly always read them with interest?

21. When something funny or terrible happens to you, do you tend to
a. Shape it up to make a good story when you tell your friends?
b. Tell it straight, just as it happened?
c. Not feel inclined to tell it at all?

22. Can you get through the day without having anything to read?
a. Yes, quite easily.
b. No, you would read anything rather than go without your quota of print.
c. Yes, if you have not got anything that you particularly want to read.

23. Do you find yourself searching about for words to pin down your experience at the moment that it is actually happening?
a. No
b. Sometimes
c. Often

24. Why do some books appeal to you a great deal more than others?
a. You enjoy the way they are written.
b. The subject matter is more interesting.
c. They are easier to get involved in.

25. What do you expect from a play in the theater or on television?
a. Very little.
b. Simply relaxation.
c. Involvement and stimulus.

26. When your husband or wife asks you "What happened today," do you
a. Say "nothing much"?
b. Tell him or her what you have done hour by hour?
c. Tell the interesting bits?

27. If you were offered a free course in creative writing, would you
a. Turn it down?

b. Hesitate, half wanting to take it up, half wanting to leave it alone?
c. Accept it eagerly?

28. Which of these statements do you *most* agree with?
a. Fiction can be truer in many ways than plain fact.
b. Fiction is nonsense and a waste of time.
c. Fiction can present facts more powerfully than a documentary can.

29. Do you ever act out scenes in your imagination?
a. Sometimes
b. Often
c. Never

30. Have you ever found yourself saying "That would make a good play"?
a. No
b. Occasionally
c. Often

31. Do you usually write down, or try to remember, vivid sayings?
a. Yes
b. No
c. Sometimes

32. What do you think is the purpose of works of literature?
a. To amuse.
b. To instruct.
c. To interest and instruct.

Now turn to page 122 and check your scores.

Literary Profile

When you have calculated your scores, make your own copy of the Literary Profile below and fill it in according to the instructions overleaf.

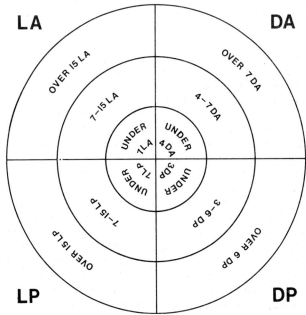

Scores

(Total your scores to find your analysis below.)

	a.	b.	c.		a.	b.	c.
1.	a. 2LA	b. 0	c. 1LA	**17.**	a. 2DP	b. 0	
2.	a. 0	b. 2LP	c. 0	**18.**	a. 1LP	b. 2LP	c. 0
3.	a. 2DA	b. 0	c. 1DA	**19.**	a. 1LP	b. 2LP	c. 0
4.	a. 2LP	b. 0	c. 1LP	**20.**	a. 0	b. 1LA	c. 2LA
5.	a. 1LP	b. 2LP	c. 0	**21.**	a. 2LP	b. 1LP	c. 0
6.	a. 1DP	b. 2DP	c. 0	**22.**	a. 0	b. 1LA	c. 2LA
7.	a. 0	b. 2LP	c. 1LP	**23.**	a. 0	b. 1LP	c. 2LP
8.	a. 2LA	b. 0	c. 0	**24.**	a. 2LA	b. 1LA	c. 0
9.	a. 2DA	b. 1DA	c. 0	**25.**	a. 0	b. 1DA	c. 2DA
10.	a. 0	b. 2LA	c. 0	**26.**	a. 0	b. 1LP	c. 2LP
11.	a. 2DA	b. 1DA	c. 0	**27.**	a. 0	b. 1LP	c. 2LP
12.	a. 0	b. 2LA	c. 1LA	**28.**	a. 2LA	b. 0	c. 1LA
13.	a. 2LA	b. 1LA	c. 0	**29.**	a. 1DP	b. 2DP	c. 0
14.	a. 2LA	b. 0	c. 1LA	**30.**	a. 0	b. 1DA	c. 2DA
15.	a. 0	b. 2DP	c. 2DP	**31.**	a. 2LP	b. 0	c. 1LP
16.	a. 2DP	b. 1DP		**32.**	a. 1LA	b. 1LA	c. 2LA

Analysis

This questionnaire deals with the two major strands, literature and drama. In all aspects of art one can conveniently measure one's degree of involvement and achievement along two scales: the *appreciation* continuum and the *participation* continuum. Your A scores refer to your appreciation factor and your P scores to your participation factor. To subdivide this further, your DA scores refer to "drama appreciation," your LA scores to "literature appreciation," your DP to "drama participation" and your LP to "literature participation."

Although it is instructive to look at individual scores, the most satisfactory picture is obtained when you consider them together. A high score in drama appreciation, for instance, with low participation scores and low scores in both literary factors would suggest an extremely one-sided approach to the literary arts. With this in mind, fill in your own copy of the Literary Profile, illustrated on the previous page. You will note that your score in each factor will place you in either the inner, the middle or the outer part of each segment. When you have filled in your score for each factor, shade in the appropriate section.

The outer parts represent a higher degree of success and achievement than those nearer the center and clearly the "best" profile will be one in which you find yourself located in the outer part of all four segments. But the chances are that you find yourself weak in one or more segments. These are the ones to concentrate on.

Drama Appreciation (DA)

Under 4DA This is a low score and suggests a weak and undeveloped sense of drama appreciation. You have probably never tried to enjoy a play and would certainly benefit from a visit to the theater. If you watch a lot of TV, try not to go for the soft option—select drama and good movies and reject "soap operas" and thrillers.

4-7DA This is an average level of drama appreciation, and the most significant thing about it is that a little effort will lead to a big improvement. Do you know of any amateur dramatics or local theater groups? Participation in them would heighten your sense of appreciation.

Over 7DA This very high level of drama appreciation, if coupled with a high participation score, suggests a deep involvement with this phase of literary arts.

Drama Participation (DP)

Under 3DP You clearly never take part in drama. If this is not due to lack of opportunity then it may well be because you are shy. Do not forget that one can contribute to the theater without actually marching around on stage! If you wanted to, you could become involved in theater via another route—dressmaking, lighting or stage managing, for example.

3-6DP You obviously do have some direct involvement with drama and if your score is high in this bracket then you may well be considerably involved. In fact you are at the point where you could convert this aspect of your life into something even more substantial by studying the theory and history of the theater. If you have a high score in the "appreciation" quadrant then you are well on your way to gaining a real sense of achievement.

Over 6DP This high score indicates a dynamic participation in the theater and drama. It is probably one of your most creative and satisfying activities.

Literature Appreciation (LA)

Under 7LA This is a low score, though you may not be surprised to find yourself with it. For some reason or another you have simply not got to grips with reading, other than of the most routine sort. Perhaps TV takes up too much of your life, or you read many magazines and too few books. Your sense of satisfaction may well increase markedly if you could only tap some of your latent ability to enjoy literature. It may be difficult at first, but here is something which may help you to set out on the right road: Think of a book which you have heard about and you have always *meant to read*. Go out today, buy it, order it or get it from your library. Once you have taken this step you have at least made a start!

7-15LA You obviously appreciate written words and literature in general. The only message for you is that there is no reason why you shouldn't really be in the upper segment of this quadrant. The appreciation of literature is for *everybody*. The more you familiarize yourself with books, the more reading you do, the more you will win from the pool of man's literary heritage.

Over 15LA You have a high level of literary appreciation and reading, and the enjoyment of books is one of the most important things in your life. You have long since learned that no matter where you are, a book is an unmatchable companion.

Literature Participation (LP)

Under 7LP With a score in this segment it is rather obvious that you do not participate actively in the literary arts, and the most likely reason for this, candidly, is that you have not really tried. The human brain is a magnificent creative device and there are few people on earth devoid of the capacity to create and convert.

7-15LP You are clearly involved to some degree in creative literature, even if it is only some simple amateur short story or poetry writing. Congratulations on at least trying. The more you keep at it, the greater your chances of success and the greater your sense of satisfaction as you find your skills maturing.

Over 15LP With a score in this range you are evidently dynamically involved in literature, not just for its own sake but possibly because you get some other rewards—perhaps because people like to read what you write and perhaps even because they pay you to do so!

Marshall Cavendish

How Tolerant Are You?

Tolerance is something we all like to think we have. But it is not easy to define: it is not just a matter of flexibility, nor simply permissiveness, nor is it the bottling up of feelings which we would otherwise have vigorously expressed. It *is* clearly tied up with empathy—the capacity to put ourselves into another person's shoes and see the world from their viewpoint. In a strange way it is also our capacity to see how other people view us. Aggressive or apparently ill-mannered behavior on the part of another individual may reflect their misjudgment of your personality and your actions, and recognizing this misjudgment in others is one of the greatest measures of tolerance.

In our complex, overpopulated world, the faults of others are often amplified because of the sheer proximity between people—not only in a physical but also in a psychological sense. Tolerance therefore is an essential quality for peaceful and harmonious living in a society which admits, within the law, so many different ways of thinking and behaving. Psychologists know that intolerance is associated with authoritarian personalities and also with narrow and limited experience of the world. But while it is easy to detect intolerance in others it is not so easy to pin it down in ourselves. This questionnaire, however, if answered honestly and accurately, will give you some pointers.

Mark your answers on a separate sheet.

1. When a friend does something you very much disapprove of, do you
   a. Break off the friendship?
   b. Tell him how you feel, but keep in touch?
   c. Tell yourself it is none of your business, and behave towards him as you always did?

2. Is it hard for you to forgive someone who has seriously hurt you!
   a. Yes
   b. No
   c. It is not hard to *forgive* him, but you don't forget.

3. Do you think that
   a. Censorship is vitally necessary to preserve moral standards?

b. A small degree of censorship may be necessary, to protect children for instance?
   c. All censorship is wrong?

4. Are most of your friends
   a. People very much like you?
   b. Very different from you and from each other?
   c. Like you in some important respects, but different in others?

5. You are trying to work and concentrate, but the noise of children playing outside distracts you. Would you
   a. Feel glad that they are having a good time?
   b. Feel furious with them?
   c. Feel annoyed, but acknowledge to yourself that kids do make a noise?

6. If you were traveling abroad and found that conditions were much less hygienic than you are used to, would you
   a. Adapt quite easily?
   b. Laugh at your own discomfort?
   c. Think what a filthy country it is?

7. Which virtue do you think is most important?
   a. Kindness
   b. Honesty
   c. Obedience

8. Do you discuss critically one friend with others?
   a. Often
   b. Rarely
   c. Sometimes

9. If someone you dislike has a piece of good luck, would you
   a. Feel angry and envious?
   b. Wish it had been you, but not really mind?
   c. Think "Good for him"?

10. When you have a strong belief, do you
   a. Try very hard to make others see things in the same way as you?
   b. Put forward your point of view, but stop short of argument or persuasion?

c. Keep it to yourself, unless directly asked?

11. A friend is suffering from depression. Everything in his life seems to be fine, but he complains to you that he always feels depressed. Would you
  a. Listen sympathetically?
  b. Tell him to pull himself together?
  c. Take him out to cheer him up?

12. Would you employ someone who had had a severe nervous breakdown?
  a. No
  b. Yes, provided there was medical evidence of complete recovery.
  c. Yes, if he were suitable in other ways for the work.

13. "Morality is relative." Do you
  a. Strongly agree?
  b. Agree up to a point?
  c. Strongly disagree?

14. When you meet someone who disagrees with your views, do you
  a. Argue and lose your temper?
  b. Enjoy a good argument and keep your cool?
  c. Avoid argument?

15. Do you ever read a periodical which supports political views very different from yours?
  a. Never
  b. Sometimes, if you come across it.
  c. Yes, you make a special effort to read it.

16. Which statement do you most agree with?
  a. If crime were more severely punished, there would be less of it.
  b. A better society would reduce the need for crime.
  c. I wish I knew the answer to the problem of crime.

17. Do you think
  a. That some rules are necessary for social living, but the fewer the better?
  b. That people must have rules because they need to be controlled?
  c. That rules are tyrannical?

18. If you are a religious believer, do you think
  a. That your religion is the only right one?
  b. That all religions have something to offer their believers?
  c. That nonbelievers are wicked people?

19. If you are not a religious believer, do you think
  a. That only stupid people are religious?
  b. That religion is a dangerous and evil force?
  c. That religion seems to do good for some people?

20. Do you react to fussy old people with
  a. Patience and good humor?

b. Annoyance?
c. Sometimes a, sometimes b?

21. Do you think the Women's Liberation movement is
  a. Run by a bunch of lesbians?
  b. An important, if overstated, social movement?
  c. A joke?

22. Would you marry someone of a different race?
  a. Yes
  b. No
  c. Not without thinking carefully about the various problems involved.

23. If your brother told you that he was a homosexual, would you
  a. Send him to a psychiatrist?
  b. Accept him, and his lover?
  c. Feel shocked and reject him?

24. When young people question authority, do you
  a. Feel uneasy?
  b. Think that it is a good thing?
  c. Feel angry?

25. Which statement do you agree with?
  a. Marriage is a bad institution.
  b. Marriage is sacred and must be upheld.
  c. Marriage is often difficult, but seems to meet the needs of many people.

26. Do you think you are right—in matters of belief rather than fact—
  a. Often?
  b. Rarely?

27. If you stay in a household which is run differently from yours—in matters of tidiness and regularity of meals—do you
  a. Fit in quite happily?
  b. Feel constantly irritated by the chaos or the rigid orderliness of the place?
  c. Find it fairly easy for a while, but not for too long?

28. Do other people's personal habits annoy you?
  a. Often.
  b. Not at all.
  c. Only if they are extreme, or you are edgy.

29. Which statement do you most agree with?
  a. We should not judge other people's actions, because no one can ever fully understand the motives of another.
  b. People are responsible for their actions and have to take the consequences.
  c. Even if it is tough on some people, actions have to be judged.

Now turn to page 125 and check your scores.

Scores

(Total your scores to find your analysis below.)

1. a. 4	b. 2	c. 0				**16.** a. 4	b. 2	c. 0		
2. a. 4	b. 0	c. 2				**17.** a. 0	b. 4	c. 4		
3. a. 4	b. 0	c. 4				**18.** a. 4	b. 0	c. 4		
4. a. 4	b. 0	c. 2				**19.** a. 4	b. 4	c. 0		
5. a. 0	b. 4	c. 2				**20.** a. 0	b. 4	c. 2		
6. a. 0	b. 0	c. 4				**21.** a. 4	b. 0	c. 4		
7. a. 0	b. 2	c. 4				**22.** a. 0	b. 4	c. 2		
8. a. 4	b. 0	c. 2				**23.** a. 2	b. 0	c. 4		
9. a. 4	b. 2	c. 0				**24.** a. 2	b. 0	c. 4		
10. a. 4	b. 2	c. 0				**25.** a. 4	b. 4	c. 0		
11. a. 0	b. 4	c. 2				**26.** a. 4	b. 0			
12. a. 4	b. 2	c. 0				**27.** a. 0	b. 4	c. 2		
13. a. 0	b. 2	c. 4				**28.** a. 4	b. 0	c. 2		
14. a. 4	b. 0	c. 2				**29.** a. 0	b. 4	c. 2		
15. a. 4	b. 2	c. 0								

Analysis

For a quick and very broad view of your level of tolerance compared to your family and friends, turn to the next page and mark your score on the "Tolerance Thermometer." Use the space on the right of it to mark the names and scores of everyone who takes the test: you may find that the results will surprise you!

For a more detailed discussion of your individual level of tolerance, read the section of the following analysis that relates to your score.

Below 30 If your score lies in this range you are a particularly tolerant person. You are exceedingly aware of others' problems and difficulties and you have a natural capacity for accepting them even when they offend you. You will be a good friend and popular with others. You may find that other people abuse this sympathetic good nature because they have nothing to fear from recriminations. Even then, you do not get really cross with them.

31-60 You are a tolerant person and people will recognize you as one. If your score is above 50 however, you are probably tolerant and broad-minded in some areas only. Actually it is easy to be tolerant if one does not hold very firm beliefs about anything. Look through the questions again and note where you picked up high rather than low scores. Were these questions where

personal comfort was directly concerned or where convictions or very strong ideological beliefs were touched upon?

61-89 You are not as tolerant as many people and if your score is higher than 80 you are basically an intolerant type of person. This will lead to clashes and short-term friendships. It will also mean that little things trouble you far more than they should and that you may waste emotional energy on what is really rather insignificant. It is very likely that you count yourself as someone with high principles tending to stick to important things rather than trivia. If you can get a wider experience of life and greater genuine contact with people, however, your tolerance temperature would come down and in the end you would feel happier for it.

Over 90 This high score indicates that you are a very intolerant person. If your score is over a hundred then you are also bossy, self-opinionated and overquick to take offense. The only kind of friends that you are likely to retain are those that are interested in your money or generosity. If you really have scored this high, ask yourself *why* you are so unable to accept the faults in others. What are the aspects of other people that offend you most? Could it be that you are really punishing yourself for faults that you see in yourself?

Tolerance Thermometer

Check your tolerance temperature. The higher your "temperature" on the thermometer, the more intolerant you are—and the closer to boiling point!

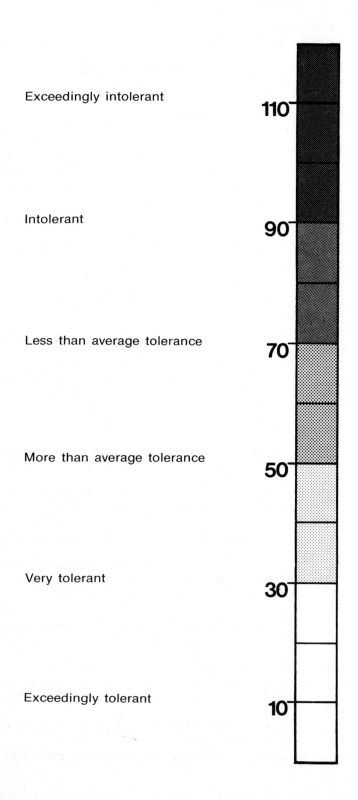

Exceedingly intolerant

110

Intolerant

90

Less than average tolerance

70

More than average tolerance

50

Very tolerant

30

Exceedingly tolerant

10

Are You a Good Judge of People?

Most of us believe that we are good, or at least better than average, at judging other people. In one classic study five highly experienced professional interviewers were asked to rank eight candidates according to their suitability for a particular job. The interviewers made their judgements independently and did not discuss the various candidates amongst themselves. The horrifying fact emerged that there was hardly any agreement amongst them and that one candidate who was ranked as "top of the poll" by one interviewer was actually placed second from the bottom by another.

What are the factors which lead to this kind of disagreement and which have made the interview a highly questionable filter for job selection? The problems are many as this questionnaire sets out to show. Prejudice is one simple stumbling block, and a particularly dangerous one because it is often unconscious. Of course it is a rare person who does not have a prejudice of some kind. After all, it is only another way of saying that we make judgements on the basis of past experience. Prejudices do not matter too much if we are aware of them. But how accurate and unbiased are you?

Mark your answers on a separate sheet.
1. Have you ever come to like someone that you initially disliked?
   a. Sometimes
   b. Often
   c. Never

2. Answer "yes" or "no" according to whether you think you can pick out the following characteristics simply on seeing someone, before you talk to them or hear anything about them?
   a. Neatness
   b. Intelligence
   c. Honesty
   d. Humor
   e. Determination
   f. Attractiveness

3. Indicate whether or not you notice the following features on meeting someone for the first time.
   a. Voice
   b. Eyes
   c. Facial expression
   d. Details of clothing

4. When you are choosing gifts for a close friend, do you
   a. Buy something that you would like yourself?
   b. Buy something that you may not like, but that you know your friend will enjoy?
   c. Buy what your friend needs?

5. Would you take *most* time and trouble over entertaining
   a. Your closest friends?
   b. Important business associates?
   c. Critical relatives or acquaintances?

6. Indicate whether you agree or disagree with these statements.
   a. Sloppy dress means a sloppy mind.
   b. Shifty eyes show that a person cannot be trusted.
   c. You can tell a person's political persuasions by their clothes.
   d. Red heads have bad tempers.

7. Do you ever find that your feelings have been hurt because someone you trusted has let you down?
   a. From time to time.
   b. No, because you are very slow to trust.
   c. Yes, more often than you would like.

8. When someone you know well behaves in a surprising way, do you
   a. Take an interest in this new development?
   b. Feel puzzled and at a loss to understand?
   c. Think they must have gone crazy?

9. Is your husband, wife or lover the same personality as they were when you first met?
   a. Yes, on the whole.
   b. No, everyone changes.
   c. No, and if I knew then what I know now I would not have got involved with him/her in the first place.

10. If you had been at school with someone who is now famous, would you
   a. Make sure that everyone you meet knows?

b. Keep quiet about it unless it comes up naturally?

c. Try to renew the acquaintance?

11. You are about to be introduced to someone that your best friend has been praising for months. Do you
   a. Feel some hostility?
   b. Look forward eagerly to the meeting?
   c. Reserve your judgement until you get to know him?

12. Have you ever come to dislike someone that you initially liked?
   a. Never
   b. Sometimes
   c. Often

13. When you meet new people, do you
   a. Usually find that they remind you of someone else?
   b. Tend to find that you base your judgement about them on what they say?
   c. Immediately begin to compare them with yourself?

14. When you read fiction, do you
   a. Prefer to read about people much like yourself?
   b. Prefer to read about people very different from you?
   c. Enjoy escaping into a world where the incidents are more important than the characters?

15. You have to appoint someone at work or to help you at home. Of the two people that you interview one is pleasant and smiling, the other promises to be efficient, but is a silent and unforthcoming person. Would you
   a. Choose the pleasant one because you feel you would prefer a little inefficiency to suffering an unsympathetic person around you?
   b. Choose the efficient one?
   c. Choose the pleasant one without considering the consequences?

16. When you meet someone who is particularly good-looking, do you
   a. Like them and be prepared to put up with more from them, as they are not to be regarded as subject to the usual rules?
   b. Feel hostile and expect them to prove themselves more than anyone else?
   c. Treat them exactly as you would someone more homely?

17. Did you invite your most eccentric relation to your wedding (or other important social occasion)?
   a. Yes, you would not hurt his/her feelings even if other people thought you were crazy.
   b. No, certainly not.
   c. Yes, you even made a feature out of it.

18. Have you ever been caught up in a wave of emotion after a stirring religious or political speech?
   a. No, you keep your wits about you at all times.
   b. Yes, but only for a short time.
   c. Yes, and the influence definitely lasted for more than a few days.

19. Have you ever been, in spite of your better judgement, fascinated by people you dislike?

a. No
b. Slightly
c. Yes

20. Have you been talked into making a bad buy by a persuasive salesman?
   a. Only once
   b. Never
   c. More than once

21. How do you feel when someone close to you reacts to a situation in a very different way from you?
   a. Fine, after all you are different people.
   b. Upset and puzzled.
   c. Convinced that your reaction is definitely the more understandable.

22. Have you ever said "Men are all the same," or, if you are male, have you ever said "Women are all the same"?
   a. Rarely
   b. Sometimes
   c. Often

23. If you fell in love with someone who was not conventionally attractive would you
   a. Keep telling your friends what a splendid person he/she is?
   b. Enjoy his/her company regardless?
   c. Cut off contact with any friends who were critical of your choice?

24. When you dislike somebody which of the following would be closest to your reason for that dislike?
   a. You resent people with all the advantages that you do not have.
   b. You only dislike qualities that deserve dislike.
   c. You dislike the traits that you do not care for in yourself.

25. When you fall in love, is it
   a. Often, then quickly lost?
   b. Slowly and for a long time?
   c. Something between a and b?

26. Do you find it hard to be critical of someone in a position of authority?
   a. Yes, after all they would not be so eminent without good reason.
   b. No, at least not in the privacy of my own thoughts.
   c. Yes at first, but once I really think about it I can be extremely critical.

27. Do people ever take advantage of you?
   a. No, never.
   b. Yes, but I do not mind up to a point.
   c. I don't know.

28. Are your friends
   a. Very much like you in their life-style, habits and beliefs?
   b. Varied?
   c. Mostly like you, though a few are different?

Now turn to page 129 and check your scores.

Scores

(Total your scores to find your analysis below.)

1.	a. 5	b. 3	c. 1

	Yes	No
2. a.	3	0
b.	0	1
c.	0	1
d.	0	1
e.	0	1
f.	3	0

	Yes	No
3. a.	3	0
b.	3	0
c.	3	0
d.	3	0

4.	a. 1	b. 5	c. 1
5.	a. 5	b. 1	c. 3

	Agree	Disagree
6. a.	0	1
b.	0	1
c.	0	1
d.	0	1

7.	a. 5	b. 3	c. 1
8.	a. 5	b. 3	c. 1
9.	a. 3	b. 5	c. 1
10.	a. 3	b. 5	c. 1
11.	a. 1	b. 3	c. 5
12.	a. 1	b. 5	c. 3
13.	a. 3	b. 5	c. 1
14.	a. 3	b. 5	c. 1
15.	a. 3	b. 5	c. 1
16.	a. 1	b. 1	c. 5
17.	a. 5	b. 3	c. 1
18.	a. 5	b. 3	c. 1
19.	a. 5	b. 3	c. 1
20.	a. 3	b. 5	c. 1
21.	a. 5	b. 3	c. 1
22.	a. 5	b. 3	c. 1
23.	a. 3	b. 5	c. 1
24.	a. 5	b. 1	c. 5
25.	a. 1	b. 5	c. 3
26.	a. 1	b. 5	c. 3
27.	a. 3	b. 5	c. 1
28.	a. 1	b. 5	c. 3

Analysis

The higher your score the more likely it is that you have a real ability to judge people. Psychologists have found that there are a number of characteristics which combine to make a person a good or bad judge of others. To help you improve your own ability and raise your score read the following discussion of the main factors influencing this capacity to judge.

1. Flexibility
This is coupled to some degree with intelligence, though there is no absolute correlation. The more flexible you are in general the more you are likely to adopt an inquisitive and openminded attitude to other people.

2. Observational powers
Many people have a surprising lack of awareness of important features in the world around them and therefore, when attempting to assess other humans, miss vital signal points. The better developed your observational powers, the more likely it is that you will be a good judge of other people.

3. Freedom from stereotypes
If you allow your mind to run along preconceived lines—with one thought always calling up the same chain of thoughts in response—your thoughts and behavior become stereotyped. Stereotyping is a serious defect when it comes to making judgements—they are always predictable and unimaginative and miss the subtle differences that can exist between people.

4. Perception of change
This is really a kind of extension of the factor relating to observational powers; to be a good judge of any situation let alone other people's personalities, one must be able to detect changes in their behavior, their statements and their attitudes.

5. Self-awareness
To be a really good judge you must have as deep an understanding as you can of your own personality structure, including your inevitable faults. This is particularly true of those faults which can cause bias—suspicion, gullibility and a tendency to identify too readily with another and cloud your own impartiality.

6. Freedom from snobbery
The snob is the worst possible judge of other people. He is also, of course, the worst possible judge of himself.

Bearing in mind these factors which might influence your judgement, now check your own score.

Under 45
You are not really a good judge of other people. Look at the above list of prime characteristics for good judgement and try to work out where you are going wrong.

46-60
You have some areas of perceptiveness, but in certain areas your judgement is rather poorer than average. Most probably, the cause of this can be found in your own prejudices: try to identify in your mind what these are, and if you can pin them down, your capacity to judge will immediately improve.

61-90
You are probably a pretty good judge of character, relatively free from prejudices and a good basic observer of human behavior. You will find it instructive, however, to look at the answers you gave to the questionnaire and identify the questions where you scored lowest.

Over 90
You are an excellent judge of other people, probably gifted with a real insight into human nature and the enormously variable range of human personality.

Even at the superficial level of a cocktail party it doesn't take very long for a good judge of character to sift through the bores and bigots and corner a kindred spirit.

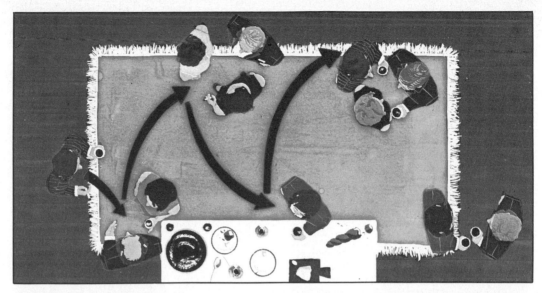

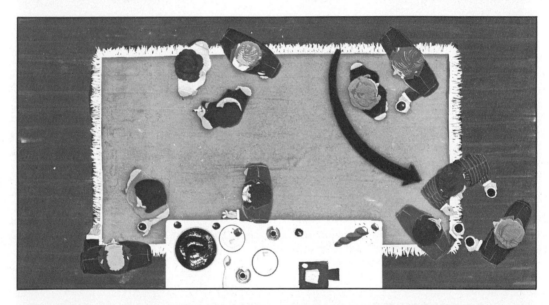

David Kinefield

130

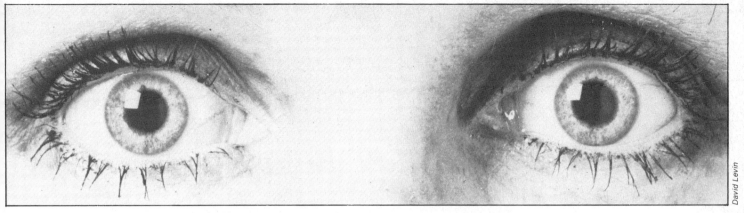

David Levin

Intuition and Insight:
How Important Are They To You?

In the Primate Research Laboratory on the island of Tenerife about half a century ago, a psychologist sat watching a chimpanzee in its cage. He had given the animal a problem to solve: How to get at a banana which had been placed a few feet beyond its reach through the bars. The psychologist had placed several objects around in the cage which the animal might use to assist it—in particular, some sticks of various sizes which could be joined together end to end. At first the animal tried to reach the banana with the longest of the single sticks without success. Then, after pacing restlessly up and down in apparent frustration, the chimpanzee suddenly paused and then determinedly picked up two sticks, fitted them together and reached out to pull in the banana. The psychologist called this the "aha" reaction—the moment of intuition and insight when the solution to the problem "suddenly came to" the animal. That animals are capable of insight and intuition may come as a surprise to many people. We all tend to believe that only humans have this power to pluck a solution to a problem apparently out of thin air without having considered the individual steps leading up to it.

How much does intuition of this kind enter into your life? And are your intuitions good ones? Supposing that the chimpanzee had put the two sticks together only to find that he got an electric shock as a result, would one still call it intuition? Answer the following questions as honestly and openmindedly as you can. Then check to see how important intuition and insight are to you.

Mark your answers on a separate sheet.

1. Which of the following statements do you feel is *most* true for you?
   a. When I try to solve a problem, I try to think of everything that might be relevant.
   b. When I try to solve a problem, I work my way systematically through all the possible answers, one at a time.
   c. I have no set plan in working out problems. I play around with a variety of ideas and something usually comes up.

2. When a good friend complains that he is not feeling well, do you

   a. Often know what is wrong?
   b. Feel able to guess what is wrong after he has told you something about the symptoms?
   c. Have no idea what it could be?

3. Do you have a kind of instinct for knowing when people are having personal problems?
   a. Yes
   b. No
   c. Only with people very close to you.

4. Would you say that all the major decisions in your life have been made on logical grounds?
   a. To some extent.
   b. Yes
   c. No—you operate by trusting your feelings.

5. If someone asks for your help in making a decision, do you
   a. Try to find out what he wants you to say before suggesting anything?
   b. Have a feeling what would be right for him and advise accordingly?
   c. Dispassionately bring logical analysis to bear on the alternatives?

6. Is it hard for you to do what you want when others try to dissuade you?
   a. No, you proceed in a way that you know to be right for you.
   b. Yes, when other people step in you get confused about what you should do.
   c. Sometimes you tend to be influenced by the judgements of others.

7. If you dreamed that a good friend of yours had died, would you
   a. Contact him immediately?
   b. Feel a bit disturbed, but think that it would be silly to act on it?
   c. Ignore it as just a bad dream?

8. Have you ever, in conversation, known exactly what is going to be said in advance?

a. Yes
b. No

9. If you checked a to question 8, which of these explanations would you give?
   a. That you knew the speaker so well that you could predict what he would say.
   b. Some kind of telepathy.
   c. That the conversation was moving in an obvious direction.

10. How do you tend to judge people when you first meet them?
   a. By the way they look.
   b. By what they say.
   c. By the "vibes" you feel.

11. Do you trust anyone else's intuition?
   a. Yes
   b. No
   c. At times

12. Do you ever have a strong feeling that you *should* do something that you don't usually do, or the other way round?
   a. Yes
   b. Sometimes
   c. Never

13. If a or b to question 12, do you ever act upon those feelings?
   a. Yes
   b. No

14. What explanation would you give for such feelings, in yourself or others?
   a. That they are some kind of warning.
   b. That they are plain silly.
   c. That they could be either.

15. Can you always be sure when people are telling you the truth?
   a. Always
   b. Sometimes
   c. Not usually

16. If a or b to question 15, how do you tell?
   a. By obvious signals, like the way they look at you and whether they blush.
   b. By how truthful they generally are.
   c. You just know.

17. The philosopher Hume said, "Reason is, and ought only to be, the servant of passion." Do you
   a. Strongly agree?
   b. Strongly disagree?
   c. Feel undecided?

18. Do you get strong impressions of the feeling of a place, like happiness or unhappiness?
   a. Yes
   b. No

19. Would you take a job with excellent pay even if you hated it?
   a. Yes
   b. No

20. Is it easy for you to understand the feelings of someone very different from you?
   a. Yes
   b. No
   c. No, but you can if you make a real effort to see things their way.

21. Before your vacation (you will be traveling by air) you dream about plane crashes. Would you
   a. Think that you were overtired and in need of a holiday?
   b. Wonder if you want to go after all?
   c. Treat the dreams as a warning?

22. You come up with an answer to a problem at work, but you cannot explain it logically. Would you
   a. Put it forward strongly?
   b. Keep quiet until you had a chance to make it convincing?
   c. Put it forward tentatively?

23. Your boss or your partner wants you to take a course of action that you sincerely believe will be disastrous. Would you
   a. Go ahead?
   b. Try to dissuade him/her?
   c. Refuse, or do something different on your own initiative?

24. Which statement do you agree with?
   a. Faith healing is scientifically impossible.
   b. There might be something in faith healing.
   c. I believe in faith healing.

25. If you found that someone you disliked seemed to be nicer than you first thought, would you
   a. Feel surprised and still suspicious?
   b. Not believe their apparent good qualities?
   c. Think that you had been mistaken?

26. Do you find that you tend to be thinking about someone just before he or she unexpectedly gets in touch with you?
   a. No
   b. Sometimes
   c. Often

27. If you checked b or c to question 26, do you think this is because
   a. It is just coincidence?
   b. Of some reason you do not understand, but not mere coincidence?

28. Do you think "women's intuition" is
   a. A polite term for a lack of logic?
   b. A reality?
   c. Simply a myth?

Elizabeth Noyes

29. When you have strong feelings about the outcome of something in advance, do you find that you have been wrong and things do not turn out the way you thought they would?
   a. Never
   b. Sometimes
   c. Often

30. Can you tolerate mysterious happenings which do not always have a reasonable explanation?

Besides words, we can also use our eyes and body to express ourselves. Intuition is a measure of how well we understand these subtle messages.

   a. No—you want to know the logical reason for everything.
   b. Yes—you do not expect to be able to understand everything.

Now turn to page 134 and check your scores.

Scores

(Total your scores to find your analysis below.)

1. a. 3 b. 1 c. 5
2. a. 5 b. 3 c. 1
3. a. 5 b. 1 c. 3
4. a. 3 b. 1 c. 5
5. a. 3 b. 5 c. 1
6. a. 5 b. 1 c. 3
7. a. 5 b. 3 c. 1
8. a. 5 b. 1
9. a. 3 b. 5 c. 1
10. a. 3 b. 1 c. 5
11. a. 5 b. 1 c. 3
12. a. 5 b. 3 c. 1
13. a. 5 b. 1
14. a. 5 b. 1 c. 3
15. a. 5 b. 3 c. 1

16. a. 3 b. 1 c. 5
17. a. 5 b. 1 c. 3
18. a. 5 b. 1
19. a. 1 b. 5
20. a. 5 b. 1 c. 3
21. a. 1 b. 3 c. 5
22. a. 5 b. 1 c. 3
23. a. 1 b. 3 c. 5
24. a. 1 b. 3 c. 5
25. a. 3 b. 5 c. 1
26. a. 1 b. 3 c. 5
27. a. 1 b. 5
28. a. 1 b. 5 c. 3
29. a. 5 b. 3 c. 1
30. a. 1 b. 5

Analysis

Psychologists know that intuition and insight occur, but have as yet no explanation for them. They appear to be leaps of understanding beyond the given information, but most intuition is probably a matter of picking up information so quickly that one is not aware of the conscious processes involved. You will have found yourself with a score lying somewhere in the range 26-150—the higher your score the more important intuition is to you. Check your score below for a more detailed discussion.

Under 50: The ultraconcrete thinker
With a score as low as this you not only appear to lack intuition more or less totally, but it seems as though you don't even want to admit that it could exist. That is a pity, for your tendency to concrete thinking will always tie you too closely to the facts and thus lead you to stick rigidly to the most unimaginative solutions to every kind of problem.

51-89: The concrete thinker
This is not a high score, suggesting that you have a basic distrust of intuition and a strong tendency towards concrete step-by-step thinking. This could be from hardheaded common sense or, on the other hand, it may be something to do with anxiety about accepting things you do not fully understand. This attitude may be a useful check to sloppy thinking, but you could also be reining in your imagination too tightly and inhibiting more creative and original thought.

90-110: The semiintuitive type
You are skeptical about the value of intuition, or at least its usefulness to you. You are right of course—intuition does not necessarily provide you with the correct answer on every occasion. But you do seem to be a bit unwilling to rely on your own insights. The trouble is that you are prepared to accept that intuition exists, but in practice you do not seem to have the mechanism for recognizing valuable intuitions when they occur. Put your feelings to the test more often; this will give you more confidence in the valid insights which you probably have.

111-135: The soundly intuitive type
This high score suggests that you certainly believe in intuition and you are almost certainly very intuitive yourself. Furthermore, your insights often pay off, saving you time and giving you that enviable reputation of being a quick and purposeful thinker. So much so, in fact, that there is a danger that you might become slightly overconfident and trust to instant judgement on too many occasions for your own good.

Over 135: The excessively intuitive type
Your score is too high. You have an almost magical belief in the intuitive power of your mind and this will certainly lead you into trouble if you do not temper it. To you it seems as though all your insights are genuine ones. Think again! Isn't it possible that you "forget" the times when intuition has led you astray?

Does Time Work For You?

If you need something done well and in a hurry, ask a busy man to do it for you. This is an old saying which packs a great weight of truth. Yet how can this be? A busy man is a man who is always doing things and, one would assume, would be the last person who could find the time to take on anything else. The key to understanding this apparent paradox comes in the phrase "finding the time." Successful busy men do not have to find the time—they know they have it and simply make it work for them. But there is busy-ness and busy-ness. We all know the kind of person who flaps around breathlessly, rushing from place to place and never seeming to get anywhere. His trouble is that he is too busy trying to find time, not realizing that it is there just waiting to be used if only he knew how.

Do you know how to make time work for you? How many hours do you waste and how many do you put to really good practical use? Is the day too long or too short for you? Do the following questionnaire carefully to find out, and perhaps get some useful tips in the bargain.

Mark your answers on a separate sheet.

1. Do you make lists of things to be done?
   a. Rarely
   b. Often
   c. Sometimes

2. If you answered b or c to question 1: What usually happens after you have made the list?
   a. You do not seem to get round to tackling the tasks.
   b. You complete the tasks methodically.
   c. You get at least some of them done.

3. Do you feel that you are very busy, but that you do not seem to accomplish much?
   a. Often
   b. Sometimes
   c. Rarely

4. When did you last take time off to relax?
   a. Within the last three days.
   b. Not within the last three months.
   c. Within the last two weeks.

5. Are you rushed at the last minute because you have wasted time?
   a. Sometimes

   b. Rarely
   c. Often

6. Would you say that you are
   a. Always punctual?
   b. Sometimes late?
   c. Very unpunctual?

7. You have a train to catch and arrive at the station just as the barriers are about to close. Would you bother to run for the train?
   a. Yes
   b. No
   c. Only if it was really urgent for you to catch it.

8. If you worked through the night, would it be because
   a. You like to work at night when there are fewer interruptions?
   b. You had got into a muddle and had left yourself no other time to work?
   c. The work was urgent and unexpected?

9. Do you feel that you are too busy to do the things you want to do?
   a. Sometimes
   b. Often
   c. Not really

10. Are you in the habit of hurrying, even when you do not need to?
   a. Yes
   b. No

11. Do you need someone else to put pressure on you before you can work flat out?
   a. Yes
   b. No
   c. Sometimes, if you are tired or the work is not particularly interesting.

12. Have you ever made a special effort to get up early in order to be on time, then somehow managed to finish up late anyway?
   a. Yes
   b. No

13. Would you prefer
   a. A lazy beach holiday?
   b. A tightly packed holiday, with lots of places to see

and lots of different things to do?
c. A mixture of relaxation and activities?

14. Do other people ask you how you manage to do so much?
a. Quite frequently.
b. No—the thought is laughable.
c. Sometimes

15. Have you ever decided to fit a regular activity, say a ten-minute exercise program, into your life?
a. Yes
b. No

16. If you answered a to 15: Did you
a. Keep it up for a few days only?
b. Keep it up for weeks or months?
c. Keep it up, but not so regularly as you planned?

17. When you have unpleasant tasks to do, do you
a. Get them over quickly?
b. Postpone them, hoping they will go away?
c. Get them done, a bit at a time?

18. Do you say "I haven't time to . . ." as an excuse
a. Often?
b. Only when it is true?
c. Sometimes?

19. As a child were you
a. Free to plan your own time to a great extent?
b. Forced to submit to a timetable worked out by your parents?
c. Free to plan your leisure activities, but made to do homework and other tasks at fixed times?

20. If you had the chance to work freelance, would you
a. Take it with pleasure?
b. Wonder if you could work without the discipline of having to go out each day?
c. Know that you would never do anything?

21. Does other people's lateness worry you?
a. Yes, it is very irritating.
b. No
c. Sometimes

22. Do you ever feel that someone is preventing you from settling down to do something?

a. Yes
b. No

23. When you have to spend half an hour waiting for something, do you
a. Find something to do or read?
b. Just relax?
c. Feel impatient and restless but do nothing?

24. In the evenings, do you
a. Flop down in exhaustion?
b. Have a good time, sometimes relaxed, sometimes energetic?
c. Go on working, or turn to domestic tasks or hobbies that you enjoy?

25. Which is your best time of day?
a. Morning
b. Afternoon
c. Evening

26. Does your busiest time coincide with your best time in the day?
a. Yes
b. No

27. Do you feel that you have tackled too much?
a. Rarely
b. Sometimes
c. Often

28. Are you in general
a. Very patient?
b. Very impatient?
c. Reasonably patient?

29. Do you finish things before you have to
a. Once in a blue moon?
b. Often?
c. Sometimes?

30. When you go on a journey, do you
a. Pack carefully well in advance?
b. Throw things haphazardly into a suitcase at the very last minute?
c. Give yourself a small but comfortable margin of time to spare?

Now turn to page 137 and check your scores.

Scores

(Total your scores to find your analysis below.)

1. a. 3	b. 5	c. 1		**16.** a. 1	b. 5	c. 3
2. a. 1	b. 5	c. 3		**17.** a. 5	b. 1	c. 3
3. a. 1	b. 3	c. 5		**18.** a. 1	b. 5	c. 3
4. a. 5	b. 1	c. 3		**19.** a. 3	b. 1	c. 5
5. a. 3	b. 5	c. 1		**20.** a. 5	b. 3	c. 1
6. a. 5	b. 3	c. 1		**21.** a. 5	b. 3	c. 1
7. a. 1	b. 3	c. 5		**22.** a. 1	b. 3	
8. a. 3	b. 1	c. 5		**23.** a. 5	b. 3	c. 1
9. a. 3	b. 1	c. 5		**24.** a. 1	b. 3	c. 5
10. a. 1	b. 3			**25.** a. 5	b. 3	c. 3
11. a. 1	b. 5	c. 3		**26.** a. 5	b. 1	
12. a. 1	b. 5			**27.** a. 5	b. 3	c. 1
13. a. 3	b. 1	c. 5		**28.** a. 3	b. 1	c. 5
14. a. 5	b. 1	c. 3		**29.** a. 1	b. 5	c. 3
15. a. 5	b. 1			**30.** a. 5	b. 1	c. 3

Analysis

Does time move too fast or too slowly for you? Using time advantageously is a real art. Your score, which will lie between 30 and 140, will give you some indication of whether you are "time's master" or its "slave." Check your score against the appropriate category below.

30-50   With a score at this low level you are one of those people who is really a slave to time. Time worries you, possibly even obsesses you. You are constantly aware of its presence and its passage, and yet paradoxically you have no idea how to handle it. The plain fact is that your life is too disorganized, or at best is badly organized. Unfortunately people like you never seem to be able to *find time* to get themselves organized and thus remain time-slaves!

51-70   You worry about time too much and you do not really know how to use it. The phrase "more haste, less speed" probably applies very precisely to you. Unfortunately you are always aware of the fact that you seem forever to be falling behind the clock and this produces anxiety which brings on even more delays. You need more organization in your life, a cooler head and a more relaxed attitude to the world.

71-95   This is a reasonable, average score. You are easygoing—perhaps a little lackadaisical, definitely unhurried, but still often successful in accomplishing what has to be done. You are not overproductive,

however, in comparison with many other people, but you are probably not bothered by this too much. You know how to relax and in fact you may enjoy life more than those scoring in the higher categories. You have come to terms with time on an equal basis: you are neither its slave nor its master.

96-120   You certainly know how to manage time. You have got an organized tidy mind and have learnt to surround yourself with people of a similar nature. People sometimes wonder at the amount of work you can get through without stress and strain. You have learnt how to use time and what it will do for a good master. Resist the temptation to go one step further and squeeze even more activities into your day, for this can be dangerous to your peace of mind. To be truly well-organized you should be able to find time to relax as well as to work.

Over 120   You have time completely under your control, responding to every crack of your whip—or so you think. Unhappily your obsession with time has meant that you have slipped back to the point where you are almost its slave. Your productivity may be tremendous, at the risk of frequent anxiety and always the tendency to bite off more than you can chew. The truth is that you are racing against time rather than controlling it. You are winning the race as far as your work is concerned but you may well have lost the ability to switch off and relax. It is never too late to learn though!

What Kind of Parent Are You?

There are few subjects so controversial as that of bringing up children – everyone has his own ideas about it, and most people believe that they have got some special key to the "truth." Part of the reason for this is that there is no other subject in which all human beings feel so personally and directly involved – the vast majority of adults become parents sooner or later, and ultimately experience "second-stage parenthood" when they have grandchildren. In addition, of course, *everyone* has been through the experience of childhood – on the receiving end of parenthood.

There is little doubt that there is a real difference between "good parents" and "bad" ones, and most of us feel fairly sure that we can reliably place ourselves in one class or another and, what is more, reliably identify all our friends and acquaintances as falling into one or other category. Unfortunately, the rules we employ tend to be very personal and, while *we* may feel supremely confident about them, it often comes as a surprise when we find them radically opposed by friends, relations – or even by wife, husband or children. The truth is that parent-child relationships – although they are of basic importance to the contentment and well-being of children and adults and have retained their importance over literally thousands of years

– have, until quite recently, received a disappointingly small amount of serious research and study. This questionnaire takes account of the rather uncertain nature of the field of research, and for this reason its results need to be treated with some caution and common sense.

As for all such tests you should complete the questionnaire on your own and for the best results you should decide *before completing it* that you are not going to discuss your results with any other person. On the other hand, a husband and wife might decide to do it independently and then discuss their results to uncover major points of agreement or disagreement. Doing the questionnaire together is likely to produce a biased result and is not recommended in this particular instance.

Special note   In general this questionnaire will be valid only for parents whose children have passed the age of three. Parents whose children have grown up and left home may still do the questionnaire, provided that they adjust the questions in their mind appropriately – for example, "Do you find that you have frequent problems over 'table manners'?" should be read as "*Did* you find that you *had* frequent problems over 'table manners'?"

Part I

The first part of this questionnaire is divided into three sections, each of which tackles one aspect of parenthood and relative degrees of failure and success. For a complete analysis and discussion of your scores on these three tests, you should wait until you have answered all the questions in Part II of the questionnaire.

Section 1: General satisfaction
Answer each question honestly by writing either yes or no against the question number on a separate sheet.
1. Would you say that you had a happy childhood?
2. Do you have more children than you would have liked?
3. Does your spouse feel that you have more children than he or she wanted? (If you don't know, answer "yes.")
4. On the whole, would you say that your marriage was a happy one?
5. Do you feel that your children would be happier if you had more money to spend on them?
6. Do you and your spouse tend to quarrel a lot?
7. Women only: Are there days when you simply crave to get away from your children?
8. Women only: If yes to 7, do you have more than one such day a week?
9. Men only: Would you say that your work seriously deprives you of contact with your children?
10. Men only: If yes to 9, can you see a realistic solution?
11. Do you feel that your children are seriously missing out on any educational opportunities?
12. Do you feel that your children are seriously missing out on any recreational opportunities?
13. Would you say that your home mostly provides a genuinely welcoming atmosphere for your children?
14. Do your children seem pleased to bring others into their home?
15. Are grandparents or other relations welcomed in your house by you and your children?

16. Are you and your spouse generally in agreement concerning your children?
17. Parents with more than one child only: Being quite honest, is there one child that you really much prefer?
18. Parents with one child only: Do you feel that your spouse is overindulgent with your child?
19. Do you feel that your children have a very marked preference for one parent over the other? (Answer "yes" if one child likes the mother and another the father.)
20. Do you feel that you bear more than your fair share of the overall responsibility for looking after and bringing up your children?
21. Do you think that your children believe that one parent is far more important than the other?
22. Being honest, if you had the chance would you change any of your children's personalities in any way?
23. Supposing that you could start your marriage and family all over again – would you change things dramatically from the way that they are at present?
Scoring: After answering this part of the questionnaire refer to the score sheet on page 140. You will end up with a certain number of S points and a certain number of Ds. The balance between Ss and Ds reflects your own general satisfaction with your relationship to your children and, as a general rule, the more Ss you have, the greater your degree of satisfaction, while the more Ds you have, the less satisfied you tend to be. Jot your S and D scores down on a piece of paper and, when you have answered both parts of the questionnaire, refer to page 143 for an interpretation.

Section 2: Problems of childhood
Answer each question honestly by writing either yes or no against the question number on a separate sheet.
1. Have your children been through prolonged or unusual periods of restless sleep?
2. Did you experience difficulties with your children

regarding toilet training?

3. Would you describe all your children as being basically contented and happy?

4. Do your children seem to play and interact contentedly with others?

5. Parents with more than one child: Does squabbling between your children often seem to get out of hand?

6. Parents with only one child: Does your child use rages or tempers to get his or her way?

7. Do you often have to force your children to "finish up their food"?

8. Have any of your children been involved in bouts of stealing at school or from friends?

9. Do neighbors tend to complain about your children's behavior?

10. Can you trust your children with money?

11. Parents of teenage children only: Have any of your children been involved in brushes with the police or illegal activities?

12. Parents with no teenage children only: Do any of your children seem unusually rebellious or disobedient?

13. Do your children confide in you readily when they have problems?

14. Do your children have a tendency for truancy or a reputation for rebellious behavior at school?

15. Do quarrels between you and your spouse seem to be having an effect on your children?

16. Do either you or your spouse indulge in any habit or practice which you suspect adversely affects relationships with the children – heavy drinking, unannounced absences from home or spendthrift behavior for example?

17. Does it ever seem that your children literally hate you?

18. Do you ever suspect that your children are "ashamed of you" as parents?

19. Parents with more than one child: Do any of your children seem to be persistently jealous of their brothers or sisters?

20. Parents with only one child: Does your child seem to be jealous when you give affection to your spouse?

21. Have any of your children had a history of "nervous" complaints for which there seems to be no physical cause?

22. Have any of your children had a serious bedwetting problem?

23. So far as you are aware, are your children genuinely popular with others? (If you don't know, answer "no.")

Scoring: This section of the questionnaire deals with typical problems associated with children and growing people. After scoring according to the instructions on page 140, make a note of your score and when you have done all the sections, carry it over for a detailed analysis on page 144. As a rough guide, the more P scores you have, the greater your share of problems associated with bringing up children, while the more Cs you have, the more successful you probably are at overcoming them.

Section 3: Attitudes to child training and rearing
Answer the following questions honestly and without spending too much time trying to work out their "hidden meaning." Then refer to the score sheet on page 140.

1. On the whole, would you agree with the expression "spare the rod and spoil the child"?

2. When "naughty" behavior or disobedience begins to appear do you make a point of trying to damp it down before it gets well established?

3. Imagine yourself in the following situation and then try to decide which course of action you would be most likely to take. Your child has begun to show unsettled behavior just before going to school, complaining of aches and pains which you suspect are caused by "nerves" rather than anything else. Do you

   a. Speak to the child firmly and say that he must go to school, like it or not?

   b. Give the child a stiff talking to, make it clear that you believe his pains are imaginary and indicate that he will be punished if the behavior persists?

   c. Administer a quick slap and tell him to be off to school without any more nonsense?

   d. Keep the child at home until he feels better and call for medical advice if the symptoms persist?

   e. Send the child to school, but resolve to see his teacher to establish what the problem is if the anxiety persists?

   f. Send the child to school, reward it later for not fussing but resolve to keep an eye on the situation?

4. In which of the following ways would you react when faced by bad behavior from your child?

   a. A quick smack or stern reprimand at the instant the act is performed.

   b. A quick smack followed by an explanation of why you administered the punishment.

   c. No punishment, but a quietly spoken reprimand.

   d. A reprimand followed by a determined attempt to reward the child if it avoids the misdemeanor on a subsequent occasion.

   e. A reprimand with promise of punishment if it occurs again.

5. State whether you strongly agree, tend to agree, tend to disagree or strongly disagree with the following.

   a. Children should be seen and not heard.

   b. A happy home is a quiet home.

   c. The majority of criminal behavior can be traced to lack of firm discipline during childhood.

   d. It is far more effective to reward good behavior than it is to punish bad.

   e. Administering a good beating not only helps the child but helps the parents as well.

   f. One should never raise one's voice in anger to a child.

   g. A good punishment for a naughty child is to send it to its room and to isolate it from others.

   h. It stands to reason that all bad behavior could be rubbed out by enough rough punishment.

   i. Firmness is the key to successful toilet training.

   j. Children will always take advantage of a parent who is not strict.

6. When you see children other than your own behaving badly do you itch to administer some painful punishment?

Scoring: Add up the total number of T scores you have gathered, and deduct from them any minus-T scores. Jot down your total and when you have finished the final section of the questionnaire, *and not before,* refer for detailed analysis to page 144. A high final T score suggests that your attitudes to training are a bit rigorous and outdated with emphasis on punishment rather than instruction.

Scores

Section 1: General satisfaction

1. yes 3S   no 0
2. yes 0   no 3S
3. yes 0   no 3S
4. yes 5S   no 0
5. yes 3D   no 0
6. yes 3D   no 0
7. yes 2D   no 0   (Women only)
8. yes 3D   no 0   (Women only)
9. yes 2D   no 0   (Men only)
10. yes 0   no 3D (Men only)
11. yes 3D   no 0
12. yes 3D   no 0
13. yes 5S   no 0
14. yes 3S   no 0
15. yes 3S   no 0
16. yes 5S   no 0
17. yes 0   no 3S (Parents with more than one child)
18. yes 0   no 3S (Parents with one child)
19. yes 3D   no 0
20. yes 5D   no 0
21. yes 3D   no 0
22. yes 3D   no 0
23. yes 0   no 5S

Section 2: Problems of childhood

1. yes 2P   no 0
2. yes 2P   no 0
3. yes 5C   no 0
4. yes 3C   no 0
5. yes 0   no 2C (Parents with more than one child)
6. yes 2P   no 0   (Parents with only one child)
7. yes 1P   no 0
8. yes 3P   no 0
9. yes 3P   no 0
10. yes 3C   no 0
11. yes 0   no 3C (Parents of teenage children)
12. yes 2P   no 0   (Parents of preteenage children)
13. yes 5C   no 0
14. yes 3P   no 0
15. yes 5P   no 0
16. yes 5P   no 0
17. yes 5P   no 0
18. yes 0   no 3C
19. yes 0   no 2C (Parents with more than one child)
20. yes 0   no 2C (Parents with only one child)
21. yes 0   no 2C
22. yes 0   no 2C
23. yes 3C   no 0

Section 3: Attitudes to child training and rearing

1. yes 5T   no 0
2. yes 5T   no 0
3. a. 0   b. 2T   c. 2T   d. 0   e. 0   f. −2T
4. a. 1T   b. 1T   c. 0   d. −2T   e. −1T

5.

	Strongly agree	Tend to agree	Tend to disagree	Strongly disagree
a.	2T	0	0	0
b.	0	0	0	0
c.	2T	0	0	0
d.	0	0	0	−2T
e.	5T	0	0	0
f.	0	0	0	0
g.	2T	0	0	0
h.	2T	0	0	0
i.	2T	0	0	0
j.	2T	0	0	0

6. yes 1T   no 0

What Kind of Parent Are You? Part II

This is the second part of the questionnaire "What Kind of Parent Are You?" The first half dealt with factors relating to general satisfaction, the management of common childhood problems, and attitudes to training, reward and punishment. The second will explore the degree to which you have accepted your role as a parent and are prepared to live up to your responsibilities. Needless to say, do your best to answer the questionnaire honestly. When you have done so check your scores against the table on page 143 and then refer to the analysis, where your scores on the three sections in the first part will also be discussed.

Section 4: Acceptance of role

Answer the questions completely honestly, writing your answers on a separate sheet.

1. Which of the following is closest to the conditions that prevail in your home?
  a. More or less total confusion with the children doing what they want, making as much noise as they like.
  b. A certain amount of noise and confusion, but periods of quiet and discipline at certain regular times – for example, mealtimes or homework.
  c. Periods of order which slide into confusion until brought together by a burst of discipline.
  d. A quiet, disciplined house with children encouraged to let off their steam elsewhere.

2. Which of the following is closest to the situation in your household as far as books and reading are concerned?
  a. Plenty of books suitable for different ages, some educational, some frivolous, and the maximum possible encouragement for reading them.
  b. Plenty of books, though mainly of an educational and "improving" kind with frivolous material excluded.
  c. Not much in the way of books, but plenty of magazines and paperbacks.
  d. Hardly any books or reading material.

3. Say which of the following is closest to the situation in your house regarding TV viewing.
  a. The TV set on more or less the whole time, whether people are watching it or not.
  b. TV on for a good part of the evening and day, except periods set aside for reading, eating, and so on.
  c. TV viewing confined to a few programs each day.
  d. The TV set rarely on, and only for highly selected viewing.
  e. No TV set in the house.

4. Which of the following is closest to your own policy regarding physical exercise for your family?
  a. The maximum encouragement of physical activity, with a concentration on sports and games over intellectual activities.
  b. Plenty of encouragement for your children to exercise, but also a deliberate attempt to make sure that physical fitness is not overemphasized.
  c. No special encouragement in the matter of exercise and physical fitness as your children take enough naturally anyway.
  d. Less encouragement and opportunity for recreation and exercise than you know your family should have.

5. Answer "yes" or "no" to the following questions.
  a. Are you or your spouse seriously overweight (say over 20 pounds more than you should weigh?)
  b. Are any of your children overweight?
  c. Do you spend a certain amount of time everyday with your children reading, talking or playing games?
  d. Are you personally known to any of the teachers at your children's school?
  e. Do you take any active part in such school activities as parent-teacher associations?
  f. Are any of your children involved of their own accord in extra school activities, such as theatricals, sports or societies. (If you don't know, answer "no.")
  g. Are any of your children actively interested in learning a musical instrument with your encouragement?
  h. Do you make sure that your children have a vacation away from home at least once a year?
  i. Do you ensure that your children pay regular visits to the dentist for checkups?
  j. Do your children seem to have more than their fair-share of dental cavities, and so on?

6. Which of the following most closely approximates to how you would behave in the following hypothetical situation? Your teenage daughter develops a taste for freakish, eccentric clothing. Do you
  a. Indicate that you disapprove and tell her that she can wear the clothes if she is not seen with you in them?
  b. Pretend to like them but try subtly to influence her taste for the better?
  c. Say "What an unusual outfit!" or something similar, but then make no further comment?
  d. Tell her simply but clearly that she must wear something more sensible and appropriate?

7. Your son, in his late teens, who is very intelligent and whom you have always hoped would become a doctor, announces his intention of "dropping out" to become an artist. Do you
  a. Talk to him firmly and tell him that he must continue his medical studies otherwise you will give him no further support of any kind?
  b. Talk to him at length and try to persuade him to change his mind by every kind of argument that seems reasonable?
  c. Tell him you think he is a fool but that it is up to him to do what he wants?
  d. Accept his decision but try to persuade him to study art in a systematic way at school or college?

8. This same son, two years after having dropped out, returns home penniless, and announces that he is giving up art and wants to return to medicine. Do you
  a. Show him the door and tell him that he has had his chance and missed it?
  b. Give him a long talking to about his silly behavior but promise to support him as long as he works hard?
  c. Try to probe for the reasons for his abandoning art studies and seek vocational guidance before you agree to support his medical studies?
  d. Express skepticism, and say you will support him for one year on a trial basis?

9. Do your children earn money at an agreed rate for doing jobs round the house?

10. If your children come to you to ask for money, do you almost always give it?

11. Has each of your children got a workspace, however small, where he or she can study in quiet?

12. Do you actively encourage your children to save money for vacations, major purchases, and so on?

13. Do either you or your spouse smoke heavily?

14. Which is closest to your own attitude to alcohol?
  a. Both you and your spouse are strictly teetotal and regularly warn your children of the dangers of alcohol.
  b. You and your spouse are generally nondrinkers and encourage your children to be nondrinkers as well.
  c. You and your spouse are moderate drinkers, but never in front of the children.
  d. You and your spouse are moderate drinkers with no attempt to shield this from the children.
  e. You and/or your spouse are heavy drinkers.

15. Do your children have regular bedtimes which they have to stick to almost always?

16. If your spouse agrees to a child's request to do something, do you *always* support this agreement, even if you would not have consented?

17. If your spouse prohibits a child from doing something, do you *always* back up this decision?

18. If your children cannot get what they want from you, do you often find that they go to your spouse to try their luck?

19. Do you make a real effort to ensure that your children have a balanced diet?

20. Are you capable, or do you feel that you are capable, of discussing sexual matters openly with your children if they ask you about them?

21. Do you insist that your children do their quota of household jobs, homework and so on before they play or watch TV?

22. Can you honestly say that you really enjoy eating out with your children in restaurants?

23. Have you or your spouse made a point of reading books (other than this book) on child care and education?

24. If you found that your child was a regular cigarette smoker (more than say 10 a day) before the age of 18 would you be worried?

25. Your 17-year-old child is drinking regularly and often comes home visibly worse for alcohol. Are you worried?

Scores

Section 4: Acceptance of role

1. a. 5A   b. 0   c. 2A   d. 2A
2. a. 0   b. 2A   c. 3A   d. 5A
3. a. 5A   b. 2A   c. 0   d. 1A   e. 3A
4. a. 2A   b. 0   c. 2A   d. 5A

	yes	no
5. a.	2A	0
b.	2A	0
c.	0	2A
d.	0	2A
e.	0	2A
f.	0	2A
g.	0	2A
h.	0	2A
i.	0	2A
j.	2A	0

6. a. 2A   b. 1A   c. 0   d. 2A
7. a. 3A   b. 1A   c. 2A   d. 0

8. a. 5A   b. 0   c. 1A   d. 0

9.	yes 0	no 2A
10.	yes 2A	no 0
11.	yes 0	no 2A
12.	yes 0	no 2A
13.	yes 2A	no 0

14. a. 1A   b. 0   c. 2A   d. 0   e. 2A

15.	yes 0	no 2A
16.	yes 0	no 2A
17.	yes 0	no 5A
18.	yes 3A	no 0
19.	yes 0	no 3A
20.	yes 0	no 3A
21.	yes 0	no 2A
22.	yes 0	no 2A
23.	yes 0	no 2A
24.	yes 0	no 3A
25.	yes 0	no 5A

Analysis

Being a good parent requires something more than reading Dr. Spock and paying attention only to those points with which you personally agree. As we said at the outset, the rules for sound parenthood have not been established to the satisfaction of all social scientists, mainly because, relatively speaking, so little research has gone into discovering them. Nevertheless, psychologists have long realized that there are a number of dimensions of behavior against which your success or failure as a parent can be assessed, and four of these dimensions have been dealt with in this multiple questionnaire. The dimensions can be summarized by the following generalizations:

1. On the whole if you are satisfied with your role as a parent, then the chances are that you are being a good parent.

2. If your children have a low record of childhood problems then the chances are that you are being a good parent by successfully negotiating those problems that do arise.

3. Overstrictness and a strong tendency to use punishment as a device to control a child's behavior is not often compatible with good parenthood.

4. General knowledge, personal involvement in the educational welfare of your children, tolerance and that rather indefinable quality, "common sense" make for good parenthood.

These are generalizations only; for a more detailed discussion of both parts of the questionnaire, check your scores in the various subsections explained below.

Section 1: General satisfaction

Your score will be made up of two sets of values – S and D. Deduct whichever is the smaller from the other, and then read off your final score below.

Over 20D This is a score which suggests a really serious state of dissatisfaction with your role as a parent and the chances are that this is reflected in a turbulent domestic situation with all the consequent disturbances in the child-parent relationship. If you really answered the questionnaire accurately and ended up with such a score, then it may be that your marriage is in such an uneasy state that you should, at the very least, seek professional marriage guidance.

11 to 20D There is not much doubt that you are highly dissatisfied with your role as a parent and are probably aware that this is causing problems or difficulties (or likely to start doing so) with your spouse and children. It may be that you are going through a trying and difficult time, in which case things may improve spontaneously. On the other hand, maybe the root of the matter is a state of tension between you and your spouse. Would frank, honest discussion between you help sort things out? If not perhaps you could consult some professional help in the form of marriage guidance or counseling.

1 to 10D It would be untrue to say that from the point of view of personal satisfaction, your role as parent was free of all problems. Clearly there are a number of things which could stand improving, and a careful analysis of the questionnaire and the points where you picked up high D scores (or failed to collect S points) may help you to identify the sore spots. If you feel that you can identify them, then give yourself a bit of straight talking-to, and as soon as you feel able, talk it over honestly with your wife or husband. It is amazing what frank discussion of this kind can achieve.

0 to 10S This is a reasonable and average score, though you are obviously aware that your relationship with your children is less satisfactory than it might be. You might find it helpful to persuade your spouse to answer the questionnaire, and if his or her score is close to your own, note whether you are both picking up Ds or losing Ss on the same issues. But you have very definite positive points regarding your role as a parent.

11 to 20S On the whole you are reasonably satisfied with your role as parent, without having reached the point of smugness or oversatisfaction. Inspect the issues which caused you to pick up some Ds though. Can you see ways to improve things there?

Over 20S You are very well satisfied with your role as parent, and the part you are playing in running your family. If your score is in the high 20s, then you might almost be a bit *over*confident. No harm for that in itself, but do not take too much for granted in case you lose the touch of dealing with real trouble – should it ever develop!

Section 2: Problems of childhood

It would be a peculiar family that did not find itself with *some* basic, and even troublesome, childhood problems, but the good parent learns how to cope with these, overcome them where possible and reduce them to insignificance. Your P score reflects the extent to which childhood problems have been affecting your family life, and your C score gives a measure of how successful you have been in coping with them. For your final score deduct whichever is lowest from the other and check against the details below.

Over 20P Unfortunately (assuming that you have filled out the questionnaire properly!) you have suffered more than your fair share of the problems associated with parenthood, and it is hard to see how your family and domestic life could be anything but confused and even unhappy. With a score at this level it is more or less impossible to offer advice – except to seek professional guidance as soon as you can.

11 to 20P This score indicates that the problems associated with raising children and family life are heavy and complex in your case. The first step is to inspect the questionnaire to see where you have been picking up on P points and failing to collect Cs. Then talk it over with your spouse in as frank and open a way as you can.

1 to 10P Your family life has more than the average share of worries. These may not be all your fault, but someone, or something, is somewhere amiss. Perhaps you and your wife or husband could go over your answers together. If you can identify problem areas, then you could be halfway to solving them!

0 to 9C You have got your share of problems, but they obviously have not beaten you down. But can you make life easier for yourself, your spouse and children by paying somewhat more attention to tackling family difficulties when they arise rather than letting them float by, or even sometimes ignoring them?

10 to 20C Where problems arise in the course of bringing up your children it looks as though you have been able to overcome them rather well. Probably this is because you have looked them in the face and dealt with them as they have arisen rather than pretending they do not exist. Chances are that if your wife or husband fills out the questionnaire you will both come up with rather similar scores.

Over 20C One is tempted to say congratulations – but a note of caution needs to be exercised. You seem to be afflicted by so few problems that one wonders if you have been shielded from reality by extraordinary good fortune! Do not get too overconfident – life (particularly family life) is full of surprises.

Section 3: Attitudes to child training and rearing

This section principally deals with attitudes to training, in particular such matters as general strictness and inclination to punish children for misdemeanors of one kind or another. Scores here are particularly easy to evaluate, for as a general rule, too much strictness indicates an inflexible and "old fashioned" attitude to child rearing which is believed to be more harmful than beneficial.

0 to 3T You do not have much inclination towards

punishment, and while this is in line with much modern theory the chances are that you are a bit overlenient. Children need some correction from time to time, and yours are likely to be no exception.

3 to 10T This is a balanced and reasonable score. You are not so soft and tolerant that you will let children get away with anything. On the other hand you have probably realized the advantages of rewarding good behavior rather than punishing the bad.

11 to 20T You have a definite tendency to be overpunitive and while this may serve to keep your children firmly under control, the chances are that when they break loose, they really go out on a limb. Try to be a fraction more moderate and aim to reward good behavior rather than trying to damp out the bad by tough action.

Over 20T You are too punitive by far and could well be scaring your children into unnatural placidity. Watch out if ever they start to rebel, for you have probably used up all your ammunition already!

Section 4: Acceptance of role

Accepting the role of parent implies not only taking a positive attitude to one's children, but also living up to the numerous responsibilities that face one in various fields such as education, recreation, guidance on social and moral factors, and so on. Any points you have picked up here are negative ones, and so the higher your score, the less satisfactorily you have adjusted to your role and the more you are probably ducking your responsibilities.

0 to 10A This is a very good score indeed, and you may be almost too good to be true! If you have filled out the questionnaire honestly, however, you have got cause to congratulate yourself – particularly if you have been getting good scores on the other sections.

11 to 20A You are probably a good parent, at least as far as accepting your parental role and living up to your responsibilities is concerned. If you have weaknesses, these should be revealed to you by studying the answers you gave and noticing where you picked up black marks.

21 to 30A This score suggests that you may be dodging your responsibilities as a parent somewhat – particularly if you are scoring in the high 20s. Take a good look at the answers which gave you black marks. Talk them over with your spouse and see if they ring true. If they do – see if you can work out how to deal with them!

Over 30A This high score (particularly if it is over 40) suggests either that you have not answered the questionnaire correctly or that you are not living up to the responsibilities of parenthood. This may be a case for marriage guidance – you will almost certainly have found difficulties in your family life.

Final Summary

While, as we have said, hard and fast rules in this important area of life are hard to pin down, the answers that you gave on these questionnaires and the final scores you achieved could well reflect areas of strength and weakness in your strategies and outlook as a parent. If you have been scoring well in all four categories – congratulations. If scores are good in some and poor in others, then use this information as a handy self-corrective guide. And – however you have scored – good luck! There is not a family on earth that cannot use some.

Are You a Victim of the Blues?

The human personality is a complex structure, partly molded by heredity, partly by the environment. On a day-to-day basis it is also subject to short-term changes caused by a mixture of bodily and mental factors. For example, stomach pains or a toothache will cause a short-term personality change in even the most optimistic human being; a piece of really good news, such as a financial windfall, will cheer up all but the most depressed.

In addition to these easily definable factors, our bodies are at the mercy of large-scale biochemical changes which affect the nervous system and can change mood and psychological state dramatically. Most women, for example, will have noticed a tendency to weepiness, touchiness or general anxiety at about the time of their monthly period; longer-term changes may occur at the cessation of menstruation, sometimes called the "change of life." Men seem somewhat less at the mercy of their body's biochemistry, but nevertheless it may still bring them periodic changes of mood at unpredictable times.

All humans are slightly different, and no personality state is absolutely right or absolutely wrong. Psychologists are slowly getting together techniques for measuring these interpersonal differences, techniques which are now sufficiently reliable to form a basis for a really useful guide to diagnosing an individual's problem and ultimately for providing treatment. One of the most striking and most easily measurable dimensions of human personality is one involving simple changes of mood – the shift from cheerfulness into depression and back again which all of us suffer from time to time. Some people seesaw more than others, while some tend to be lodged more permanantly at the cheerful or depressed ends of the continuum. This questionnaire is designed to give you some idea of where you stand on that continuum. Remember, though, that it is a guide only – a self-test questionnaire not designed or suitable for administering to other people. The more honest and careful you are in answering it, the more reliable and meaningful the results are likely to be.

Mark your answers on a separate sheet.

1. If you had to make a prediction about the future of the world, which of the following seems closest, in your view, to the way things are going to turn out?
   a. Man faced many worse crises in the past than he is facing now and, as in the past, will overcome them in triumph in due course.
   b. Man will make a real effort to solve his present problems, but he may have a tough time doing so.
   c. Man is at a crisis point of a kind he has never met before and there is a very real possibility that he will be unable to survive.
   d. Man is unlikely to be able to solve his present problems and his civilization will probably be destroyed.
2. Which of the following is closest to your present sleep pattern?
   a. I sleep easily without drugs and wake refreshed most mornings.
   b. I can get to sleep fairly well and usually wake refreshed but occasionally use a drug or a drink to help me.
   c. I have periods when sleep is difficult and then I have to resort to drugs. On other occasions my sleep is normal and refreshing.
   d. I am a poor sleeper and definitely rely on drugs in order to get to sleep.
3. If you feel down in the dumps can you pull yourself together, "put a smile on it" and carry on with what you were doing?
   a. Always
   b. Sometimes
   c. Never
4. Which of the following is closest to the way you would rate yourself regarding changes of mood?
   a. I am more or less constantly in a good humor.
   b. I am pretty well always in a good humor but have occasional, though not very many, bouts of feeling depressed.
   c. Sometimes I feel in a good humor, sometimes I feel depressed – about fifty-fifty.
   d. I have periods of good humor, but on the whole I tend to feel depressed.
   e. I feel depressed most of the time.

(For questions 5 to 15, say whether each statement is "definitely true," "true on the whole," "untrue on the whole" or "definitely untrue" for you.)

5. I feel tired, even when I haven't been working.
6. It is difficult for me to make decisions.
7. I seem to be losing weight.
8. Women only: I find myself crying a lot over little things.
9. Men only: Little setbacks depress me more than I feel they should.
10. My heart seems to beat unusually quickly.
11. I feel that I am not really needed or useful to anyone.
12. I feel at my best in the mornings.
13. My appetite is much the same as it always has been.
14. I don't find it difficult to relax.
15. I don't find it difficult to do the things that I used to.

16. Which of the following is closest to how you feel?
   a. I lead a very full and active life and get a great deal of enjoyment from it.
   b. I lead a reasonably full life, but of course I have my ups and downs.
   c. I don't lead as active or useful a life as I would like.
   d. My life seems pretty empty and useless.
17. Do you sometimes get the feeling that you "know" you are going to go into a depression?
18. When you are in a depressed state or feeling blue, which of the following things can you usually do (if any) and which not (if any)?
   a. Cook yourself a meal.
   b. Answer the telephone.
   c. Read a novel.
   d. Watch television.
   e. Go out to a dinner party.
   f. Go shopping.
   g. Write a letter.
   h. Decide which clothes to wear.
   i. Get on with routine office or housework.

j. Pursue a favorite hobby.

19. Most people get periods of depression at some time in their lives. Which of the following is closest to the way in which depression affects you?

- **a.** I don't often get depressed, and if I do it doesn't seem to bother me in any way.
- **b.** I occasionally get depressed and find it a bit of a nuisance.
- **c.** I have definite periods of depression and they interfere with my working and social life a little.
- **d.** Periods of depression have a marked affect on my work and social life.
- **e.** Periods of depression interfere very seriously with my social and work life.

20. Do depressions or the blues sometimes come upon you for no obvious reason?

21. Have you ever been prescribed any drugs by a physician because of depression?

- **a.** Never
- **b.** Once or twice
- **c.** Frequently

(For questions 22 to 31, say whether each statement is "definitely true," "true on the whole," "untrue on the whole" or "definitely untrue" for you.)

22. I feel that I have made a real contribution to the happiness of at least one other person.

23. I don't enjoy sex as much as I used to.

24. I feel generally optimistic about the future.

25. My mind isn't as clear as it was once.

26. I have difficulty sleeping.

27. I have a lot of trouble with constipation.

28. I suffer a good deal from depressive states.

29. I am more irritable about things than I used to be.

30. My life seems rather empty.

31. I don't enjoy things as much as I used to.

Now turn to page 147 and check your scores.

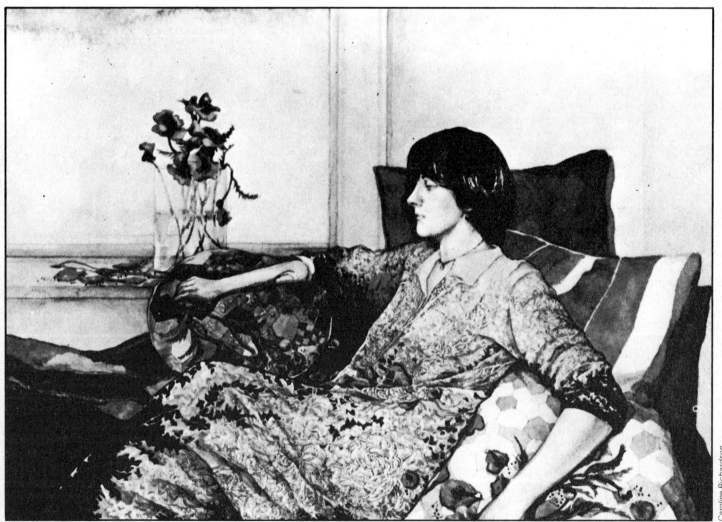

Caroline Richardson

Scores

(Total your scores to find your analysis below.)

1. a. 0 b. 0 c. 1 d. 4
2. a. 0 b. 0 c. 1 d. 3
3. a. 0 b. 1 c. 3
4. a. 0 b. 1 c. 2 d. 4 e. 5

	Definitely true	True on the whole	Untrue on the whole	Definitely untrue
5.	4	2	1	0
6.	3	1	0	0
7.	3	1	0	0
8. Women:	4	2	1	0
9. Men:	4	2	1	0
10.	4	2	1	0
11.	4	2	1	0
12.	3	1	0	0
13.	0	0	1	3
14.	0	0	1	3
15.	0	0	1	3

16. a. 0 b. 1 c. 2 d. 4
17. yes 2   no 0

	yes	no
18. a.	0	2
b.	0	3
c.	0	3

	yes	no
d.	0	4
e.	0	1
f.	0	2
g.	0	1
h.	0	2
i.	0	1
j.	0	2

19. a. 0 b. 1 c. 2 d. 3 e. 5
20. yes 2 no 0
21. a. 0 b. 1 c. 3

	Definitely true	True on the whole	Untrue on the whole	Definitely untrue
22.	0	1	2	4
23.	3	1	0	0
24.	0	0	1	3
25.	3	1	0	0
26.	4	2	1	0
27.	4	2	1	0
28.	4	2	1	0
29.	3	1	0	0
30.	4	2	1	0
31.	3	1	0	0

Analysis

The points in your total for this questionnaire are essentially "depressive" points, and the greater number of these that you have collected the more likely it is that periods of depression are a significant factor in your life. Before reading the relevant comments for your own score, however, it is important to realize that for most people – even those who end up with a very high score and are subject to frequent bouts of depression – the score on this test will vary from day to day. It will also depend on the mood that you are in at the time that you take the test. Therefore the fact that you come out with a high score does not necessarily mean that severe depression is with you always. Conversely, if you come out with a score which seems particularly low to you (and makes you seem less depressive than you feel yourself to be!) then this may mean that you took the test while in an "elated" personality swing. Do not be troubled by this, for personality swings are characteristic of almost all human beings!

0-10 This is a very low score and indicates, without much doubt, that your personality is more or less totally free from any kind of depressive illness. Your outlook on life may well be basically optimistic, cheerful and free from irritating mood swings. Happy person that you are! However, a personality type like yours is often extremely insensitive to less fortunate people and you should do everything that you can to be more tolerant and aware of those others in your life who may be more troubled by occasional depressive bouts than you are.

If you have come out with this score and yet feel that, though it applies to you at the moment, it would be quite uncharacteristic of you at other times, then you may have what is known as a cyclothymic personality – that is someone with pronounced swings of mood. There is no harm in this unless the mood swings are *very* extreme, when you may find the depressive half of your personality a bit difficult to bear.

11-30 There is a depressive side to your personality, but it is certainly hardly anything to worry about. You suffer the normal ups and downs of life, and occasionally react to these with a sense of gloom or pessimism. But on the whole you get the better of them and enjoy yourself in just about everything that you do. On the other hand you have enough insight to know what depression can mean when it touches you, and therefore to have sympathy with others less fortunate than yourself.

31-50 On the whole you are a well-balanced personality, but you know what depression is and it certainly touches you from time to time. The chances are that, if your score is less than 40 it will not have much practical effect on your life, except that occasionally you will find yourself difficult to live with, and others may find this too. If your score is closer to 50, then depression, in bouts, will probably actually interfere with your life from time to time, making work seem a bit of a grind and social occasions not worthwhile. Even so, on balance, you are probably a happy sort of person who gets plenty out of life and enjoys the greater portion of it.

51-75 You probably have more than your fair share of depressions and these may be difficult to bear at times. Probably these are associated with, or can be traced to, a fairly major event in your life – the death of a close friend or relative, a major upset at work, a physical illness or "the change of life." If this is the case, then you should gain comfort from knowing that this is called a "reactive depression" and that recovery from it is almost 100 percent. If you cannot so readily trace the source of your depression then it may be due to some unconscious conflict or long-term stresses at home or at work. If so, and the depressions seem difficult for you to bear at times, then you should not hesitate to confide fully in your physician or general practitioner.

Over 75 Any score in this range indicates a fairly severe degree of depression in your psychological make-up. The chances are that it is cyclic and alternates with moods of good humor – perhaps even extreme good humor. Personality seesawing of this kind is often due to major biochemical changes in the system which, fortunately, frequently respond to drug therapy. You should consult a physician about this if you do find that you suffer from extreme depression. There is no need to make life any tougher for yourself than it need be!

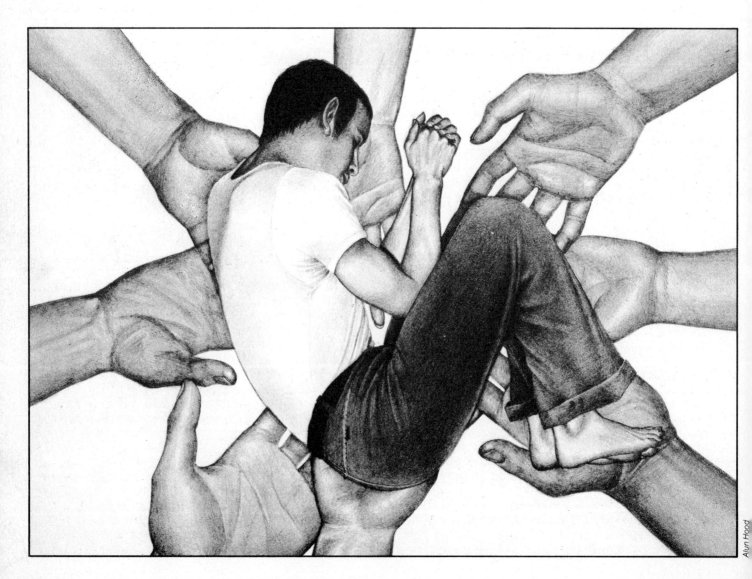

What is Your Real Age?

Shakespeare wrote of the seven ages of man, implying that we all move from cradle to grave in a series of uniform steps. In our teens we are adolescent, in our 20s adult, in our 40s middle-aged, and in our 70s we are old and decrepit. Perhaps this generalization is true for a certain proportion of humanity but it is certainly not true for everyone. We all undergo momentary changes of "personal age"—one day we feel raring to go and behave like teenagers, another day life seems boring and hard and we seem to have more than our fair share of aches and pains. Doctors have long realized that the chronological age of an individual is no guarantee of how fit they will be or how well they feel.

Age is largely an attitude of mind and it is not simply a matter of how much vivacity and general perkiness we feel from day to day. Some people become rooted in their childhood, their adolescence or other phases of their life, and whereas it is good to be "young at heart" in some respects, it is not always good to bring childish attitudes to bear on the problems of adult life. This questionnaire, by probing your attitudes, emotions and other patterns of behavior, will give you an indication of whether you act your real age in the way you face up to the problems of life. Before you begin the questionnaire however, take a gentle warning. This test can be very revealing and it will also take a certain amount of personal courage on your part for you to go ahead with it to the end. The first twenty questions are fairly straightforward—you answer those yourself. But Part 2 is not for the fainthearted. It contains ten questions about yourself which you must get *someone else* to answer. But first tackle Part 1 on your own.

Mark your answers on a separate sheet.

1. Which is most true for you?
   a. I am often attracted to people who have a stronger and more assertive personality than mine.
   b. Usually I am drawn to people who appear to like and admire me.
   c. I am often attracted to people who seem to need me.

2. You are trying to explain a great idea to a friend, who disagrees or does not understand. Would you
   a. Go on explaining?
   b. Feel hurt or angry, and stop talking?
   c. Stop to reconsider the idea?

3. If, in the middle of an evening with friends, you began to feel low, would you
   a. Excuse yourself and go home as soon as you could?
   b. Prefer to be miserable in company, so stay till the last possible moment?
   c. Bluff your way through the evening hoping that no one will notice?

4. When you are confined to bed with a bad cold, do you
   a. Like to be fussed over?
   b. Like to be left alone?
   c. Like some attention, but prefer to have books and other pastimes brought to you so that you can amuse yourself?

5. Which statement is most true for you?
   a. I like the kind of food my mother always used to cook for me.
   b. I enjoy most things if they are well cooked.
   c. The food I enjoy best is cooked by me.

6. After a trying day at work, would you be most likely to
   a. Go out to have a good time and forget your worries?
   b. Go home hoping to be soothed there?
   c. Go and tell a friend what a bad time you have had?

7. You have been needling a normally placid friend and he or she suddenly shouts at you. Would you
   a. Feel put out?
   b. Shout back?
   c. Reckon that you asked for it, and try to make up?

8. Someone you have just met tries to instruct you, laboriously, in something you know a lot about. Do you
   a. Tell him that you already know that?
   b. Say nothing, but just shut off?
   c. Wait till he has finished, then reveal your expertise?

9. If you were given a moderate sum of money (say as much as you earn in a month), would you
   a. Save it?
   b. Spend it on something you don't need but have been hankering after?
   c. Buy something for the house?

10. What kind of leisure activity interests you most?
    a. Anything that brings you into contact with other people.
    b. Escaping from the pressures of work into sheer pleasure.
    c. Organized sport, or useful activities, like gardening or carpentry.

11. If a friend said something insulting, would you
    a. Feel outraged and cut off contact with him?
    b. Feel hurt, however ridiculous the comment was?
    c. Wonder what had got into him?

12. Would you say that the person you most care about
    a. Needs you more than you do him/her?
    b. Needs you about the same as you do him/her?
    c. Doesn't need you nearly so much as you do him/her?

13. You are becoming very involved with someone an old friend of yours already knows well. The friend expresses some concern and appears to be trying to warn you. Would you
    a. Listen objectively to what he had to say?
    b. Tell him to mind his own business?
    c. Reject everything he says?

14. How do you react to an unexpected gift?
   a. By wondering what you can give in return.
   b. With unmixed pleasure.
   c. By wondering what the giver wants.

15. You have arranged the holiday of your life, but it is a month away. Would you
   a. Feel so excited that the time in between would seem empty and drag?
   b. Spend quite a lot of the time dreaming about what you are going to do?
   c. Get on with the rest of your life in the meantime?

16. At the last minute a friend cancels an engagement with you, without giving a convincing explanation. Would you think that
   a. He/she had found something better to do?
   b. He/she might be in some kind of trouble?
   c. He/she was a bit thoughtless, but it wouldn't worry you much?

17. When you get interested in something, do you
   a. Work hard at it and pursue it for a long time?
   b. Throw yourself into it, but quickly burn out your initial enthusiasm?
   c. Sometimes a, sometimes b—depending on the interest?

18. Which statement is most true for you?
   a. If I had had the right opportunities I could have done far more than I have.
   b. I've always worked hard and earned all I have.
   c. I spend a lot of time doing things I don't want to do.

19. A friend points out an annoying characteristic you did not know you had. Would you
   a. Feel indignant?
   b. Worry and feel self-conscious for a time?
   c. Ask other friends if it's really true?

20. You have been interested in getting to know someone and finally asked him/her to a party. He/she turns down the invitation, would you
   a. Feel that you have been foolish?
   b. Wonder what you could have done to put him/her off, but not feel too upset about it?
   c. Shrug your shoulders and tell yourself that there are lots of other people about?

Part 2
To complete the questionnaire properly you now need the help of a partner—a close friend, wife, husband, lover or parent will do, or anyone who knows you really well. From now on the questions are directed towards this partner (the "you" in the questions applies to him now) and he must answer them as honestly as he possibly can. Make sure he is a close enough friend to give his honest opinion—not just the one he knows you would prefer to believe.

21. You are entertaining friends that you know your partner (the subject of the quiz) dislikes. Does he usually
   a. Try to be pleasant and sociable?
   b. Get out of the way?

   c. Stick around, radiating hostility?
   d. Make a terrible scene with you after they've gone?

22. When you both work on a task together, do you find that your partner
   a. Tends to be bossy?
   b. Leaves most of the work to you?
   c. Works well as a team with you?
   d. Works well, so long as you boost his morale?

23. Before an important interview, does your partner
   a. Behave in a very agitated way?
   b. Prefer not to talk about it?
   c. Discuss with you possible questions and answers?
   d. Demand a lot of support and encouragement?

24. After a disagreement, does your partner
   a. Calm down quickly and apologize?
   b. Keep on trying to justify his position?
   c. Pretend that nothing has happened?
   d. Sulk for a day or two?

25. How does your partner react to the things about you that annoy him/her?
   a. By constant nagging?
   b. By occasional nagging?
   c. By teasing you perhaps with some sarcasm?
   d. By ignoring them?

26. When you feel bad-tempered does your partner
   a. Keep asking you what is wrong?
   b. Show anxiety and ask you if it's his/her fault?
   c. Leave you alone until you come round?
   d. Tell you to snap out of it?

27. If you had to tell your partner bad news, would you
   a. Brace yourself to tell him straight out?
   b. Choose your moment carefully?
   c. Try to put off telling him?
   d. Find him fairly easy to tell but fear repercussions?

28. You are going out together and your partner thinks that you are inappropriately dressed. Would he/she
   a. Insist that you change?
   b. Suggest that you change?
   c. Probably say nothing?
   d. Refuse to go out unless you change?

29. You have both arranged to go out. Problems arise (like babysitting) which means that only one of you can go. Which is more likely to happen?
   a. You would end up at home, with no discussion?
   b. You would both discuss what should be done?
   c. Your partner would offer to stay at home?
   d. You would both stay at home?

30. If your partner complained that you had been seeing too much of your friends, would it be because
   a. He/she felt neglected?
   b. You seemed to be having all the fun?
   c. Your partner felt jealous?
   d. Your partner wanted to see more of you?

Now turn to page 151 and check your scores.

Scores

(Total your scores to find your analysis below.)

Part 1

1. a. 1X b. 3X c. 5X
2. a. 5X b. 1X c. 3X
3. a. 3X b. 1X c. 5X
4. a. 1X b. 5X c. 3X
5. a. 1X b. 3X c. 5X
6. a. 5X b. 1X c. 3X
7. a. 1X b. 3X c. 5X
8. a. 3X b. 1X c. 5X
9. a. 3X b. 1X c. 5X
10. a. 3X b. 1X c. 5X
11. a. 5X b. 1X c. 3X
12. a. 5X b. 3X c. 1X
13. a. 5X b. 3X c. 1X
14. a. 5X b. 1X c. 3X
15. a. 1X b. 3X c. 5X
16. a. 1X b. 5X c. 3X

17. a. 5X b. 1X c. 3X
18. a. 1X b. 5X c. 3X
19. a. 5X b. 1X c. 3X
20. a. 1X b. 3X c. 5X

Part 2

21. a. 1Y b. 2Y c. 3Y d. 4Y
22. a. 3Y b. 2Y c. 1Y d. 4Y
23. a. 3Y b. 4Y c. 1Y d. 2Y
24. a. 1Y b. 3Y c. 2Y d. 4Y
25. a. 3Y b. 2Y c. 1Y d. 4Y
26. a. 2Y b. 3Y c. 4Y d. 1Y
27. a. 1Y b. 2Y c. 3Y d. 4Y
28. a. 1Y b. 3Y c. 2Y d. 4Y
29. a. 1Y b. 2Y c. 4Y d. 3Y
30. a. 2Y b. 3Y c. 4Y d. 1Y

Analysis

You should have two sets of scores, the first the result of answering Part I on your own, and the second the score provided by your partner's answers.

PART 1

You will have achieved a score somewhere between 20X and 100X. Depending upon your score you will find that your real age can be classified into three life eras—childhood, adolescence and adult or parenthood. In fact the division is not as precise as it seems. We all have a bit of the child in us, we all have a bit of adolescence and we are all adult to a greater or lesser degree. The categorization here will help to tell you which of the three "eras" is strongest in your case.

20X-45X Your real age is still, in balance, that of a child. In all probability you are a person with a strong feeling of helplessness and with a strong need for emotional support at critical times. You probably seem to yourself far more helpless than you actually are, but that is the way you feel. You tend to depend on approval from others and you are always anxious to please and to hear from others that you have pleased them. This may sound rather negative, but it is not necessarily so. The childish aspect of your personality may make you unrealistic in lots of ways but it could be that you feel happiness more keenly than "maturer" people. Very likely you have a positive interest in sports, get great pleasure from games and still have in your heart a childish capacity to enjoy things.

46X-75X With a score in this range you are in balance an adolescent at heart. It is a characteristic of the adolescent personality that there is a conflict between a need—almost a crushing need—for independence and an equally overpowering need for support and protection. The adolescent desires above all to break away from the confines of his home life and yet at the same time has an underlying anxiety about the rigors of the world outside. Whatever your chronological age, this adolescent ambivalence is still a strong vein in your character. You are ambivalent not only about responsibility—you cannot make up your mind whether you want it or not—but also about authority. You do not know whether to accept or reject it. You tend not to be realistic in assessing situations, jumping from optimism to pessimism with great rapidity. Possibly your strongest feature is a creative side to your nature, for you may well retain the adolescent's view that all things are possible and that the world is your oyster.

76X-100X Whatever your age—in point of fact you are almost certainly over 25—you are an adult at heart. This will mean that your solutions to day-to-day problems of living and your general tactical approach to life is mature and realistic. You have a strong rational streak to your nature, hating pointless arguments and tending to reject idealism. You see yourself as essentially a powerful figure at least to the extent that you feel able to control others and care for them at the same time. If you are a parent you are probably strongly aware of your parental responsibilities. But there are drawbacks. By taking on responsibility you may also take on too much. You may find that your adult role means that you have to sacrifice your independence. Are you also losing out on the fun of life a bit?

PART 2

If you have been brave enough to get someone to answer Part II for you and have the courage to look at their responses, then you should score yourself a big tick for having an adult approach to life. Not everyone would be prepared to have taken the risk that you have and you deserve congratulations whatever your score on either part of the questionnaire. This second part assesses what kind of *child* you are at heart, for we all have a streak of childishness in us. This is true no matter how high your score on the first part of the test. Clearly no hard and fast rules can be laid down but depending on your score—it should lie between 10Y and 40Y—you can get a rough, and perhaps revealing, image of the personality of the child that still remains inside you.

Recognize the child in you if you can and by doing so take a step forward to real adulthood.

10Y-15Y (The Good Child) Your childish persona is dominated by the wish to please others and to keep the peace at all costs.

PAF International

16Y-23Y (The Helpless Child) Your childish persona tends to be fearful and uncertain. Above all what it wants is to be "looked after."

David Humphrey

24Y-32Y (The Angry Child) The strongest streak here is frustration. The child in you does not know how to get what it wants. It may also feel guilty about its rages.

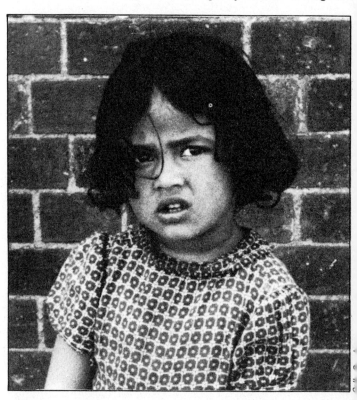

33Y-40Y (The Dumb or Stubborn Child) The child in you is basically angry, but it is not the kind of anger which shows up in a good old-fashioned tantrum. The chances are that its only weapon and the way it gains attention is emotional blackmail.

How Emotional Are You?

Mary Evans

How much are we controlled by our intellect and by the powers of reason and how much by the more "animal" emotions? Human beings differ as to how much they are in control of their emotions and how much their emotions are in control of them. The balance is partly determined by temperamental factors (largely inherited), partly by a phenomenon which psychologists call "level of arousal," partly by training and partly by experience. To reach an emotional equilibrium you have to recognize the strength of your emotions and exert a reasonable degree of control over them, making sure that your emotional responses are relevant to the situation. This questionnaire will help you to decide how the balance lies in your case. Does emotion work *for* or *against* you? Answer these questions as honestly as you can and check your score at the end.

Mark your answers on a separate sheet.

1. If you could choose, would you prefer to work
  a. In close contact with lots of people?
  b. With a few people?
  c. On your own?

2. When you read for relaxation, do you
  a. Choose factual books, history, travel, biography, informational reading?
  b. Prefer books with some informational content plus fictional element, like historical novels or novels with a detailed social background?
  c. Enjoy most of all escapist reading, like romantic or fantasy novels?

3. How do you react to horror movies?
  a. With boredom
  b. With fright
  c. With amusement

4. Which statement is most true for you?
  a. I think very little about other people's affairs.
  b. I am interested in the lives of people I know well.
  c. I am very interested in the details of other people's lives and I enjoy hearing all the latest news.

5. Do you find on visits to the country or beach
  a. That you are glad of the relative peace and quiet?
  b. That natural scenes give you a good feeling?
  c. That you wonder why you don't go more often?

6. Do you cry, or feel like crying, at a movie?
  a. Often
  b. Sometimes
  c. Never

7. When you greet your friends, do you usually
  a. Nod and say hello?
  b. Smile, shake hands and say hello?
  c. Give them a hug?

8. If you met a tedious stranger on a plane who tried to involve you in listening to the story of his life, would you
  a. Ruefully reflect that you always meet that sort?
  b. Listen with real interest?
  c. Cut him short and get back to your book?

9. Would you consider writing to a Problem Page?
  a. Certainly not
  b. Perhaps
  c. Yes

10. During a job interview, you are asked some rather personal and private questions. Do you
  a. Feel angry and upset and refuse to answer?
  b. Calmly answer what you think is relevant?
  c. Answer, but feel uncomfortable about it?

11. You go into a coffee shop for a quiet cup of coffee, and find that the girl next to you is in tears. Would you
  a. Want to say something comforting, but feel shy?
  b. Ask her if you can help?
  c. Move your seat?

12. After a dinner party at their place, a couple you are friendly with start to quarrel acrimoniously. Would you
  a. Feel upset and helpless?
  b. Get out quickly?
  c. Try to reconcile them?

13. Do you give your friends gifts
   a. Only at Christmas and birthdays?
   b. On impulse, whenever you feel particularly warm towards them?
   c. When you feel guilty or neglectful towards them?

14. Someone you have just met says complimentary things about you. Do you
   a. Feel embarrassed?
   b. View him/her with caution?
   c. Feel flattered and disposed to like him/her?

15. If you come to work in a bad mood because things at home have been difficult, do you
   a. Continue to feel and show your annoyance?
   b. Put your troubles aside while you work?
   c. Try to be reasonable, but find yourself rather irritable?

16. When an important relationship in your life breaks up, do you
   a. Feel bad, but go on with your life as near to normal as possible?
   b. Feel prostrated for at least a short time?
   c. Shrug it off and block feelings of grief?

17. You open the door to a stray kitten. Would you
   a. Take it in and look after it?
   b. Close the door quickly?
   c. Take it in, try to find it a home, but ultimately deliver it to be painlessly killed if you can't find a home for it?

18. Do you
   a. Ruthlessly throw away letters and old mementos almost as soon as you get them?
   b. Keep them for years?
   c. Sort out such possessions every couple of years?

19. Do you suffer from feelings of guilt and remorse?
   a. Yes, even about events long over.
   b. Occasionally
   c. No, you see no point in regrets.

20. When you have to talk to someone who is obviously shy or tense, do you
   a. Feel uneasy and pick up some of their shyness?
   b. Feel empathy, and try to draw them out?
   c. Feel mildly irritated?

21. Do you prefer children
   a. When they are small and helpless?
   b. When they have grown up?
   c. When they can talk and have definite personalities of their own?

22. Your partner has complained about the time you spend at work. Would you
   a. Explain that it is for the benefit of both of you, ultimately, and continue as before?
   b. Try to spend more time at home?
   c. Feel torn between conflicting demands and try to satisfy both?

23. At the end of a particularly good performance at the theater, do you
   a. Applaud energetically?
   b. Feel constrained about applauding?
   c. Join in the applause, but feel rather silly?

24. When you get the bulletin from your old school or college, do you
   a. Look through it before throwing it away?
   b. Read it carefully and keep it?
   c. Toss it unread into the rubbish bin?

25. You see someone you are pretty sure you recognize across the street. Would you
   a. Walk on?
   b. Cross over to say hello?
   c. Wave, but if he doesn't respond, walk on?

26. You hear a report that a friend has misunderstood an action of yours and is angry with you. Would you
   a. Get in touch very soon to explain?
   b. Leave him to work it out himself?
   c. Wait for a natural opportunity to get in touch, but say nothing about the misunderstanding?

27. What do you do with gifts you don't like?
   a. Get rid of them fast?
   b. Keep them lovingly?
   c. Hide them and bring them out only when the giver comes to see you?

28. Do demonstrations, rituals or patriotic occasions
   a. Leave you cold?
   b. Move you to tears?
   c. Embarrass you?

29. Are you ever afraid without apparent or real cause?
   a. Frequently
   b. Occasionally
   c. Never

30. Which statement is most true for you?
   a. I am wary about trusting my feelings.
   b. My feelings are my main guide in my actions.
   c. Feelings do not matter—consequences do.

Now turn to page 155 and check your scores.

Scores

(Total your scores to find your analysis below.)

1. a. 3	b. 2	c. 1
2. a. 1	b. 2	c. 3
3. a. 1	b. 3	c. 2
4. a. 1	b. 2	c. 3
5. a. 1	b. 3	c. 2
6. a. 3	b. 2	c. 1
7. a. 1	b. 2	c. 3
8. a. 2	b. 3	c. 1
9. a. 1	b. 2	c. 3
10. a. 3	b. 1	c. 2
11. a. 2	b. 3	c. 1
12. a. 2	b. 1	c. 3
13. a. 1	b. 3	c. 2
14. a. 2	b. 1	c. 3
15. a. 3	b. 1	c. 2
16. a. 2	b. 3	c. 1
17. a. 3	b. 1	c. 2
18. a. 1	b. 3	c. 2
19. a. 3	b. 2	c. 1
20. a. 2	b. 3	c. 1
21. a. 3	b. 1	c. 2
22. a. 1	b. 3	c. 2
23. a. 3	b. 1	c. 2
24. a. 2	b. 3	c. 1
25. a. 1	b. 3	c. 2
26. a. 3	b. 1	c. 2
27. a. 1	b. 3	c. 2
28. a. 1	b. 3	c. 2
29. a. 3	b. 2	c. 1
30. a. 2	b. 3	c. 1

Analysis

You will find yourself with a score somewhere between 30 and 90. For a rough idea of how you rate on the emotional scale, turn the page and fill in your score on the "Emotional Thermometer" overleaf. Use the space to the right hand side of the page to mark in the scores of your family and friends: you may find some of the results surprising to say the least!

But the thermometer can only give you a rough guide. For a more detailed discussion, read the analysis below. From a questionnaire of this kind it is impossible to go into very fine detail and for this reason scores are classified into three groups, which we term the Cerebral type (score between 30 and 50), the Balanced type (score between 51 and 69) and the Emotive type (score between 70 and 90).

The Cerebral Type

If you scored in this group you are basically of the type known as "cool, calm and collected." You rarely get excited about anything (or you rarely *seem* to) and even the most difficult or demanding situation never seems to push you into violent action. Even if you do get angry you tend to do so in a controlled and "seething" way. This may save you from getting into fist fights or slanging matches, but it may also mean that your anger tends to get bottled up and to last far longer than it should. Your main weakness is that you will be unresponsive to (or, if your score is very low, perhaps even incapable of accepting) emotion in others. You may find yourself with a restricted love life and you may have acquired the reputation of being a bit of a "cold fish." It would do you good to loosen up.

The Balanced Type

This is an average score. You are a person who, in common with the bulk of mankind, tends to find periods when emotions overwhelm you, but also periods when they seem to be kept pretty well under control. Even in the worst circumstances, if you really grit your teeth, you can stop yourself from flying off the handle. It is very unlikely that you have ever had a really big row with anybody—domestic tiffs not included. You will probably be free and easy in love affairs, getting emotionally entangled on some occasions but perhaps surprising yourself from time to time at how "realistic" you can be. You are the kind of person who enjoys a love affair while it is going well but *can* give it up if necessary.

The Emotive Type

There is no doubt about it, you are highly emotional with a very strong tendency to allow emotions to get the better of you. Many is the time you will have said to yourself "Why did I do that?" or "How could I have said such a thing?" If you are a woman you are a ready prey to tears and scenes, though you probably recover from these with amazing rapidity. If you are a man, you will be aggressive and dominant, inclined to shout a bit and throw your weight around. You also probably have tempestuous love affairs which may end as quickly as they begin and which may bring all kinds of problems with them. It is not easy to tell someone like you to cool down a bit—it is simply not in your nature—but if you could somehow persuade "your head to rule your heart" more directly you might find life a bit smoother. And so might some of your friends and those closest to you!

Emotional Thermometer

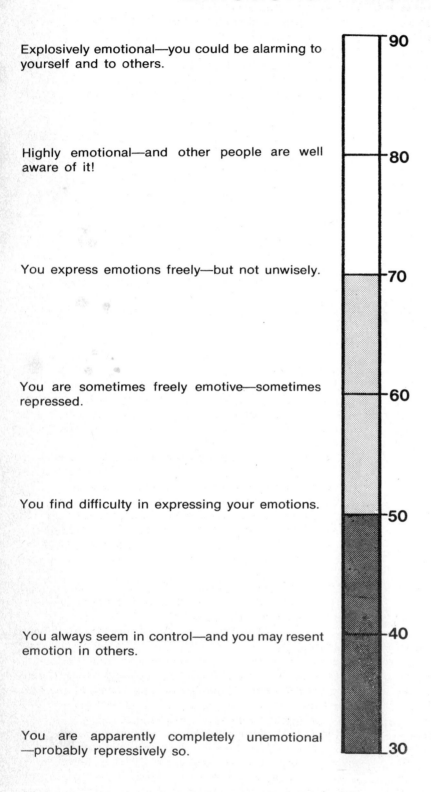

Explosively emotional—you could be alarming to yourself and to others.

Highly emotional—and other people are well aware of it!

You express emotions freely—but not unwisely.

You are sometimes freely emotive—sometimes repressed.

You find difficulty in expressing your emotions.

You always seem in control—and you may resent emotion in others.

You are apparently completely unemotional —probably repressively so.

90

80

70

60

50

40

30

Test Your Self-confidence

Watch a toddler take his first shaky steps, a child bounce a ball against a wall, an adolescent try balancing tricks with a bicycle. Watch any animal at play, any human exploring and manipulating his environment. What you are seeing is living organisms acquiring mastery over the world around them and, by doing so, building confidence in their ability to protect themselves in a treacherous world. But self-confidence is not simply a matter of acquiring muscular or, as psychologists call them, ''psychomotor'' skills. It is not only the *physical* movement that we need to learn to control. There is also a psychological environment, a vital area involving communication between people, rules of social behavior and tricks and strategies devoted to establishing one's position in the pecking order of civilization. Self-confidence in all these areas is something we seek out almost instinctively. It is a quality we think we see in others though we are so often aware of the lack of confidence underlying our own actions. In fact, people who seem capable, self-assured, enviable may just be presenting a mask, to the world and are often quite terrified underneath.

How do *you* rate as far as self-confidence is concerned? Remember that it is partly situational—in familiar tasks we may be at ease and yet become alarmed in new circumstances. One person may feel few qualms about talking to an audience of hundreds and yet may shy away from intimate encounters. Another may feel most at ease in small groups. Check out your level of self-confidence in this questionnaire and establish the sorts of situation in which you feel happiest.

Mark your answers on a separate sheet.

1. You are attracted to someone of the opposite sex and want to get to know him/her. Would you
 a. Get someone else to introduce you?
 b. Make the first contact yourself?
 c. Do nothing but hope that you will be noticed?

2. Your partner tries to talk about sexual feelings and preferences. Do you
 a. Respond easily and share your feelings?
 b. Feel uncomfortable, but gradually let yourself be persuaded to talk?
 c. Refuse to talk, or change the subject?

3. How do you feel when your partner shows an interest in someone else?
 a. Threatened and jealous.
 b. Pretty sure that you are the most important person in his/her life.
 c. Slightly worried.

4. When someone loves you, do you
 a. Feel afraid that as he/she gets to know you the loving will stop?
 b. Accept it as your due?
 c. Feel glad and do your best to please?

5. At the end of a love affair, do you
 a. Feel completely rejected and shattered?
 b. Feel bad, but get over it quickly?
 c. Feel bad for some time, but know that you will recover?

6. If you lost or damaged someone else's valued possession, would you
 a. Avoid admitting what you had done?
 b. Accept that it was an unfortunate accident?
 c. Own up, but dread the consequences?

7. If you are attracted to someone other than your partner, do you
 a. Feel guilty even if you do nothing about it?
 b. Feel that it is a normal occurrence?
 c. Feel guilty only if you do something about it?

8. Is it easy for you to show your appreciation of your partner?
 a. Yes
 b. No
 c. Not always

9. If your partner goes on holiday, or a business or family trip without you, do you
 a. Wish him/her a pleasant time and not worry?
 b. Feel slight misgivings?
 c. Fantasize about possible infidelities?

10. If you are angry with your partner, do you
 a. Feel afraid to make a scene?
 b. Feel free to show your feelings, knowing that it will work out in the end?
 c. Be unsure of your right to be angry, but show something of it?

11. In conversation, someone states as a fact something that you know is incorrect. Would you
 a. Correct him immediately?
 b. Feel awkward, but point out the error tactfully?
 c. Let it go?

12. Your friends are planning an outing that you would enjoy, but have not asked you to join them. Would you
 a. Assume that they want you to go along?
 b. Ask them if you can come too?
 c. Feel hurt and left out?

13. If you give a party, do you
 a. Have a good time?
 b. Have a miserable evening because you worry about how well it is going?
 c. Start off worried, but relax as the evening goes on?

157

14. Do you talk about yourself?
  a. Rarely, because you are afraid of boring others.
  b. Yes, if you are asked about yourself.
  c. Rather a lot of the time.

15. When friends come to you for advice, do you
  a. Feel inadequate to give it?
  b. Tell them exactly what you think?
  c. Feel hesitant, but hope that you can do some good?

16. Two guests at a dinner party are becoming more quarrelsome every minute. Would you
  a. Take some action, like engaging one of them in conversation yourself?
  b. Leave them for your host to deal with?
  c. Feel deeply embarrassed?

17. You are looking for a house in a street which is not clearly numbered. Would you
  a. Ring the first doorbell and ask for help?
  b. Wander about for a few minutes, before approaching any house?
  c. Walk up and down the street hoping for enlightenment?

18. Two missionaries of a religious group that you do not belong to turn up on your doorstep while you are busy. Would you
  a. Send them away without another thought?
  b. Get trapped in some kind of discussion?
  c. Send them away apologetically?

19. You discover after a shopping trip that the fruit in the bottom of the box is unripe. Would you
  a. Sigh and do nothing?
  b. Mention it timidly next time you are in the store?
  c. Complain firmly and ask for a replacement?

20. You are lunching with some friends and you feel much less (or more) hungry than the others. Would you
  a. Order exactly what you want without feeling that you have to apologize?
  b. Feel that you are obliged to do the same as your companions?
  c. Have what you want, but feel obliged to explain or make a joke of it?

21. One of your friends or colleagues has criticized you. Would you
  a. Take it calmly?
  b. Feel a bit defensive?
  c. Feel very hurt and angry?

22. Do you react to interviews by
  a. Feeling terrified?
  b. Feeling excited by the challenge?
  c. Feel nervous but hopeful?

23. Could you carry through an unpopular policy at work or in the home?
  a. Yes, so long as you thought it right.
  b. Only if you had no choice.
  c. Probably not at all.

24. Which statement is most true for you?
  a. I have a lot to offer in my work and I expect this to be acknowledged.
  b. Sometimes I think I have a lot to offer, but I need to be reassured.
  c. I am constantly afraid that my inadequacy in my work will be found out.

25. How often have you decided against buying something to wear, though you really liked it, because you thought it might be too young/too exotic/too noticeable for you?
  a. Never
  b. Often
  c. A few times

26. At a public meeting or lecture, you want to ask a question. Would you
  a. Take the first possible opportunity to stand up and ask?
  b. Rehearse the words in your head, and come out with it at last?
  c. Never dare to ask?

27. You have to make a speech at something like a PTA meeting. Would you
  a. Make a few notes, and ad lib?
  b. Write down every word?
  c. Write down the main points, and perhaps the opening and conclusion?

28. An interviewer from a local TV or radio station approaches you asking for your comments on an event. Would you
  a. Take the opportunity with gusto?
  b. Refuse to speak?
  c. Feel nervous, but willing to try?

29. If you found that you disagreed with a group of your colleagues about an issue at work, would you
  a. Make your standpoint clear to them?
  b. Raise mild objections to their plans?
  c. Keep quiet?

30. If the same sort of disagreement arose with your boss, would you
  a. Make your standpoint clear to him?
  b. Raise mild objections to his plans?
  c. Keep quiet?

Now turn to page 159 and check your scores.

Scores

(Total your scores to find your analysis below.)

1. a. 3P	b. 5P	c. 1P
2. a. 5P	b. 3P	c. 1P
3. a. 1P	b. 5P	c. 3P
4. a. 1P	b. 5P	c. 3P
5. a. 1P	b. 5P	c. 3P
6. a. 1P	b. 5P	c. 3P
7. a. 1P	b. 5P	c. 3P
8. a. 5P	b. 1P	c. 3P
9. a. 5P	b. 3P	c. 1P
10. a. 1P	b. 5P	c. 3P
11. a. 5S	b. 3S	c. 1S
12. a. 5S	b. 3S	c. 1S
13. a. 5S	b. 1S	c. 3S
14. a. 1S	b. 3S	c. 5S
15. a. 1S	b. 5S	c. 3S
16. a. 5S	b. 3S	c. 1S
17. a. 5S	b. 3S	c. 1S
18. a. 5S	b. 1S	c. 3S
19. a. 1S	b. 3S	c. 5S
20. a. 5S	b. 1S	c. 3S
21. a. 5W	b. 3W	c. 1W
22. a. 1W	b. 5W	c. 3W
23. a. 5W	b. 3W	c. 1W
24. a. 5W	b. 3W	c. 1W
25. a. 5W	b. 1W	c. 3W
26. a. 5W	b. 3W	c. 1W
27. a. 5W	b. 1W	c. 3W
28. a. 5W	b. 1W	c. 3W
29. a. 5W	b. 3W	c. 1W
30. a. 5W	b. 3W	c. 1W

Analysis

As a result of answering this questionnaire you will have acquired three sets of scores—P, S and W—with a maximum of 50 in each group. First, check your rating in each of these groups to see which aspects of your nature are most richly endowed with self-confidence, then tot up your three scores and place yourself on the Confidence Scale below.

Your P Score
This relates to your confidence in purely personal relationships. The higher your score the more confident you are when it comes to handling the nitty-gritty problems which go on between men and women, lovers and really close friends.

10P-20P Personal relationships are obviously among your weak points. Your lack of self-confidence probably leads you, paradoxically, into conflict situations. You may be stubborn, but this stubbornness is really a sign of weakness rather than strength.

21P-40P This is a reasonable, average score, and if your score is in the 30s, then you show a good measure of self-confidence in personal situations. This will lead on the whole to a harmonious domestic life.

Over 40P You are exceedingly self-confident and your partner and closest friends may well find themselves dominated by you and your decisions. Watch out that you don't hurt them, though, through thoughtlessness.

Your S Score
This refers to confidence in social situations, at parties and in ordinary informal gatherings of the kind that we all find ourselves in from time to time.

10-24S Unfortunately you lack self-confidence in social situations. You are probably an introvert and you very likely hate parties and get-togethers because you feel inadequate in them. Nine times out of ten feelings of inadequacy of this kind are unjustified however. Try to overcome them because otherwise you will miss out on much of the social fun of life.

25S-40S You enjoy some social settings, and if your score is in the 30s you probably go out of your way to go to parties and to meet strangers wherever you can. You may be a good host or hostess and enjoy your command of the social scene.

Over 40S This high score suggests unusual self-confidence in social situations. Fine—but beware that you do not overdo it. You may be absolutely sure that you are always the "life and soul of the party," but this could make you extremely overbearing if you do not put the brakes on.

Your W Score

This score relates to your self-confidence in the vital field of work and to how well you manage to deal with other public situations.

10W-20W For some reason you lack self-confidence in a working environment, and this may be handicapping your chances of advancement. Do you perhaps feel unsure about your academic abilities or your lack of qualifications? Would night school or a part-time college course help you here?

21W-40W You are confident in working and public situations, but not overconfident. This is a good thing, for work and public life is largely a matter of give and take. If your score is in the 30s you may well hold a responsible position at work or if you are at the beginning of your career, you certainly have a good chance of being promoted into one.

Over 40W You are a bustling, self-confident go-getter who knows how things ought to be done and feels impatient if they are not just so. You might turn out to be a Captain of Industry but there is a danger in being quite so confident in your work. Be careful that you do not become far too self-confident to be a tolerant and understanding boss.

The Confidence Scale

Total your three scores (P, S and W) and read your individual analysis.

30-50 You are very seriously lacking in self-confidence. There may be a good reason for this but the chances are that it is a neurotic trait which could be overcome.

51-75 You are rather lacking in confidence and this may take a lot of the fun out of life for you. But look at your individual scores—is this weakness general or mainly in two areas? What has gone wrong? Bad experiences in life or something in your temperament? Try to build on positive qualities and wherever you can get reassurance from friends.

76-109 This is a reasonable average range. You probably have areas of strong self-confidence where you feel totally in command and others where you are really weak. Alternatively, there may be overall fluctuations because of mood. Actually you are probably better liked than people scoring in the 110+ range because you are *not* totally hard-headed and thick-skinned. Try to be realistic about what you really *can* do and increase your confidence in appropriate situations.

Over 110 This is a very high score and if you are over 125 then the chances are that you are overconfident. This will not make you popular but, by one of those quirks of fate, your self-confidence is so high that your unpopularity will not bother you.

Real or fake? This man seems full of confidence but how much does that depend on his "props"?